French Philosophies
of the
Romantic Period

BY
GEORGE BOAS

BALTIMORE
THE JOHNS HOPKINS PRESS
1925

Copyright, 1925,
By The Johns Hopkins Press
Baltimore, Maryland

The Lord Baltimore Press
BALTIMORE, MD., U. S. A.

French Philosophies
of the
Romantic Period

To my Mother

Les philosophies sont intéressantes seulement comme des monuments psychiques propres à éclairer le savant sur les divers états qu'a traversés l'esprit humain. Précieuses pour la connaissance de l'homme, elles ne sauraient nous instruire en rien de ce qui n'est pas l'homme.—*Le Jardin d'Epicure.*

CONTENTS

CHAPTER ONE
PAGE
PREFACE vii
THE PHILOSOPHICAL SITUATION AFTER THE REVOLUTION 1

CHAPTER TWO
THE FORTUNES OF IDEOLOGY.................. 23

CHAPTER THREE
THE NEO-CHRISTIANS 70

CHAPTER FOUR
THE INTRODUCTION OF FOREIGN THINKERS...... 154

CHAPTER FIVE
THE RISE OF ECLECTICISM.................... 197

CHAPTER SIX
THE RISE OF POSITIVISM..................... 254
CONCLUSION 306
APPENDIX 310
INDEX 321

PREFACE

The following essays on French philosophies of the Romantic Period attempt to study the philosophic background of one of the most interesting political and cultural periods in French history. Politically France was adjusting herself to normal life after the upheaval of the Revolution; she was experimenting with new and indeed unheard of political fashions. One of the steadiest dynasties in Europe was to be replaced by a series of short-lived governments, differing not only in structure from their predecessors but in the very ends which informed them. Culturally France was no less the scene of experimentation. If the æsthetic revolution did not appear so soon as the political, it was no less intense and there were times when it looked as if it might be almost as bloody. What was called first " the new spirit " and later " romanticism " divided the world of art into sects as hostile to one another as émigrés and Jacobins.

Behind the political and æsthetic changes lay certain beliefs. Whether the beliefs determined the changes or the changes the beliefs we shall not take upon ourselves to settle. What this book is concerned with is making the proper correlation. Such a concern has had an unfortunate effect. It has neglected at times the philosophies to the advantage of the motives behind them or before them and given the philosophers the air of men who were not wholly sincere in the carrying out of their life's interest.

The pages which follow have another characteristic which may prejudice philosophers against them. They do not form what is often called a "critical exposition" of their subject matter. I have not been blind to the logical errors of these men's thinking; nothing would have been easier than to point some of them out. But only when the pompousness or insolence of the author grew intolerable have I yielded to the temptation of suggesting how little ground there was for his self-appraisal. I have not been interested in the truth and falsity of these ideas; I have been interested in their rise and decline. This book is a portrait, not intentionally a caricature, and has no moral purpose. It is addressed not only to students of philosophy but to students of civilization in general. If anyone wishes to pursue his investigation of these philosophies further, the footnotes will suggest ample material to be examined.

Begun in 1921 this manuscript was completed in 1924. Were I to begin it now I should undoubtedly attack the problem differently, emphasizing certain points which are here obscured, obscuring perhaps certain which are not here emphasized. Some of the chapters would have new footnotes referring the reader to publications which have appeared since I ended actual writing. But on the whole I find little in it which I should feel inaccurate.

My warmest thanks are due to my friend and colleague, Professor A. O. Lovejoy, who, though he would not agree with some of the opinions expressed here, has aided me in every way to get them into print; to Professors Charles Cestre and Lévy-Bruhl of the Sorbonne for their numerous kindnesses to me and to their fellows in France who helped make my stay in their country pleasurable and profitable.

G. B.

BALTIMORE, May 1925.

Voltaire and Rousseau in the Panthéon is evidence that the people thought—falsely or truly—that they were somehow connected causally with the events then going on. As for the lesser lights, a report of the Prefecture of Police of the 4th of Vendémiaire, Year IX (26 September 1800) when the Revolution was calming down, reads, "There is going to appear under the title, 'Etrennes de l'Institut national et des Lycées,' a literary review of the Year VIII, 1 vol. in-12, 204 pages, printer Moller. At the head of this collection is a very satirical letter to the Institut which is utterly outrageous. It would seem that this organization is merely an assembly of men conspiring against sane morals, enemies of true philosophy (very evidently that according to the author to which royalism attributes the birth of the Revolution); in short a crowd of atheists, etc., etc."[2] A year after the Prefecture of Police is less friendly. It reports, "The philosophers are complaining that people are trying to attribute to them all the evils of the Revolution and the destruction of their former institutions. They are saying that the scorn which people affect towards them is discouraging talent and knowledge, and that it will end by delivering them over to the indiscretion of the priests, who even now are not sparing their feelings in their speeches and who soon will point them out to the people as the authors of all the evils which they have suffered, and that, in this way, they will draw to them the general hatred of the

[2] Aulard; "P. sous le Consulat," P. 1903, I 675.

public. Following such complaints they permit themselves most often remarks against the government."³

Some men of course had sense enough to see that a philosopher or even several, cannot make a popular movement. The *Décade,* the philosophical review of the time, protested on the ground that the philosophers had suffered too much from the Revolution to have been responsible for it—a strange argument—and *La Minerve Française* (Vol. III), the paper of Benjamin Constant, in a review published some years later of the Abbé Georgel's "Mémoires pour servir à l'histoire des évènements de la fin du 18ᵉ siècle," protests that the guilt of kings, of the upper classes, of the ministers had more to do with starting the Revolution than the philosophers had. But perhaps the justest remark on this subject is by Professor Aulard made in another connection but applicable here, "If they tried to destroy Christianity, it was not because Voltaire had said, 'Ecrasez l'infame,' or because the Abbé Raynal had constructed the theory of the rights of the State upon individual conscience: It was because the Catholic priest was conspiring with the enemy from without."⁴

If the philosophers were to suffer from Napoleon's rise, the Church was to benefit. For the Church had always been the friend of the monarchy. What was

³ *Id.,* II 590, Report of the 5th of Brumaire, Year X.
⁴ Aulard; "Le Culte de la Raison et le Culte de l'Etre Suprême," 3d ed., P. 1909, p. 15. See also Roederer's defence of philosophy, quoted by Picavet; "Les Idéologues," P. 1890, p. 122 n. 1.

needed in France, as Napoleon saw it, was men who would teach that the enduring commands respect and obedience, that the passing is of no moment. It was on the Eleatic rock that the Church had founded her power far more than on the restless lake of Galilee, and as she had been the foe of the philosophers from Voltaire to Destutt de Tracy, so she was the friend of whatever power would make for order, for stability, for permanence, for unity.

In reading the works of the philosophers of the Revolution, of either the intellectualists or the sentimentalists, one is puzzled to know whether their opposition to the Church was the effect of their philosophies or whether it was the inspiration. Both might easily be true.

The followers of Condillac, the Idéologues, believed in the cognitive primacy of sensations, which—as Cabanis was going to show—varied with age, sex, temperament, climate, diet, health, and the like. He had laid out his work as early as 1798 before the Second Class of the Institut, in a memoir read on the 7th of Pluviôse, " Considerations on the Study of Man, and Upon the Relations of His Physical Organism to His Intellectual and Moral Faculties." To such men ideas were merely compounds of sensations, and when they wished to understand an idea, they analysed it into the sensations of which it was composed.[5] Early in the Revolution one of their group, Arbogast, has proposed that this method

[5] See Destutt de Tracy's memoir on the metaphysics of Kant, "Mem. de l'Institut National des Sciences et Arts: Sciences Morales et Politiques," IV 578.

should be used even in composing elementary school books. It alone, he felt, could keep the youth of the land from the shadowy method of abstract principles, of vague and general ideas which had reigned hitherto.[6] A section of the Institut existed for no other purpose than the breaking down of ideas into their elementary parts.

If all ideas were made of such matter, then the ideas of God, freedom, and immortality, or, if you choose, divine right, authority, hereditary rule, might be inferred to be nothing more than sensory complexes. Habit, repetition, might be seen to have fixed them in the minds of men, so that they had no more enduring value than any other habit, that of wearing wigs or carrying swords. To be sure, if it could be shown that some sensation corresponded to them, as the sensation

[6] Arbogast; "Rapport et projet de décret sur la composition des livres élémentaires destinés à l'instruction publique," P. n. d. "Analysis is to the sciences, it is to teaching, what liberty is to political institutions; both make a man feel his worth and contribute to his perfection. Analysis pertains to all the branches of human knowledge; throughout it is the instrument which guides one to inventions and discoveries; it alone gives that rectitude of judgment, that feeling for truth which characterizes the man who is truly educated.

"The analytic method should, then, reign everywhere in well ordered studies. One should never offer a single idea, a single word, unless analysis has made it exact and precise. One should never present any result which does not derive from a preceding analysis. Let us beware of that shadowy method which has ruled in the greater part of text-books, of those abstract principles which have misled men up to the present, of those vague and general ideas which have been too often realized, although they do not exist in nature."

of a color corresponds to our idea of a color, the case might be easier. But the Church, for one, did not wish the truth of its doctrines to be based on anything as personal as sensations which one might or might not have. It had made that clear in its constant opposition to all forms of mysticism. The State was in the same situation. What could the Church do in such circumstances? What happened to such doctrines as vicarious atonement, the Trinity, inherited guilt, whose dependence upon a realistic logic had been well enough illustrated in the twelfth century? What happened to the privileged position of the Clergy, their supervisory power over education, their monopoly of truth? Their high estate depended upon their peculiar knowledge of God and His ways, and if that dwindled to a mosaic of sensations, colored by age and temperament and attainable by the least clerical of souls, what was to become of them?

The followers of Rousseau, the sentimentalists, shrank in horror from this sensationalism. Something in their hearts told them that God dwells in the beauty of the landscape and in the vastness of the sky. Robespierre himself, not their least picturesque adherent, cried out in the Assembly that he would have been lost in the struggles and intrigues of politics if he could not have lifted his soul to that Eternal Being who seemed to him "to watch over the French Revolution in an especial manner."[7] The mystics, who may be grouped

---

[7] Quoted in Joyau; "La Philos. en Fr. pendant la Rév. (1789-1795)," P. 1893, p. 256.

with the sentimentalists, followed the same lead. Bernardin de Saint-Pierre and Saint-Martin as well, both named by the supposedly atheistic Assembly as guardians for the Dauphin, were on the best of terms with the Deity. Bernardin de Saint-Pierre saw His hand even in the shaping of melons for the knife; Saint-Martin saw little besides Him in the world.[8] Robespierre had no great difficulty in making the Convention decree that "the French people recognize the existence of the Supreme Being and the immortality of the soul."[9] So our own Benjamin Franklin, author of a treatise in defence of polytheism in his youth, pleaded for the offering of prayers in the Continental Congress, on the ground that God—who had won the war for the colonists—had been wronged by their omission.[10]

But in spite of their pronounced opposition to atheism, this group too was hostile to the Church. The same decree of the 18th of Floréal, Year II, which recognizes that God exists, adds that the cult worthy of Him is the practice of manly virtues. It says nothing about Catholic worship. It was no concession to the Clergy. In presenting it for consideration, Robespierre turned towards the ecclesiastical representa-

[8] But see Franck; "Philos. Mystique en Fr. à la Fin du 18⁰ siècle," P. 1866, esp. ch. vi.

[9] From a contemporary reprint. The text can be found in Aulard; "Le Culte etc.," ch. xxiii.

[10] See "The Debates in the Federal Convention of 1787 etc.," reported by James Madison, ed. Hunt and Scott, N. Y., 1920 (Pub. of the Carnegie Endowment for International Peace), p. 181.

tives and cried, " Fanatics, hope for nothing from us . . . ; ambitious priests, do not expect that we shall work to re-establish your empire." [11] How could men who saw God in their hearts accept the revelations of a priesthood? For them the source of religious insight was within the individual; it was a personal affair; its authority came from the feelings of the believer; its Church was the Church Invisible. For the Catholic, religion is a social affair; the individual is subject to error in reading both his Bible [12] and his heart; [13] its authority comes from the institution of which Christ's vicar is the head; its church is visible and militant.

Thus the Church found both her theory of knowledge and her religious discipline assailed.

But there were reasons other than those of logical consistency which made it probable that any philosophy formulated as an expression of the Revolution would be anti-clerical. If the monarchy was to go, the Church must go. That was obvious to political leaders of almost all philosophical persuasions. When one saw how thoroughly the Church had grown over the State, like ivy over an ancient tree, one did not need to be told in order to see that to cut down the tree was to cut down the vine.

[11] Quoted in Aulard; "Le Culte etc.," p. 272 n. 1.
[12] Denziger's "Enchiridion" (ed. of 1921), no. 1429, the Errors of Quesnel (no. 79); cf. no. 1606, 1608 and the *Encyl.* of Gregory XVI, *Inter. praecipuas*, no. 1630.
[13] *Id., Index systematicus,* I c.

AFTER THE REVOLUTION

It has been held that the aim of the Revolution was above all to de-christianize France,[14] and when one remembers that the civil constitution of the Clergy was passed before the King was beheaded, one sees some reason in the charge. But even if this had not been its aim, it could scarcely have been avoided. How to de-christianize France and have anything left was a problem easier to state than to solve. Where was the State and where the Church? The Church was not merely a religious institution. Her members had peculiar economic privileges and political power. She alone had buildings in which to hold divine service; a book attacking her could not be published in France; she controlled the education of the youth; she owned, according to popular belief, one-fifth of the land of France; her revenues from all sources, including perquisites, were nearly two hundred million livres; the property of the Clergy was exempt from taxation and the only contribution which they made to the State was voluntary gifts, consisting of a quinquennial grant of sixteen millions, used in large part to pay debts contracted at an earlier date.[15] Her peculiar wealth had, for that mat-

[14] See Joyau; *Op. cit.*, which criticizes it harshly on that account; Michelet, who praises it for the same reason. Paul Janet; "La Philos. et la Rév. Fr.," P. 1875, p. 94, says that for Michelet there are only two periods of history, the Christian and the Revolutionary.

[15] Pressensé; "l'Eglise et la Rév. Fr.," P. 1867, p. 8. Pressensé refers his readers to Rodot's "La Fr. avant la Rév., son état politique et social en 1787" and to "La Fr. ecclésiastique" for 1788, for the facts about the quinquennial grants. I should like to add the more accessible volume of Robinet, "Le Mouvement Relig. à P. pendant la Rév.," P. 1896, I 151.

ter, been satirized long before the Revolution. The *Persian Letters* are not dumb on the subject and Usbek writes to Rhedi that the Catholic dervishes never cease taking and never begin giving."[16] No other institution, it is needless to say, enjoyed such a position.

That was more antipathetic to the reformers than the beliefs of the Church. For years before the Revolution scepticism seems to have been fashionable and no dignitary of the Church of any importance was simple-minded enough to show the world more than the form of Christianity. The Archbishop of Narbonne, for instance, is said to have explained the resistance of the upper clergy in '91 as due not to their faith but to their honor as gentlemen.[17] It was not, then, the mere religious scepticism of men of whom only a part were sceptics, which overthrew the Church; for if the weight of scepticism had been enough, the Church would have crashed to earth with no propulsion from without. French society owed her a grudge. Scepticism and the philosophers helped to articulate and sanction it.

Accordingly one finds that Catholicism is given as hard a blow as the monarchy which it seemed to support. But it is Catholicism as a political institution, and not as a religion, which the Revolution tried to over-

[16] Letter cxvii.
[17] Taine; "Les Origines de la Fr. Contemporaine: l'Ancien Régime," II, liv. iv, ch. iv. The reader should be warned, of course, against Taine as an historian—see Aulard; "Taine, Historien de la Rév. Fr.," P. 1907. I do not find this particular assertion, however, contradicted by Aulard.

throw at the start. "The idea of attacking the dogma, of trying to destroy Catholicism, was made popular only in that so critical period from April to December 1793, when the Revolution had to struggle at once against the Vendée and against Europe. It was then believed that religion was the soul of the coalition against France," says Professor Aulard.[18] Up to that time the estates of the Clergy had been sold (10 October 1789) and the Civil Constitution of the Clergy passed (12 July 1790), but as late as June 1793 the Convention decreed that "the salary of the Clergy is part of the public debt." Law means little when not observed, to be sure, but it is important to note what it was thought good to include in the law.

It is only thereafter that there comes measure upon measure to destroy not only the outward manifestations of Catholicism in buildings, in art, in ceremony, but the very faith of the people. Priests are encouraged to marry, the church bells are made into cannon, the gold and silver of the altars are taken to the Mint, and finally the churches are turned into temples where first Reason, then the Supreme Being, are worshipped.[19] But this story is worn thread-bare and has no place here. We should not forget however that the methods of the Revolutionists were not new. Many of the de-

[18] "Le Culte, etc." p. 19.
[19] The story of the rise of the revolutionary cults is best and most briefly told in Aulard: "Le Culte etc." But no one, wishing to read the whole story should omit Mathiez: "La Théophilanthropie et le Culte Décadaire," P. 1904 nor the work of Pressensé already cited.

crees of the Convention are paralleled by analogous decrees in the Theodosian Code.[20] In fact, one does not have to go to Rome for a precedent. The Revocation of the Edict of Nantes was no less one. It ordered that all places of worship of the Protestants be demolished; forbade assemblies of any sort for the exercise of Protestant worship; forbade the practice of Protestant worship in one's own house individually; ordered all ministers of Protestantism to embrace Catholicism or leave France within two weeks; offered apostate ministers a continuation of certain exemptions from taxation; offered inducements for such ministers to take the degree of Doctor of Laws; forbade schools for the instruction of children in Protestantism; ordered all children born of Protestant parents to be baptised and educated in the Catholic faith under a minimum penalty of five hundred livres fine; returned property to Protestants who came back to France within four months after the publication of the Revocation and confiscated that of those who did not; and forbade all Protestants to leave the country.

One might venture to say that any attempt to supplant one religion by another in a legal way would afford as close if not so piquant an analogy. The attempted destruction of Catholicism is like a reproduction of the attempted destruction of paganism, and

[20] *De Apostatis* and *de Judaeis, Caelicolis, et Samaritanis,* "Theodosiani Lib. XVI," ed. Mommsen and Meyer, Berlin 1905, I xvi 7 and 8. Cf. Dill; "Roman Society in the Last Century of the Western Empire," 2d ed. rev., Lond. 1919, ch. i and ii.

just as the old Italian peasant illegally worshipped in isolated shrines the nymphs of his woods and streams, so the Breton peasant stole off under cover of darkness to confess to his priest or to have his marriage solemnized. In the one case the destruction was fairly thorough and took centuries to be completed. In the other it seemed superfical and endured for half a decade.

It fell to Napoleon's lot to play the rôle of Julian the Apostate. And characteristically enough he played it with greater effect than his Roman prototype.

He turned first to the philosophers. The sentimentalists were easy enough to conquer. Their vague ruminations were hardly worth noticing. The President of his Legislature and later Grand Master of the University, Fontanes, as early as 1786 had seen how weak a head was Bernardin de Saint-Pierre's,[21] the professor who, in the words of Anatole France, "retired after his first lecture to find out what he had to say and never came back to the platform."[22] The Emperor had little to fear from him. Appreciating his ability as a writer, he gave him a pension of six thousand francs to prove it. But he said that he should have been chased out of the Institut for having written on the harmonies of nature. He knew that this man was harmless and left him to enjoy his young wife, his

[21] Letter to Joubert in "Les Correspondants de J. Joubert," P. 1883, p. 47.

[22] "Le Génie Latin," p. 238. This should be corrected by Maury; "Etude sur Bernardin de Saint-Pierre," P. 1892, pp. 200-206.

garden, his pension, and his cross of the Legion of Honor. There was, moreover, a certain bond of sympathy between the Emperor and the poet-philosopher. They both hated the descendants of Condillac.[23]

This group he railed at without end. They were "these miserable metaphysicians," "inexhaustible nonsensemongers."[24] He railed at them because he feared them. As a member of his Conseil d'Etat, Pelet de la Lozère, says, he feared them and the Republicans much more than the Royalists. Theirs was the work he must undo. And as they were neither Royalist nor Jacobin and could give him no cause to guillotine them or to deport them, he vented his spleen in diatribes and in using Destutt de Tracy's name, Idéologue, as a synonym for all that was vain and trivial, a meaning which it has kept to this day.[25] But his sneers left his victims unharmed.

The development of his unfriendly sentiments towards the Idéologues is coincident with his rise to power. As a young lieutenant of artillery, he had sworn to obey the constitution of the National Assembly.[26] As a young general fresh from the Egyptian

---

[23] Maury; *Op. cit.* 224.

[24] These remarks were originally written in the *Journal de P.*, 15 pluviôse IX and republished in Fontanes's journal, *le Mercure de Fr.* on the following day. They are constantly quoted and can be easily found in Picavet; *Op. cit.* p. 23 or Gauthier; "Mme. de Staël et Napoléon," P. 1902, p. 64.

[25] Lerminier; "De l'Influence de la Philos. du XVIIIe Siècle sur la Legislation et la Sociabilité du XIXe," P. 1833, p. 277.

[26] Conveniently quoted in Fournier; "Napoleon I," tr. by Annie Elizabeth Adams, N. Y., 1911, I 36.

Campaign he had been by no means unwilling to accept membership in the Institut and humbly had gone to Auteuil to pay his respects to the widow of Helvétius.[27] In this early period he had been on terms of friendship with Destutt de Tracy, whom he had invited to accompany him to Egypt. After the Treaty of Campo-Formio he replied to Garat's compliments, " The true victories, the only ones which leave no regrets, are those over ignorance. The most honorable as well as the most useful occupation for nations is to contribute to the extension of human ideas."[28] This was well enough for a modest and precocious officer fresh from foreign wars, when simplicity of demeanor would excite the enthusiasm of the masses. But later when he saw that his love of ideas might not be compatible with his love of power, his attitude changed. He grew to see in the Idéologues a set of sanctimonious dreamers, incapable of fruitful action. Yet without their aid, their planning and preparing, their moderate liberalism, their willingness to experiment, their freedom from prejudice, their optimism in the face of discouragement, not even the 18th of Brumaire would have succeeded.[29]

[27] Picavet; *Op. cit.* p. 221 n. 2. See Jules Bertaut; "Mme. Helvétius," R. de la Semaine, VI, 30 June 1922, for a lively account of this charming woman. For a more careful study, see Guillois; " Le Salon de Mme. Helvétius," P. 1894.

[28] I translate from the text in Garat's paper, *le Conservateur*, No. 122, 11 nivôse VI (31 Dec. 1797), p. 972. It is also quoted by Picavet; *Op. cit.* 221.

[29] Fournier; *Op. cit.* II 248.

As a young lieutenant of artillery Napoleon had sworn to obey the constitution of the National Assembly. But under the Constitution of the Year VIII the Declaration of the Rights of Man has disappeared. Two years later personal prerogatives begin to accrue to him; he appoints senators and has the power of pardon; he names the presidents of the *assemblées de canton*. Again two years and he is Emperor of the French with his power hereditary in his male descendants and derived not only from the constitutions of the French Republic but from the grace of God. Meanwhile he has closed the Ecoles Centrales, the invention of the Idéologues, and has substituted for them the Imperial University.[30]

"My principal aim," he said in 1806, "in establishing a teaching body, is to have a means of directing political and moral opinion."[31] The decree of March 17, 1806, is a good illustration of how he thought it should be achieved. "All the schools of the Imperial University," it reads, "will take as the basis of their teaching, first, the precepts of the Catholic religion; second, fidelity to the Emperor, to the imperial monarchy, depository of the happiness of peoples, and to the Napoleonic dynasty, conserver of the unity of France and of all the liberal ideas proclaimed by her constitutions; third, obedience to the statutes of the teaching body which has for its object uniformity of

---

[30] Picavet; *Op. cit.* 29.
[31] Pelet de la Lozère; "Opinions de Napoléon . . . recueuillies par un membre de son conseil d'état," P. 1833, Séance du 20 mars 1806, p. 167.

instruction and which tends to mold for the benefit of the state citizens attached to their religion, their prince, their country, and their family; fourth, all the professors of theology will be held to conform to the provisions of 1682 concerning the four propositions contained in the declaration of the Clergy of France of that year " (*i. e.*, Gallicanism).[32]

The idea of uniformity of instruction and of molding the young according to a preconceived plan was utterly different from that which informed the schools of the Idéologues. In them written lectures were forbidden and after the discussion by the lecturer, the students debated the problems involved in his talk.[33] The words "liberal ideas" in Napoleon's plan alone suggest this régime. So changed is everything else that their presence must be a cynical joke. Whereas the Ecoles Centrales, again, had men as different as Volney and Bernardin de Saint-Pierre on their teaching staff, the Imperial University had a catechism prepared with the collaboration of the Papal Legate. The catechism, which is worth reading begins:

"What are the duties of Christians towards the princes who govern them, and what in particular are our duties towards Napoleon I, our Emperor?

"Christians owe to the princes who govern them, and we in particular owe to Napoleon I, our Emperor, love, respect, obedience, fidelity, military service, the tribute ordered for the preservation and defence of the

[32] Duvergier; "Lois, Décrets, etc.," P. 1826, XVI 267.
[33] For the bright side of the medal, see Picavet; *Op. cit. passim;* for the dark, Maury; *Op. cit.* 202. Cf. Sainte-Beuve; "Chateaubriand et son Groupe Littéraire," P. 1861, I 61.

empire and of his throne. . . . To honor and to serve the emperor is then to honor and to serve God Himself.

"Are there not special motives which ought to bind us more strongly to Napoleon I, our Emperor?

"Yes; for it is he whom God has aroused in difficult circumstances to establish the public worship of the holy religion of our fathers, and to be its protector. He has restored and preserved public order by his profound and active wisdom; he defends the state by his powerful arm; he has become the anointed of the Lord by the consecration received from the Sovereign Pontiff, head of the Church Universal.

"What should one think of those who might fail in their duty towards our emperor?

"According to the Apostle Paul, they would be resisting the established order of God Himself, and would be making themselves worthy of eternal damnation."[34]

This is a far cry from the republican catechisms published during the Revolution.

"What is the communion?" asks the Citoyen Poitevin in his.

"It is the association proposed to all rational peoples by the French republic to form in the future but one great family of brothers, who know not nor enshrine either idol or tyrant."[35]

There can be no doubt that Napoleon's is more conducive to a stable government. It not only insists on

---

[34] A fuller English translation of this can be found in F. M. Andersen; "Constitutions and other Select Documents illustrative of the History of Fr.," 2d ed., Minneapolis, 1908, p. 312. Compare Napoleon's words to Queen Louise of Prussia, "There is a Providence which directs all, of which I am merely the instrument," in Blennerhassett; "Mme. de Staël et son Temps," P. 1890, III 209.

[35] "Catechisme républicain etc.," par le Citoyen Poitevin, P. n. d., p. 6. Cf. Aulard; "Le Culte etc.," p. 336.

unity but upon national and dynastic loyalty to preserve it. It makes the individual exist for the group, not the group for the individuals in it. The Emperor in exile said that the Consulate was a first step towards a goal which he had always had perfectly clearly before his eyes, a step towards accustoming the people to unity.[36] This may not have been true at all; yet it is true that freedom of thought would have accustomed them to diversity. His hope was in the former as the hope of all rulers has ever been.

He acted, however, as if that had been his goal. For he rid himself as far as possible of those elements which would disturb his victory. In 1803 he dissolved the Second Class of the Institut, the class devoted to the study of moral and political sciences. It was that class, with its six sections given over to the analysis of sensations and ideas, to ethics, to social science and legislation, to political economy, to history and geography, which worried more than any other the heart of him who, as conqueror of Italy, had told the professors of Pavia that the arts and sciences which "honor the human mind" "ought especially to be revered in free governments."[37] He was himself, as everyone knows, a member of the Institut and in 1800 was unanimously named president of the class of phy-

[36] "Mémoires de Napoléon," 2d ed., P. 1830, VI 144. Cf. Napoleon's famous conversation with Benjamin Constant during the Hundred Days, *La Minerve Fr.*, VIII 100.

[37] Reprint of the *Moniteur,* 22 messidor IV (10 July 1796), XXVIII 347.

sical sciences and mathematics.[38] The thought that the great general would condescend to sit with mere men of learning was overpowering to the Parisian public. The papers never mentioned the fact without titillating.[39] "After one of the last private sessions of the Institut," said the *Gazette de France* (17 thermidor VIII), "the Consul talked familiarly with his colleagues for more than an hour. Many questions were put to him about his last campaign in Italy. The Consul answered them with that *sang-froid,* that modesty which characterize the great man. The conversation was so interesting that it was prolonged for some time. The Consul was so gracious, so charming, that he almost made his colleagues forget that they were discoursing with the first magistrate of a great state." The Institut was no less pleased than the public. The Second Class printed at the head of its memoirs for the Year XI—the year in which it was dissolved, " Was there ever a more beautiful sight than that of the chief of an immense republic seated by chance among scientists whom he makes his equals, and modestly sharing with them their work and their deliberations, while a simple citizen, enjoying as president the honor of the chair, is seated above the hero who holds with firm hand the reins of the most powerful of empires, extends his influence over the destinies of all Europe, and makes respected upon the whole surface of the globe this fair great nation, too long unhappy, restored

[38] *Gazette de Fr.* 4 germinal VIII, in Aulard; " P. sous le Consulat," I 233.

[39] See Aulard; " P. sous le Consulat, " I 7, 62, 81, 252, 582.

to happiness by him? *Unus qui nobis . . . restituit rem."* [40]

There was some reason for Napoleon's hostility to the Second Class. It is freely admitted by the historian of this body that its members were anti-imperialistic and anti-deistic.[41] Among them sat Volney, opponent of all of Napoleon's innovations, especially the Concordat, in spite of all efforts to win him over; Naigeon, the atheist; Ginguené, editor of the *Décade* which was to be suppressed in 1807; Daunou, who had helped to plan the Institut for the Directory, one of the most obstinately honest men of the time and persistent liberal.[42] Bernardin de Saint-Pierre was a friend, of course, but he had little influence.[43] Irritated perhaps by the indifference of these men to passing things—and here Bernardin de Saint-Pierre sinned with the rest—Napoleon wrote to Ségur that if they discussed politics in their meetings, he would break them like a *mauvais club*. And finally, by his consular decree of the 3rd of Pluviôse, Year XI (23 January 1803), the Second Class disappeared from the Institut, which was forbidden to occupy itself with moral and political science, except in their relation to history, "especially very ancient history."

[40] "Mém. de l'Institut: Sci. Mor. et Pol." IV 2.
[41] J. Simon; "Une Académie sous le Directoire," P. 1885, p. 470.
[42] Picavet; *Op. cit.* 403 n. 1.
[43] Maury; *Op. cit.* 217, with the report on the *concours*, "Quelles sont les institutions les plus propres à fonder la morale d'un peuple."

Underneath Napoleon's hatred of these men, as underneath his hatred of Mme. de Staël, was an appreciation of his inability to use them as he saw fit. "To me," he boasted to Daunou,[44] "men are tools." If the Idéologues had been willing to serve as such, all might have been well. But they were not all of the temper of Garat, who turned his coat with the rapidity of a conjurer.[45] They persisted in following the light as they wished. And Napoleon understood finally that they had defeated him. For in 1808 he said to Fontanes, "Fontanes, do you know what excites my wonder most in the world? It is the impotence of force to organize anything. There are only two powers in the world, the sword and the mind. . . . In the long run, the sword is always beaten by the mind."[46]

But his defeat was not complete. For he succeeded in breaking the power of the particular group of philosophers whom he hated, though philosophic reflection went on more or less steadily. "In 1810," says Lerminier, a contemporary, "nineteen years after the Constituant, no one remembered either the Revolution or philosophy." Napoleon was in part at least responsible. For he introduced and countenanced and encouraged the fashion, which was only too easily acquired, of sneering not only at the Idéologues, but at philosophy in general.

[44] Picavet; *Op. cit.* 403 n. 1.
[45] See the enlightening but often unfair " Dictionnaire des Girouettes," P. 1815, p. 175.
[46] Gautier; *Op. cit.* 405.

CHAPTER TWO

THE FORTUNES OF IDEOLOGY

Ideology had practically run its course with the suppression of the Institut. Napoleon's prestige had made it the fashion to use the word as a term of reproach, and any airy fancy might be called "ideology" irrespective of its origin. The members of the school, to all intents and purposes out of the political arena, retired to the garden of Helvétius in Auteuil, bequeathed by Mme. Helvétius to Cabanis, who shared with Destutt de Tracy, the headship of the group. Their retirement must not be interpreted as absolute seclusion. Destutt de Tracy, for instance, was still a senator. It means simply that their influence in affairs of state was neither sought nor imposed.

As far as French thought is concerned, the teachings of Cabanis were to survive largely in literature and in the work of Auguste Comte. They entered Germany where we shall not follow them through Schopenhauer. We shall see them gaining literary ground in Stendhal and in that long list of "physiologies" which begins with Brillat-Savarin and runs through to the '80's. In Auguste Comte we shall see them gaining philosophic ground, linked, however, to the pseudo-science of Gall and Spurzheim, for the founder of positivism was not always happy in his choice of scientists. Destutt de Tracy, on the other hand, has two disciples, who alter his work but still carry on his tradition. The first is Laromiguière, whose influence is hardly important and who—though he lived well into the nineteenth century and gained great popularity—is really an eighteenth century figure. The second is Maine de Biran, who, beginning in Ideology, ends in Christian mysticism. He is the initiator of the important voluntaristic tradition in French nineteenth century philosophy.

Although the doctrines of the Ideologists are presented with a thoroughness which I could scarcely hope to equal in the work of Picavet, " Les Idéologues," it is perhaps desirable to give here a brief synopsis of the main tenets of the school in order to clarify the position of their successors.

The name " Ideology " was invented by Destutt de Tracy to denominate that study which was to supplant metaphysics. It was a study which was obviously inspired by Condillac's sensationalism, although Destutt does not agree with all the details of Condillac's system. Unlike the Germans, he says,[1] who profess philosophy as one professes religion, the Idéologues adopt merely their master's method. This method, he continues, " consists in observing facts with the greatest care, in inferring from them only the surest consequences, in never giving to simple suppositions the sta-

[1] Destutt de Tracy; " De la Métaphysique de Kant," *Mem. de l'Institut: Sci. Mor. et Pol.,* IV 549. Cf. his memoir, " Sur la Faculté de Penser," *Id.* I 302 and his " Elémens d'Idéologie," Pt. I, 2d ed., P. An XIII—1804, xvi.

bility of facts, in undertaking to bind truths together only when they are linked naturally and without gaps, in admitting frankly what one does not know, and constantly preferring absolute ignorance to every assertion which is merely probable." [2] So far the method seems to consist in a sort of radical empiricism and agnosticism. It requires greater precision and this Destutt de Tracy proceeds to give. In treating general ideas, he says, a good method is to decompose them, " to examine the elementary ideas from which they are extracted, and to go back to the first facts, to the simple perceptions, to the sensations from which they emanate, if one could reach that point; if not "—and here his agnosticism appears again—" one must wait, suspend judgment, and renounce the attempt to explain what is not known clearly." This study of ideas, " which is only logic treated reasonably," is what he called " ideology."

That the only method worthy of serious consideration was analysis would have disturbed only Catholics. But that analysis will reduce all ideas to sensations was a more difficult matter to admit. Destutt de Tracy, however, insisted on this point and drew from it a consequence which separated his philosophy and that of Cabanis from that of their contemporaries.

That point he announced in the preface to his " Elémens d'Idéologie " (An XIII—1804). " Ideology is a part of zoology " (p. xiii). This text may be said

[2] " Métaph. de Kt." 550, 578, 594.

to account for the reaction of the early nineteenth century to his school. For people during the Empire were no longer willing to admit that they were on a level with the brutes. They had a more lofty conception of the human spirit. To them ideology, rightly or wrongly, was a strict denial of what the Church had always taught, for instance. To the Church the zoological aspect of humanity was disgraceful. The thinking processes to her were an elevation towards God, and any attempt to identify them with the purely animal function was to widen the breach between man and his Creator—an end which was not repugnant to the taste of Destutt and his followers.

The sensationalism of Ideology emphasized the animality of the human mind. Whenever we think, whenever we judge, remember, desire, we " feel a sensation," says Destutt (*op. cit.* 22-25). The only difference which he finds between thinking and feeling is one of time. Sensations which are no longer in process of production are thought; while they are being produced, they are felt. But the material of consciousness is absolutely homogeneous—it is perception of sensations. All of this material naturally comes to us through our sense organs. Whence Destutt is able to fortify his original proposition that ideology is a part of zoology. It is at this point that Cabanis begins his work.

Destutt de Tracy divides consciousness, what he calls the faculty of thinking, into four elementary faculties, sensibility, properly so-called, memory, judgment, and will (ch. I). Sensibility is the faculty of receiving impressions (p. 30) through the nerves (p. 32). The impressions are not only external, such as colors, sounds, and so forth (p. 33), but are also internal, such as visceral (p. 36) and kinesthetic sensations (p. 37), the feelings of well-being and malaise (p. 38). Memory is a kind of internal impression (ch. III). Judgment is simply a sensation of relation (ch. IV) and will is the sensation of desire (ch. V). The will, he says (p. 71), " in only like our other faculties, a result of our organism, but it has this peculiarity, that it is always the cause of our happiness or unhappiness."

Now all the "ideas" or thoughts which we experience are complex, but if we could experience a sensation for the first time without remembering others like it, or judging it, or desiring it, we should have the experience of a simple sensation. But, as a matter of fact, this never happens and our minds are full of complex ideas. We unite similar sensations, discarding their differences, to form what we call " general ideas." But we must never fall into the error of thinking that these general ideas have other than a mental existence (ch. VI).

If we are thus limited to a life of sensations, how does it happen that we have any notion of the objects which produce the sensations? It is certain, says Destutt (p. 123), that the internal sensations tell us nothing except that we exist. The same holds true for tastes, odors, and sounds (p. 124). Even sight (p. 126) and touch (p. 128) upon examination turn out to be as secretive as the other senses when it is a question of their revealing a non-sensory cause. Destutt concludes that it is through our powers of movement and the feeling of resistance (p. 152) that something beyond ourselves makes itself felt. One can make the simple experiment of a voluntary movement. Suppose one wills to push through a solid block of stone. The obstacle is stubborn and resists. But since we cannot both will a movement and will its annihilation at the same time, we conclude that something not ourselves exists to obstruct our will. It is thus that Destutt hopes to escape from subjectivism. It will be noticed that the external world is not revealed in direct sensation but by a process of reasoning about our sensations.

It is worth remarking that what Destutt de Tracy felt to be a philosophic absurdity was at that very time being utilized by Fichte as the cornerstone of his metaphysics. The self-obstruction which Destutt felt that the will could never voluntarily incur was for his German contemporary the secret of the cosmic drama. This material world which met our volition with resistance furnished for Fichte not evidence of an objective something hostile to and different in kind from the active Ego, but a construction of that Ego created for its own moral ends. More curious than the fact itself is the environment in which the fact arose. The Frenchman was faced with a world in which a will, Napoleon's, had conquered all resistance to such an extent that the superstitious looked upon it as something more than human. The German, on the contrary, was surrounded either with human beings too placid to abandon their preconceived ideas or, later in his life, broken by foreign invasion and humiliation.

We see that Destutt de Tracy appreciated the importance of the will. It was an appreciation shared not only by his contemporaries in Germany but also by some of those in France. But Destutt kept the discussion to a quasi-psychological level instead of generalizing it into a metaphysical theory. He had already asserted that the will was merely a kind of impression—the sensation of desire. This definition he continued to maintain even in his treatise on the will, in which he might have been expected to indulge in greater liberties.[3] It is because of this definition that later philosophers were to object most strongly to Ideology. For desire is something " passive," and they were to insist that the will be " active," if man's moral force and obligation were not to be weakened or even eliminated. Destutt, however, saw no more need of making his theory of knowledge fit a desirable or traditional ethics than he saw of making it fit a traditional theology. He coldly founded our idea of personality and property, our needs and means of satisfying them, our ideas of right and wrong, on his peculiar type of will. He would found upon its law the laws of economics and politics, also, but unfortunately we cannot follow him there.

It is fairly obvious, I take it, why Destutt's theory should die out. He makes two points especially impor-

[3] "Elémens d'Idéologie: IVe et Ve Pties. "Traité de la Volonté," P. 1815.

tant, the analysis of complex ideas into simple ones, as far as that is possible, and the significance of the data of sensation. The method of analysis was his substitute for what his predecessors had called "Reason." It was the weapon of the philosophical opposition. Its enemies were bound to be not only the Catholics but all reactionaries, for it gave the individual the power to substantiate his own beliefs. Nor does analysis show us grounds for accepting what authority wishes us to believe. It does not permit us to put credence in suprasensory truths. For in such theses as the reactionaries had to propose, there was always a grain of mystery beyond which analysis could not go, and beyond which the human mind was forced to go, unless it was willing, as Destutt's was, to suspend judgment. Destutt could afford to be agnostic at a certain point; the reactionaries could not.

The insistence that sensory data were fundamental for true knowledge gave the reactionaries another ground for complaint. What sensation could account for the truth of the doctrine of the Trinity? Sensations have always seemed low to some people, perhaps because they require a body, perhaps because they do not show us all the things in which we enjoy believing. It was their lowness more than anything else which inspired most of the opposition to them. Had the sensationalists been willing to circumscribe the field of knowledge so as to exclude knowledge of right and wrong, all might have been well. Destutt, as we have seen, refused to do this, and put the basis of morality on the same plane as that of logic. But reactionaries wanted morality to be on a higher plane. Even when Victor Cousin, who as a youth had written enthusiastically of analysis,[4] made morality theistic but rational, they rebelled. They wanted it beyond the reach of reason. There were ineradicable differences of what one can only call temperament which made the Idéologue carry his sensationalism to the limit without fear of consequences and prevented the Catholic from giving up even the first inch of ground. It was, in other words, not the logical outcome of their philosophies which interested these men so much as their practical outcome, although they would have fought to the last to prove that their particular practical outcome was alone logical and consistent.

The zoological aspect of ideology was more apparent in the work of Cabanis than in that of Destutt de Tracy. For in his "Rapports du Physique et du Moral de l'Homme" (2d ed., p. 1843), he states definitely that the physical is the same thing as the mental "considered under certain particular points of view" (p. 73). He traces his beliefs from what he calls the discovery of Locke that all ideas come from sensation (p. 45). But if sensations are the last term in psychology, physical sensibility is the last term in biology. There is neither knowledge nor life without sensation. Like his colleague, he says, "If we experienced but one sensation, we should have but one idea; and if to this sensation were linked a determination of the will whose effect was hindered by a resis-

[4] "De Methodo sive de Analysi," 19 July 1813.

tance, we should know that independently of us there exists something; we could know nothing more" (p. 74). But since sensibility varies among individuals according to sex and what he calls "temperament," in the same individual according to age or health, in all by climate and the totality of physical habits or what one might call the mode of living (p. 75), it is of utmost importance to study these variations if one is either philosopher, moralist, or legislator.

There were terrifying conclusions to be drawn from the work of Cabanis. The Ego, as in Destutt, is simply the feeling of effort due to the operations of the will; we have several Egos, but usually refer the egoistic feeling to the common center of all sensations (p. 442). We find that the source of happiness consists in nothing more than "the free exercise of the faculties, in the feeling of force and ease with which one puts them into action" (p. 181). Even the happiness, which is based upon so physical a ground, turns out to be a kind of stoical virtuousness, justified by self-interest (p. 51). The "faculties of man" are "assuredly nothing but the more generalized statement (*énoncé*) of the operations produced by the play of his organs" (p. 230). Such conclusions and others like them could not but be repugnant to thinkers of a spiritualistic turn of mind.

But there was another objection to Ideology which occupied the contemporary thinkers. Ideology seemed to mean that man was "passive," the mere statue of Condillac quickened into life by the stimulus of sights and sounds and smells. The feeling is well expressed by the Abbé Bautain writing much later, in 1839, when he says,[5] "The man of to-day with moral needs more profound, conscience more enlightened, ideas more vast, views which tend towards the universal, sublime presentiments, burning anxiety—the man of to-day is no longer his (Condillac's) man nor his statue. He no longer recognizes himself in a sensation-machine, in an ideological mannikin or in a mass organized to feel." After all it was the human will which seemed at that time to be productive of most of the changes, at least in history. How could one convince men who had seen a group of commoners overturn the government of France and an unknown adventurer from Corsica conquer almost all of Western Europe, that they were the playthings of forces external to themselves? What was particularly impressive in the history of this time was the progress made by man in spite of external obstacles. The existence of Napoleon alone would have been inducement enough to think that some account must be given of humanity which would place his initiative in an important place. It was this task which the non-Catholic philosophers attempted above all others.

II

Of the two disciples of the Idéologues who had an influence in the nineteenth century as metaphysicians, Maine de Biran and Laromiguière, it is the latter who is the less wayward. A professor in the Imperial Uni-

---

[5] "Philos.-Psychol. Expérimentale," Strasbourg et P., 1839, I xxi.

versity, a man of letters, he preserved the self-assurance of one who is used to charming audiences and a reading public and advanced but cautiously into new realms of philosophic enquiry. The philosophies then in vogue in Germany, for instance, left him cold, and in one of the later editions of his major treatise, "Leçons de Philosophie," he thought that he had settled the question of the merits of Kantianism by proving that it is nothing but a new form of scepticism. He had no doubts about the validity of his own teachings. He had on the contrary, a full confidence that what he advocated could not be false, for his method was correct and his principles were sound. If he had any doubts at all, it was about the more ultimate problems such as the interaction of soul and body and about the value of life.[6]

His writings were not extensive. He opened his literary career, when still a Doctrinaire, with " Eléments de Métaphysique " (1793), a work which he later suppressed. In 1796 appeared his two memoirs, " Sur la détermination de ces mots: *Analyse des Sensations*" and " Extrait d'un mémoire sur la détermination du mot *Idée*" which earned the praise of Cabanis. In 1805 appeared his " Paradoxes de Condillac, ou Réflexions sur la Langue des Calculs." From then on he kept silent until in 1811-1812 he gave his famous lectures which were printed as " Leçons de Philosophie." It is upon this that his fame rests and six editions of it were called for between

[6] "Leçons de Philos." P. 1815, I 93.

1815 and 1844. This last edition, which was posthumous, contains a few minor writings until then unpublished. The apparent charm of his published lectures was but a reflection of the charm of his speech. "Auditors of all ages," says Janet,[7] " pupils and masters, followed these brilliant, clear, and methodical lessons. M. de Fontanes came to one of them, the lesson on definition. The charm of M. Laromiguière's words was, according to the testimony of his auditors, irresistible. 'Who will again give us,' says M. Counsin, ' these improvisations, of which the happiest style affords but a weakened image, these incomparable lectures, wherein the grace of Montaigne, the wisdom of Locke, and sometimes also the suavity of Fénelon were effortlessly united with supreme clearness.'"

These traits, chosen with Cousin's habitual eclectic enthusiasm, indicate how highly Laromiguère was regarded by his contemporaries—though Cousin was speaking after his predecessor's death. They do not indicate, however, Laromiguière's contribution to the history of French philosophic ideas.

As we have suggested, the main alteration which he made in Ideology was the introduction, or better the extension of the rôle of "activity" in epistemology. There seemed to be obviously powers in the soul of man which were not mere mosaics of passively received sensations. Destutt himself had admitted that no perception was produced from a sensory stimulus

[7] "Laromiguière," *La Liberté de Penser, R. Philos. et Littéraire,* 1848, I 261.

until activity had been excited.[8] Cabanis had insisted, as one of the major portions of his thesis, that though we might all have the same sensations—by which he means only external sensations—yet our ideas differ, since our individual constitution influences them and differentiates them from the ideas of our fellows. We count for something in the makeup of our knowledge. Laromiguière's pupil, L. J. J. Daube, a professor in the Ecole Centrale des Hautes-Pyrenées, thought that he was distinguishing sharply between sensation and activity in his study, the " Essai d'Idéologie " (1803). " I am active," he says, " when I am myself the cause of what takes place within me. I am passive when the cause of what takes place within me is not I. That being posited it is evident that I am passive in sensation, since its cause is without me; that it does not depend on me to procure myself agreeable sensations when I am experiencing disagreeable ones; without which I would never be disagreeably affected. I am active, on the contrary, in attention, since it depends on me whether I shall give it or refuse it. But is it not absurd to say that an active faculty is only a passive faculty transformed?" That was exactly what, he maintained, the classic Condillacist was saying. He tried further to prove the independence of sensation and attention by pointing out that the intensity of a sensation varies with the stimulus, whereas the intensity of a feeling attended to varies with the attention we voluntarily give it.

[8] " Métaph. de Kt." p. 551.

It was with a similar distinction that Laromiguière's epistemology took its start.[9] "We have," he says in his "Leçons" (Ed. of 1815, I 91 f.), "two sorts of facts in inverse order, first, the action of the object on the organ, of the organ on the brain, and of the brain on the soul; second, the action or reaction of the soul on the brain; communication of the motion received by the brain to the organ, which flees from the object or approaches it." These types of experience are activity and passivity. But so sure is Laromiguière that people since Condillac have forgotten this truth, that in spite of the fact that the distinction was known and made much of in early Greek philosophy, he goes into the matter at some length, winding up by saying, "All mankind knows, then, and cannot not know, that there is a difference between seeing and looking, between listening and hearing; it knows, in other words, that we are now passive, now active, that the soul is by turns passive and active."

Just what activity is Laromiguière does not say. But he recognizes the seeming impropriety of not defining it. He excuses himself on the ground that it is a primitive idea in his system. "The definition of an idea is . . . possible only when one has an anterior idea from which one derives what one proposes to define. Whence it follows that the fundamental idea of a science is and can never be defined. . . . We shall

[9] Janet maintains that Daube's book was the source of L.'s main idea. V. *Op. cit.* 257 n. 1. Daube continued to combat L., who in his early work, "Elémens de métaph." had sustained Tracy's point that sensation is active.

not define 'attention' nor the activity of the soul, because in the soul nothing is anterior to its activity: I mean nothing anterior from which activity might derive its origin." (*Leçons* I 156 f.) He would probably, if pressed, have fallen back on the definition of activity given by his pupil, Daube, although the use of the word "cause" would leave the modern reader, but not the reader of his day, dissatisfied.

Laromiguière seems to have felt no uneasiness about his distinction between activity and passivity and saw in the innateness of activity a basic fact for the understanding of the human mind. With it and passivity as a foundation, he was able to build up the superstructure of the human faculties, and having provided for an active faculty in the inventory of his elements, he is not at a loss to account for one when he comes to the composites.

The human intelligence for Laromiguière seems to be concerned with three interests, discovering facts, grasping their relations, reducing them to a system. This is quite in accord with the tradition of Condillac who also saw the world as an arrangement of elementary "facts"; in the tradition of Bacon, if you will, and perhaps in the tradition of Socrates himself. A world which can be understood by the accurate grouping of particulars under general laws is a world which has place alone for classification, systematizing, rearrangements. It was a proper philosophy for times when the historical sense had not been highly developed. Laromiguière was not insensible to the charm of this philosophy. " System," he wrote [10] " when it is carried to its perfection, is the highest degree of knowledge to which the human mind can rise. It offers a whole science in a single fact, in a single idea, in a single word which represents this idea or this fact. But how rare are good systems! "

Accordingly, when you have an idea given you, one of the best ways to grasp its meaning is to analyse it. This, as we have seen, is in agreement with the tenets of Ideology, and was in fact a simple acknowledgment of the justice of the Institut's existence in part. The Institut existed for the coordination and analysis of knowledge; its *raison d'être* was the faith of Idéologues in the very ideas which Laromiguière carried over into the nineteenth century. Laromiguière never lost sight of this fundamental point. He retained it in his " Leçons " unchanged and assigned to metaphysics no other rôle than that of going back to the origin of our ideas (*Leçons* I 271).[11] His colleague, Daunou, had assigned this rôle to logic, giving to metaphysics " the less extended " function of finding " the most precise and striking proofs of the existence of God and of the future life." [12] But for Laromiguière such a function is futile since its execution is impossible.

[10] *Mem. de l'Inst.* I 458.
[11] Cf. " Leçons " I 270; also *Mem. de l'Inst: SMP.* I 460.
[12] See his " Plan d'Education présenté à l'Assemblée nationale, au nom des Instituteurs de l'Oratoire," P. 1790, p. 14 n. 2.

The Condillacist point of view made it almost inevitable that Laromiguière should love symmetries. He had divided the primary faculties of the understanding into attention, comparison, and reasoning, to each of which he assigned the satisfaction of one of the primary needs of the understanding (*Leçons* I 101). He must now investigate the will, and to that too he will assign three faculties, on a parallel with the faculties of the understanding (*Leçons* I 167). To attention corresponds desire, the faculty which attracts one to an object; to comparison corresponds preference, by which the value of an object is decided; to reasoning corresponds liberty, the power to act or not to act. Facile and attractive as the analysis is, it makes one puzzle over what there was beyond its facility to convince men of its truth.

The obvious answer will be that Laromiguière had restored to the soul a certain autonomy which it seemed to lack in the reign of Condillac.[13] This meant, whether men understood it or not, a satisfaction of that egoism which reached its height in German phi-

[13] See Janet; *Op cit.* (p. 361): "L.'s title to fame in contemporary philosophy is to have restored to activity its true rôle in the human soul. I do not mean to say that he studied it as profoundly as it could have been studied, nor even that his discussion of the system of Condillac is as decisive as he thought. But is it not a great deal, after an entire century had repeated with Condillac that the human soul was only sensation, to return to the soul its independence, its initiative, the power to act or to react?" Cf. p. 366: "There are no innate ideas [in L.'s system] for all our feelings have their cause in experience; but the soul is not a *tabula rasa;* it is originally and essentially a force, an activity."

losophy and was soon to burst forth along with many other things in French romanticism. Why people should have demanded that their egoistic yearnings be satisfied, one can only answer with a guess. Perhaps it was the success of Napoleon and the Revolutionists before him, perhaps it was the increasing success of the natural sciences which, like these political successes, showed people that they could secure the independence of authority without incurring some enormous penalty—at least in this world. Be all this as it may, the assertion of the human will was fashionable at this time and people would listen to any philosopher who told them in technical language what they had heard only in the whisperings of their hearts.

By appointing Laromiguière to a chair in the Faculté des Lettres, the Emperor gave official sanction to a type of thinking which was his personal abomination. He had founded the University, he said, as a means of directing moral and political opinion. It was possible that he was not so aware as Fontanes was of the nature of Laromiguière's teachings. For it is hard to see how anything in the "Leçons" would make a man a better imperialist. Was Napoleon not misled by the subject matter of these courses into thinking that they were harmless? Laromiguière said nothing about politics and taught a mild form of idealistic ethics. As his most acute critic has said, his doctrine was rather a work of literature than of philosophy.[14] Yet his method was as dangerous to authori-

---

[14] Janet; *Op. cit.* 367. Cf. Mignet; "Not. historique sur la vie et les travaux de M. L." *Mem. de l'Inst.*, 1856, XXVI 84.

tarianism as that of his predecessors. He preached, as they did, introspection and the analysis of ideas. If the Second Class of the Institut was an organization harmful to the state, so was the doctrine of Laromiguière. Perhaps Napoleon suspected this after some time, for Laromiguière withdrew from his chair. No one has definitely discovered the exact cause of his withdrawal. Picavet, who has studied the case more thoroughly than most writers, hesitates to lay the blame upon the government, quoting Laromiguière's friend, Saphary, to the effect that sickness was the cause. It may very well have been sickness, but it is not to be forgotten that if Napoleon did not interfere with the liberty of teaching in this instance, it was one of the very few cases in which he did not.

III

The revolt against passivity shows itself most strikingly and most effectively in Maine de Biran, a man who begins as a disciple of the group at Auteuil and ends as a Christian mystic. As early as 1794 he said of himself, " I should like, if ever I were capable of undertaking anything continuous, to see how far the *soul is active,* how far it can modify external impressions, augment or diminish their intensity by the attention it gives them, examine to what extent it is master of attention." [15] He continued the search

[15] " Maine de Biran, Sa Vie et ses Pensées," P. 1857, 123. Hereafter " Pensées."

throughout his life, until he succeeded, according to Jules Simon,[16] in bringing about the ruin of the philosophy which had been dominant in France for the past fifty years.

Maine de Biran's interest in activity is practical. That is, he wished to find out how far the soul is active not for any epistemological end in itself, but in order to found upon his discoveries an ethics.[17] Moralists, he maintained, are persistently telling us to control our passions and direct our emotions, but they never justify their program by establishing the possibility of its realization. He for his part felt himself to be the prey of his thoughts and dreams, even though he was less passionate than other men.[18] He felt the need of a guiding philosopher.[19] "At times," he said,[20] "I feel myself burning for goodness, I adore virtue; at others I feel myself but lukewarm, I relinquish my hold and become indifferent to duty." If only there were some-

---

[16] " M. de B.," *Revue des Deux Monde* (hereafter *RDM*), 1841, IV 658. Cf. Ravaisson; " La Philos. en Fr. au dix-neuvième Siècle," 5ᵉ ed., P. 1904, p. 15 : " To re-discover activity under the passivity of sensations, which since Hume seemed to explain all. was to re-discover the spirit itself under the material world. Strengthened by this discovery, philosophy was soon to free itself from physics, under which Locke, Hume, and Condillac himself had, so to speak, crushed it. Two men especially aided in bringing this about: Maine de Biran and Ampère."

[17] " Pensées," 124.
[18] *Id.*
[19] *Id.* 126.
[20] *Id.* 128.

one to analyse the will as Condillac analysed the understanding![21]

But this could not be done, he maintained,[22] without an equal understanding of man's physical organism. He was convinced that the body counts for more than we usually suspect in the determination of our mental states, and, like a good disciple of Cabanis, he pictured to himself in his notebooks the possible physiological causes of certain of his moods.[23] "If we recognized that our troubled state, our state of anxiety, is almost purely physical, we should look upon it as an illness, and having tested that which can guarantee us or prevent us from falling into it so often, we should put these means into practice."[24] He insisted then upon the value of full self-consciousness, just as he would later on.

The thoughts indicated above were written in 1794 and 1795. At that time their author was administrator of the Dordogne. His time for study was limited and it was not until 1798 that he could return to his home and his reflections. These were then directed by the Institut's *concours* of 1799 to the question of " the influence of habit upon the faculty of thinking." It can be easily seen why this question was of a certain importance to the Idéologues. Habit is, they believed, that which makes us formulate general ideas, since it is the constant repetition of experiences which gradually

[21] *Id.*
[22] *Id.* 132.
[23] *Id.* 138.
[24] *Id.* 140.

forms our intellect; habit is the cement which binds our elementary sensations together. The quotation from Bonnet which Maine de Biran put at the head of the essay which he submitted, " What are all the operations of the soul but movements and repetitions of movements? " put the matter in a nutshell.

It was somewhat of a problem to account for activity in the behavior of a such a soul, for movements in the eighteenth century were looked upon as the continuation of previous movements whose origin went back at least to God. But Maine de Biran would content himself with something which stopped far short of absolute spontaneity. He was not as yet stubbornly advocating that each active soul is a first cause. He was satisfied if the soul could be shown to have merely some effect in the productions of consciousness. Thus, following Destutt de Tracy,[25] he maintains that active and passive states are fundamental and irreducible—a point of view like that of Laromiguière and Daube. One is passive in sensation or affection for " it is evident that [one] exerts no power on the modification, that one has no means at hand either to interrupt or to change it."[26] One is active in voluntary movement. " It is in truth *I* who create my modification, I can begin it, suspend it, vary it in every way, and the consciousness that I have of my activity is for me as evident as the modification itself."[27] Activity and passivity are thus again linked with the problem of causation.

[25] " Habitude," *Oeuvres,* ed. Tisserand, II 22 n. 1.
[26] *Id.* 20.
[27] *Id.* 21.

This problem was not so difficult for Maine de Biran as for us. He believed that we have an immediate consciousness of a causal operation when we exert effort.[28] It is effort which became the keynote of his whole philosophy; which revealed to him the secrets of the most trying problems of his day. But, as he developed, the concept of effort developed with him.

It is effort which explains why the resistance of the external world to our movements gives us an idea of its existence, an idea, it will be recalled, of Destutt de Tracy's. If we did not meet the resistance of physical objects with the force of our movements, they would no more exist for us than if they did not meet the force of our movements with their resistance. It is a situation like that expressed in Newton's third law of motion. There are two forces at work when we exert pressure on a physical object, our pressure and the object's resistance, both of which are needed to produce our consciousness of the object. As he says in a manuscript note to the Institut's copy of his memoir, " Effort is a mean term between the action and the effect, or between the motor force which be-

---

[28] *Id.* 25. Janet in " Un Précurseur de M. de B.," *R. Phil.*, 1882, XIV shows how much M. de B. may have owed to the obscure Rey Régis's " Hist. Naturelle de l'Ame," Montpellier 1789, not to be confused with Dr. Charp's (La Mettrie's) book of the same name. Like Régis Biran believes in (a) the psychical importance of effort, (b) the motive force of the soul as against the Cartesian doctrine of inertia, (c) the difference between the movement of our organs from without and from within (p. 371). He differs however in founding his whole psychology on effort; Régis sees in effort simply one psychic fact (p. 372).

longs to the individual and the resistance which *belongs to the body:* It is their means of communication." [29] Later on he reproduced this triad in the physical external world, the psychical internal world, and their means of communication, the Ego. Not to anticipate, he was here carrying a step further Destutt's attempted escape from subjectivism, by examining the fact of resistance to which Destutt had called attention and describing it in terms of inner experience.

In the second place, effort revealed to the individual his will. For movements which are performed without effort are involuntary unless they have become habitual. Whenever effort is exerted Maine de Biran believed that the will expresses itself and, he said in another development of Destutt, the human personality is revealed.

But even now he went to the extent of maintaining that in the activity of the will man perceives or knows, and that without this activity of the will, knowledge or perception would be impossible.[30] Thus he achieved that revolt from sensationalism which Destutt had begun but which people in general still maintain was to be undertaken. If it was not noticeable, it was because the Maine de Biran of the " Memoir on the Influence of Habit " had not as yet seen the metaphysical consequences of the doctrine. One who was living in the Ideological atmosphere could hardly have been expected to. But what he had begun to understand was that the analysis of consciousness into sensation and

[29] " Pensées," 25 n.
[30] *Id.* 26.

their products and something non-sensory in origin made further clarification necessary.

His opportunity came in the *concours* of 1803-1804, " How should we decompose the faculty of thinking and what elementary faculties should we see in it?" His memoir, which was crowned, discarded sensationalism once and for all. He had already distinguished two psychical elements, the active and the passive. He now proposed to give an introspective account of the active elements. The main fact, needless to say, which he discovered was " an actual exercise of certain organic instruments." He later amended this to read, " The primitive fact for us is in no wise a sensation alone, but the *idea* of a sensation, which takes place only insofar as the sensible impression concurs with the personal individuality of the Ego."[31] But here again he had not made a striking advance beyond the doctrines of Destutt, in spite of the general opinion of historians, for Destutt too had maintained that a sensation did not become a perception until it had excited activity. When Maine de Biran, moreover, maintained that " a being reduced [to passive sensibility] not only could not acquire any idea of objects external to him, but also could have no consciousness of his own sensitive being, that he would not be an individual person and that he could never say, ' I,' "[32] he was practically repeating what Destutt had said before in his " Traité d'Idéologie." And when he argued that self-consciousness, or consciousness of the Ego, can arise only

[31] " Fondements," I 39; *cf.* I 214.
[32] *Id.* I 23.

through the exercise of a "suprasensory and supra-organic" activity, an act of will which is beyond and above sensation,[33] he went back at least to Rousseau's argument in the "Profession de Foi du Vicaire Savoyard," to the epistemological importance of which he seems to have been blind.

At the risk of being more tedious than even scholarship requires, let us digress for a paragraph or two to clarify this historical matter. In the "Profession de Foi" Rousseau had argued among other things for a recognition of what he called the intuitive method. By the intuitive method he had proved to his own satisfaction that he existed and that he was affected by sensation, the cause of which was external to him. He then went on to say in an important passage,

"To perceive is to feel; to compare is to judge; to judge and to feel are not the same thing. By sensation, objects are given to me separate, isolated, such as they are in nature; by comparison I move them, I transport them, so to speak, I put them one upon the other to pronounce upon their difference or their likeness, and in general upon all their relations. According to me the distinctive faculty of the active or intelligent being is to be able to give some sense to this word 'is.' I look in vain in the purely sensitive being for this intelligent force which superimposes and which then pronounces judgment. . . . This passive being will feel each object separately, or it will even feel the total object formed of the two; but having no force to lay one against the other, it will never compare them, it will not judge them." "Comparative ideas," he continues, "greater," "less," for instance, "are certainly not sensations, although my mind produces them only on occasion of my sensations."

[33] *Id.*

It is because of the mind's activity that error is possible and communicated between individuals.[34]

So much would suggest Biran's point that the Ego is outside of sensations and "superior" to them. But Rousseau goes even further and distinguishes between motion imparted to an object and motion initiated by the object, and applies the distinction just as Biran

[34] The matter may be extended in a foot-note by the following quotation from the famous "Hermes" of James Harris (*Works of James Harris, Esq.*, new ed., Lond. 1803, II), originally produced in 1751. "By an Energy as spontaneous and familiar to its Nature, as the seeing of Color is familiar to the Eye, it [the soul] discerns at once what is MANY in ONE; what in things *Dissimilar* and *Different* is *Similar* and the *Same.*" (p. 361.) There follows a note, "This CONNECTIVE ACT of the Soul, by which it views ONE IN MANY, is perhaps one of the principal Acts of its most excellent Part. It is this removes that impenetrable mist, which renders *Objects of Intelligence* invisible to the lower faculties. Were it not for this, even the *sensible* World (with the help of all our Sensation) would appear as unconnected, as the words of an Index. It is certainly not the Figure alone, nor the Touch alone, nor the Odour alone, that makes the Rose, but it is made up of all these, and other attributes UNITED; not an *unknown* Constitution of *insensible* Parts, but a *known* Constitution of *sensible* Part, unless we chuse to extirpate the possibility of natural Knowledge.

"What then perceives this CONSTITUTION or UNION? . . . Can it be any of the Senses? . . . No one of these, we know, can pass the limits of its own province. Were the Smell to perceive the union of the Odour and the Figure, it would not only be Smell, but it would be Sight also. It is the same in other instances. We must necessarily therefor recur to some HIGHER COLLECTIVE POWER, to give us a prospect of Nature, even in these her *subordinate Wholes,* much more in that *comprehensive Whole,* whose sympathy is universal, and of which these smaller Wholes are all no more than Parts."

does, the first to sensations—passive modifications of the organism, the second to the will, which alone can cause movement. "In a word, all motion which is not produced by another can only come from a spontaneous voluntary act. Inanimate bodies act only by movement and there are no real actions without will. This is my first principle. I believe then that a will moves the universe and animates nature. This is my first dogma." When he is asked how he knows all this, he answers, "Only by immediate intuition."

Though Biran had read and written on the "Profession of Faith," he failed to see in it the statement of the very principles which he was later to discover for himself. On the contrary, his reflections on the "Profession" limit themselves strictly to questions of morality. He makes no comment whatsoever on the epistemological importance of the work.[35] His Rousseauist doctrines came more probably from Kant unless he thought them out entirely by himself. For we find him quoting with approval from Kant's early dissertation, "De mundi sensibilis atque intelligibilis forma et principiis," "An intellectual conception abstracts from everything sensible and is not abstracted from the sensible, and perhaps should more rightly be called ABSTRAHENS

[35] See "Premier Journal," *Oeuvres*, I. Nor have other writers up to the present. Even Alexis Bertrand, who sees the common master of Kant and Biran in Rousseau says that it is R.'s interest in the inner life which makes him their common master and not his theory of a transcendental ego. See "Psychol. de l'Effort," P. 1889, p. 32. Gertrude C. Bussey, in an article, "Anticipations of Kant's Refutation of Sensationalism," *Philos. R.*, 1922, XXXI 564, shows the similarity of Kt. and the Vicar.

than ABSTRACTUS," which he notes as the beginning of the whole critical philosophy.[36]

For Biran, then, the primitive fact of knowledge has become the Ego, which does not depend upon any sensory impression. It is *sui generis* and discovered by a peculiar inner sense. If the wrong sense is employed, the Ego will not be found. If other philosophers had not been too abstract and analysed the Ego way, or had not been too little abstract and had not failed to reach the Ego by analysis, they would have agreed with him, he says.[37]

[36] *Oeuvres Inédites,* I 306. He had two enthusiastic Kantians among his friends, Stapfer, the Swiss ambassador and Ampère. Yet A. wrote him in 1812, after having cited Kt. almost from the beginning of their correspondence, " You have no idea of Kt., which the ' Hist. des systèmes de philos.' and the work of Villers have thought only to disfigure for contrary motives. He was mistaken in his conclusions; but how profoundly did he note the fundamental facts and the laws of human intelligence! Blindly you go back in this respect to what MM. de Tracy and de Gérando say, who have treated him as Condillac treated Descartes and often Locke: twisted his expression to make him say the exact opposite of what he did say." (" Philos. des Deux Ampère," 2ᵉ ed., P. 1870, p. 297) Naville credits Stapfer with having introduced Biran to Kt; see his " M. de B., Sa Vie Intime et ses Ecrits," *RDM,* 1851, XI 259. Couailhac in his " M. de B." P. 1905, p. 291, says that Biran was ignorant of Kt. when he constructed his system. His use of a Kantian terminology does not prove a fundamental knowledge of Kant's works, for the Berlin Academy's announcement of its *concours* of 1807, in which he received honorable mention and a medal, makes use of such a terminology freely and Biran adopted it for himself. The general knowledge of Kant in France is discussed below in the text.

[37] " Pensées," 141, 142, 197.

THE FORTUNES OF IDEOLOGY 53

By 1805 Maine de Brian had made the acquaintance of Ampère, the physicist, whose correspondence and conversations were to prove so great an aid to him in formulating his philosophy. Ampère's metaphysical theories were begun, at least to a certain extent, in conversation with his Lyonnais friends, one of whom was a M. Roux, a Kantian from Geneva.[38] The correspondence between Ampère and Maine de Biran turned largely upon our knowledge of the Ego and its implications.

Ampère argued that "the sensitive system, insofar as there has been no effort, can give only sensations or intuitions and the images which they leave after them. . . . When there is effort, the consciousness of effort or *autopsia* (*i. e.*, self-consciousness) . . . furnishes a new element absolutely different from all others, which is perceived in distinction from them but in combination with them."[39] Throughout his letters there is a constant insistence upon the fundamentality of activity and passivity and on the intuition of the Ego in the experience of effort. They agree, said Ampère in 1805, on all points but one. Biran did not distinguish between the feeling of effort and the muscular sensation, whereas for Ampère they were utterly different.[40]

It is doubtless because of Ampère that Biran was led to emphasize the importance of the Ego in knowledge. For Biran came more and more to approach his friend's conceptions as time went on. He soon began to inter-

---

[38] "Deux Ampères, 197.
[39] *Id*. 207.
[40] *Id*. 200.

pret reality in egoistic terms. This seems to have been one of the tasks of his unfinished "Fondements de la Psychologie." It was a task analogous to the Kantian deduction of the categories. But whereas Kant's categories are not so much characteristics of the Ego as of its knowledge of the world, Biran's are simply the characteristics of the Ego transferred to the world. His categories are "substance," "cause or force," "unity," and "identity." They are, he thought, Locke's simple ideas of reflection which Locke had failed to analyse sufficiently. There are various ways in which they might be derived, one suspects. For instance, they might be as in Kant—if I read him correctly—the subject's uniform manner of understanding the world. Or they might be discovered in the world as a sort of egoistic projection. Or they might be created, as Fichte's non-Ego was created, for moral reasons. There are a number of possible explanations. But Biran leaves the question unanswered.

"We cannot follow in detail," he says,[41] "all the divers applications which the human mind makes of these two primary and regulative ideas [substance and force], transforming them to combine them with phenomena or images of things without. It is enough for us to have shown the true origin which they have in the primitive fact of consciousness, which is itself only the exercise of a particular sense, that of effort and of resistance. It is enough that one should conceive how these ideas, however much they may be removed from their source, may always be brought back to it by reflective analysis."

[41] "Fondements" I 253.

He contented himself with saying that the mind discovers its own durable, identical, unified, forceful character, intuitively and primitively, and thus authorizes itself to make use of such terms as "substance," "unity," "identity," and "cause."[42] As his editor, Naville, remarked, "He arrives at the redoubtable problems raised by Kant and passes over them as if he had not seen them."[43]

He was not without misgivings, however, for he said in his journal (1816), "I have been on a visit with my friend Ampère, who is ill. I discussed with him the passage from the consciousness of our activity, which gives us the first idea of a productive, efficient cause, to the belief in external causes. I thought formerly that it was enough to experience a passive impression of which the *Ego* had first been the cause, in order to relate immediately this passive impression to a foreign cause. I see to-day more difficulties in this, and I find between the individual feeling of the Ego's causality and the belief or universally necessary notion of cause, an abyss which cannot be crossed by the help of analysis alone and by analogy or induction, as I used to think. From this conception, 'I am not the cause of such a passive modification,' to this, 'There is necessarily a cause of all which is done without me,' there is no possible passage by reasoning. One can say only that it is natural that we should perceive or that we should conceive of things which do not depend on the Ego. . . . We exist as an Ego, or as an indi-

[42] *Id.* I 299.
[43] *Oeuvres Inédites,* I c.

vidual person only insofar as we are causes; it is then natural that we should be able to conceive of nothing or realise it outside of ourselves except in the same manner." [44]

In the meantime he was working steadily on special problems. His group of friends who formed a little Philosophical Society, Thurot, Degérando, Cuvier, Royer-Collard, Guizot, Ampère, and later Cousin, were meeting weekly.[45] At one time they debated the question whether sensations can be experienced without experiencing the Ego, Biran and Ampère taking the affirmative, Royer-Collard and Cuvier the negative.[46] At another time Royer-Collard and Guizot, although maintaining that the Ego is both subject and object for itself, yet maintain that it is an "object of belief (*croyance*)" "like all substances which we neither perceive nor feel by the intermediary of any sense, but which we believe to exist really and absolutely"; Maine de Biran on the other hand insists that this notion of absolute reality is a deduction from the primitive fact of experience.[47]

At the same time these questions begin to grow flat and stale and we find Biran, under the stimulus of Joseph de Maistre's "Essai sur le principe générateur et conservateur des sociétés politiques," admitting that the introspective method, by which he had set such store, has led him astray from questions of morals,

[44] "Pensées" 219.
[45] *Id.* 154.
[46] *Id.* 152.
[47] *Id.* 155.

questions which occupied his youth.[48] "How shall I derive from the principles of philosophy which I have followed moral obligation, duty?" he writes in 1815, while still working on the "Fondements"[49] and rejoicing over Napoleon's defeat at Waterloo. And when April weather sends his blood coursing through his veins, he who had once considered that ethics was closely related to medicine, now writes that his soul is tugging at the bodily tether. *"In interiore homine habitat veritas,"* he quotes from St. Augustine, and adds, "These experiences of an inner sense make me doubt whether there is a real action of the will on ideas or internal perceptions, or if the will, spreading itself over the organism, has not for its unique effect the repression of this organic influence and thus the obstruction of this obstacle to the intuition of the spirit."[50]

This was break enough with the Idéologues who believed the will to be nothing other than a kind of sensation. But soon we find Maine de Biran acknowledging the break.

"About fifteen years ago," he wrote in 1816, "seduced by the commendation of a learned socity, and yielding to the instigation and advice of several of its members who had the ascendency of age and fame upon me, I decided after long hesitation to have printed a work on habit, crowned by the class of moral and political sciences of the former Institut. This work is that of a young man in whom the imgination predominates over the reflection, who has almost no

[48] *Id.* 190.
[49] *Id.* 192.
[50] *Id.* 202.

idea of the difficulties and the first questions of the science which he is undertaking, who does not yet suspect our power of knowledge nor what we never know in the science of our own being, who trusts to hypothetical explanations of facts inexplicable in their nature, or which have no relation to the things imagined to explain them. Thinking about this more maturely, I have delivered a severe censure upon this premature production, and the painful feeling, the kind of shame which I attach to it, as to everything which shows signs of imperfection, has prevented me from publishing since this time three other memoirs crowned by learned societies, steadily waiting for greater maturity and perfection, in a system of ideas which I still feel to be quite incomplete. However, time is passing, life is gliding away, and I have arrived at the age when man feels that there is no further growth, no physical and intellectual progress to hope for, when he should hasten to make the best of what he has acquired which is soon perhaps to escape him by a series of imperceptible wanings. I do not wish to begin to die in my own eyes and in those of the intellectual world without having expounded the particular point of view from which I have seen the world, and the discoveries which I believe I have made since the publication of my essay on habit; I do not wish this imperfect work of my youth, without reflection and presumptuous in its ignorance, to remain as the sole title by which I shall be judged too unfavorably by the real metaphysicians who will read me, and, what I fear more, too much to the taste of young adepts who may be lost on my account in a path whose dangers and attractions I have recognized too late. It is my rigorous duty to point out the rocks against which I have stumbled and to indicate the surer route which has led me away from them." [51]

With the writing of this page in his journal, there is the composition of an article on Laromiguière for

[51] *Id.* 220.

the *Archives Littéraires* (July 1817), finally issued as a brochure, for the review judged it too long and too profound.[52] This again is an open statement of his divergence from the ideas which first inspired him. In it he attempts to prove that Laromiguière, in spite of his division of the faculties into active and passive, has really gone no farther than Condillac himself towards the justification of activity. He centers his attack on Laromiguière's theory of attention, denying that it is different from sensation. Real active attention is voluntary and free, he maintains, whereas Laromiguière's can be neither, since attention is a "reaction of the sensibility upon itself" and freedom and volition develop later.

The emphasis upon the spontaneity of attention is characteristic of Biran's thoughts at this time. His years of introspection and his early desire to see how far the soul is active, had bred in him a devotion to the non-material world typical of the mystic temperament. From wishing to see how far the soul is active, he had been led to see more and more activity in the

[52] It was reissued in 1829 along with an article by Cousin on the same subject, with the following publisher's announcement. "At a time when the partisans of M. Laromiguière join with the writers of the *Quotidienne* and the *Gazette* and with those of the materialistic party to attack, God knows with what weapons, the new philosophy, the violence of the pupils naturally attracts the attention to the principles of the master's system." Hence the publication of the brochure. It is not without interest to note that the followers of L. were still supposed to be the radicals, just as the followers of the older Idéologues had been. The "new philosophy" attacked both by them and the Catholics is, of course, Eclecticism.

soul, for he was becoming gradually more religious. We find him transforming his old metaphysical language into the language of Christian worship. He noted as early as 1811 moments in which his soul "exercised its faculties" with no organic obstacle, much as one might say that Aristotle imagined the soul to do in thinking about thought.[53] Six years later, after criticising the Stoics adversely for declaring that the reason can dictate its rules of conduct to the will, he decides that the will is *conscius et compos sui* and that its principles of action come from "something higher" than the reason.[54] He has gone another step a few months later when he declares not only that the human person is essentially dependent though willing, but that it is indescribable, ineffable. His friend, Morellet, has asked him, "What is the Ego?" And Maine de Biran, instead of answering, "That which we feel in muscular tension," writes, "I could not answer. One must put himself in the intimate point of view of consciousness and having then present this unity which judges all phenomena while remaining invariable, one sees the Ego; one no longer asks what it is."[55] It is perhaps superfluous to invite the reader's attention to the similarity between this passage and famous passages from Bergson.

By the next year Maine de Biran had gone so far as to point out what takes the place in his system of the mystic way. There are three stages to his journey

[53] "Pensées" 145.
[54] *Id*. 234.
[55] *Id*. 253.

of the human soul. In the first, man is nothing for himself and everything for his fellows; he thinks only of them and of the appearance he will make in their eyes. In the second, he separates himself from the external world in order to judge it, but he utilizes it nevertheless as the end of all his spiritual exercises. In the third, however, both the external world and self-interest drop out of view. The invisible world, God, becomes the object or goal of his thought. The two extremes meet. They meet in the lowest form of intellectual activity where there is no effort and consequently no Ego, and in the highest, where their individual's effort is lost in the person of God. The Ego is found between these terms. " The soul can find in itself, or in the thought of God, of the infinite, means of strength, of elevation, of peace which remain the same even when the machine grows weak and the whole organism bends before discouragement, sadness, ennui. There is whither one should aspire instead of surrendering, as I have done up to the present, to the instinctive impressions which make up my whole life, even my inner life. I have been giving in to the call of these impressions, I have found happiness in them alone; others have succeeded them; one must seek strength elsewhere. In my best moments until now I have been alone with myself. 'Poor counsel wherein God hath no place,' said Fénelon. The presence of God creates the way out of ourselves and that is what we need. How reconcile this with my psychological theory of the Ego?" [56]

[56] *Id*. 292.

He did not reconcile it. The effort which he first saw as a muscular strain developed into a mystical longing for something as far from the soul of man as the moon from the arms that reach for it. He was in the hands of that desire which would not give him peace. His voluntarism is but another expression of the *mal du siècle* which no discipline seemed able to cure. Maine de Biran hoped to cure it by his mysticism. He tried to lead what he called " the third life," which was the life directed by the faculty of love, still an effort but now an effort to attain repose in God.[57] In his early days he had thought to solve this problem by the addition of the life of volition to that of sensation; now he finds this solution inadequate. More and more he tries to lead his third life, cultivating " activity, meditation, and prayer," [58] that he may find the happiness which he has so long been seeking. At the very end of his days, two months before his death, he writes, " *Miserere mei, Domine, quoniam infirmus sum. . . . Lumbi mei impleti sunt illusionibus et non est sanitas in carne mea.* Wisdom, true strength, consists in walking in the presence of God, in feeling oneself sustained by Him; otherwise, *vae soli!* " [59]

That was the end of Maine de Biran's reflections. He had arrived at a goal which seemed antipodal to the point from which he had started. But he had arrived there by the consistent driving forward towards the happiness which his busy life had not been able to

[57] *Id.* 399, 411.
[58] *Id.* 414.
[59] *Id.* 220.

give him. For him philosophy was a practical means of regulating life, not of describing certain facts; he knew at the outset of his thinking the kind of return which he asked of it—spiritual repose. The problem was to find rational justification for it.

It was not his mysticism which was adopted by later thinkers. For one reason or another they did not go so far. Yet there is ground for legitimate suspicion that a voluntarism, like any other anti-rationalistic theory, ought to lead one near to mysticism if not directly to it. Ravaisson perhaps of all his readers came the closest to the same result. But even he stopped short of it.

It was on the contrary Maine de Biran's method of introspective analysis, in spite of his own confession of its impotency, which was of immediate consequence in French philosophies. In later days his emphasis upon the will became the more fertile doctrine. Yet these are both but fragments of the Biranian philosophy and are not, strictly speaking, representative of the whole. For his philosophy is not a body of propositions, a system, like Spinoza's. It is rather a drama. It is more to be compared to a Chinese painted scroll whose significance emerges as it is unwound, than to a simple wall picture of the West, which can be appreciated as a whole in a relatively small space of time. The meaning of the details in Biranism can be most truly interpreted only in relation to the rest of his life. They mean much more to him as a person than they do to the other details in his reflections.

The voluntarism of Maine de Biran is not like that of Nietzsche, the glorification of creative power. It may be true, as Picavet says in his article in the *Grande Encyclopédie,* that Biran was a voluntarist because he was physically a weakling. But his will is the will which struggles against the brute creation with no necessary hope of accomplishing anything beyond its own negation.

His influence made itself felt at first through his conversation in the Philosophical Society, for his work was not published to any great extent until Cousin's edition of 1841. His friends were fairly enthusiastic over him: Ancillon called him " notre maître à tous " ;[60] Cousin called him the most original of French thinkers.[61] Jules Simon found him half responsible for Royer-Collard's teaching,[62] although a reading of the " Pensées " would lead one to think that they seldom agreed in conversation. Sainte-Beuve points out how a Catholic, Father Gratry, the Positivists, the Eclectics, and Spiritualists like Ravaisson and Lachelier—whom he quotes to this effect—derive or could derive their philosophies from Maine de Biran.

" Pauvre Maine de Biran," he writes,[63] *" toujours en quête de son point d'appui qu'il ne put jamais recontrer ni atteindre, le voilà devenu, sans qu'il s'en soit douté, un guide en matière de certitude, un fondateur!"*

[60] *Oeuvres Inédites,* I lii.
[61] *Oeuvres Philos.* IV vi; " Premiers Essais," 3ᵉ ed., P. 1855, p. 19.
[62] *RDM,* 1841, IV 649.
[63] *Causeries du Lundi,* XIII 323 n.

IV

Ideology, if it led to little in philosophy, had two interesting effects upon literature. The doctrine of the analysis of sensations intensified the interest of writers in self-scrutiny and undoubtedly molded the genius of Stendhal; the physiological doctrines of Cabanis inspired a new genre of social satire.

Henri Beyle was educated in the ideological Ecole Centrale of Grenoble. His teacher of literature was an Idéologue, basing his work, the analysis of the art of thinking, on the ideas of Locke, Condillac, and Helvétius.[64] His teacher of logic carried out the program of "general grammar" prescribed by the preface of Destutt's "Traité," using the text-books of Lancelot, Bauzée, Dumarsis, Condillac, and Harris's "Hermes."[65] How orthodox was his teaching can be seen in his remarks on the distribution of prizes of the Year VI. "General grammar," he said, "is the reasoned science of the general and immutable principles of language . . . its study is founded upon that of logic, or rather it is itself true logic. . . . The acuteness which this study communicates to the mind, the habit it gives of combining and comparing ideas, binds it intimately to mathematics and by it to all the exact sciences."[66]

Beyle's interest in Ideology grew. In 1802 he sent to his mistress a copy of Condillac's "Logic"[67] and he wrote in his "Life of Henri Brulard" that about this

---

[64] See Arbelet; "La Jeunesse de Stendhal," P. 1919, I 264.
[65] *Id.* 281.
[66] *Id.* 282.
[67] *Id.* 283. N. 1.

time he wished to become a philosopher. " I read a great deal . . . the tragedies of Alfieri, forcing myself to find pleasure in them. I revered Cabanis, Tracy, J-B. Say. I often used to read Cabanis whose vague style cut me to the quick (*me désolait*)."[68] He found in Cabanis's account of the "melancholy temperament" a portrait of himself.[69] He found in Destutt de Tracy a guide to right thinking,[70] and regretted that he was never successful in pleasing either him or Madeleine Pasta, about both of whom he was enthusiastic.[71] He hated the "empty ideas of Plato, Kant, and their school"[72] and their *"phrases louches"* almost as much as he hated Chateaubriand, "that king of egoists."[73]

M. Delacroix in his "Psychologie de Stendhal" has already shown with what fidelity Beyle utilized the teachings of Cabanis in his psychology of art, love, and of "human temperaments." Thus he based the experience of musical beauty on the tension of nerves in the ear.[74] "The so touching virtue preached by the so beautiful phrases of the 'Génie du Christianisme' is reduced to not eating truffles from fear of having cramps in the stomach."[75] But it goes without saying that he does more than slavishly reproduce the ideas

[68] " Henri Brulard," I 12.
[69] *Id*. I 17, 137, 269.
[70] *Id*. I 239; II 60.
[71] *Id*. II 24, 67.
[72] " Promenades dans Rome," P. 1829, I 241.
[73] " H. B." I 6; cf. pp. 7, 242, 269, 310.
[74] Delacroix; p. 188.
[75] " De l'Amour," P. 1822, II 154.

of his masters in his novels and essays. Their influence on him is of a more general nature.

He might be said, that is, to belong to the ideological tradition though he is more than an Idéologue. He employs, for instance, psychological analysis. But psychological analysis is found in French literature at least as early as Montaigne and has continued through Marcel Proust to our contemporaries. What differentiates Beyle's analysis from that of his predecessors is the theory of knowledge which is its foundation. His peculiar gift of selecting the correct sensation at the most telling moment is nothing short of amazing and accounts in large measure for the irony of many of his passages. Montaigne, after all, was interested in his own reactions to the world. Beyle is interested in writing a novel. One would be very rash to say that he wrote the " Chartreuse de Parme " for other than literary reasons, for he had none of the pretensions of a Zola. His use of ideology is directed towards a literary end. It is doubtful whether he would even have maintained the analytic pose had he not found it amusing. He said himself often enough that he was writing not for his own day but for 1935. Ideology for him was a study in disillusion showing him of what clay our loftiest notions are built and giving him that crackling style and mild contempt for his more romantic characters which are exactly the literary gifts which we most admire to-day.

He joins to his analysis of sensation an admiration for activity which carries him beyond Ideology. Beyle's characters do not languish in mountain retreats nor meditate beside flowing waters. They are forever dashing about energetically, as often as not to no end. It is as if their author felt that the lowliness of sensations could be balanced by loftiness of will. At any rate his enthusiasm for Napoleon and his disgust for himself are perhaps expressed in the youthful Julien and Fabrice whose age is no obstacle to their ambitions. The comedy hidden in Destutt's theory of resistance and effort is here brought into the open. The author of the "Chartreuse de Parme" is not blinded by the dust of battlefields and broad highways. He loves the action that takes place upon them, but he can evaluate it.

The fundamental paradox in Destutt's theory is that we learn of the existence of the external world by the resistance it gives our efforts to understand it. A paradox may be either sublime or grotesque. Beyle was great enough to accentuate the grotesqueness of the situation. He not only constructed his two major novels with a fundamental contrast, but developed individual scenes after the same pattern. One could hardly maintain that either Julien or Fabrice were inherently interesting people. They belong to the family of heroes whose English branch descends from Ernest Pontifex, if not from Tom Jones. Unfortunately for the interest of this book, we cannot trace their progeny in France.

Almost contemporaneous with "De l'Amour" (1822), whose author called it "un livre d'idéologie," appeared Brillat-Savarin's "Physiologie du Goût" (1825), which is about as physiological as "De l'Amour" is ideological. Its author, surely one of the most accomplished writers of any country, prides himself on his knowledge of medicine and physiology. His physiological notions came from Cabanis's disciple, Richerand. It would be pitiable to maintain that his famous aphorisms, " Tell me what you eat and I will tell you what you are," and " The discovery of a new dish does more for the happiness of humankind than the discovery of a star," are based on any deep conviction of a metaphysical nature. Yet they do reveal the same general attitude towards the world as that of the man who voiced the equally exaggerated opinion, that " the brain in a way digests impressions; it secretes thought organically." [76]

The " Physiologie du Goût " is the beginning of a long series of " Physiologies," including Balzac's " Physiologie du Mariage " (1828), which was a direct imitation, and Sophie Gay's " Physiologie du Ridicule." The series broadened out in the '40's with twenty or thirty physiologies, of the butcher, the baker, the candlestick-maker. They were the type of literature foreshadowed in La Bruyère's " Characters," except that where La Bruyère's types were psychological, the types of the physiologies were economic, a difference between the seventeenth and nineteenth centuries which is not insignificant.

[76] Cabanis; "Rapports," p. 123.

CHAPTER THREE

THE NEO-CHRISTIANS

During the Revolution, while the Idéologues were elaborating their theories in France and developing their practical consequences, the partisans of the old régime sat in a ring about their mother country awaiting their return to power and justifying it in their books. In England, in Holland, in Switzerland, in Germany, they plotted and schemed and allied themselves with the enemies of France until they saw how useless such action was. Then they began to put their ideas into writing. In 1796 and 1797 arose a new group of literary productions which were to do for the counter-revolution what the Philosophers had done for the Revolution.[1]

In Hamburg Mallet du Pan produced his "Correspondance politique," and Rivarol, the Abbé de Pradt and others collaborated on the *Spectateur du Nord*. At Neuchâtel appeared Joseph de Maistre's "Considérations sur la Révolution Française," not the work of a Frenchman, but very influential in the counter-revolution. At Constance appeared the Vicomte de Bonald's "Théorie du Pouvoir," a book which Sainte-Beuve says had very little effect at the moment of its appearance, although its author went so far as to beseech Siéyès to

[1] See Sainte-Beuve; "Causeries du Lundi" (hereafter *CL*) IV 429.

give it publicity by denouncing it if necessary.² The whole edition was sent to Paris and there seized by order of the Directory,³ but the book was well known among the group to whom it was addressed and helped establish its author as one of the leaders of the Catholic royalists. There is a legitimate suspicion that all these productions were by no means the spontaneous outbursts of the *émigrés*. Louis XVIII had a finger on events and a firm finger. One has only to read the correspondence between him and Joseph de Maistre to see how in at least one instance he directly inspired what was written.⁴

But Bonald was to win the reputation not so much of a political scientist as of a philosopher.⁵ His bitter acrid style was not such as could win the hearts of his fellows, as Lamennais's could, nor dazzle his opponents, as Maistre's could. But he did have the power of presenting his ideas systematically and of giving them the appearance of fact.

Philosophically he feels at one with the great Catholics of the Middle Ages. Like them he believes that that which is unified and permanent is that which alone commands respect. The multiple and the changing are not mere appearance; they are evil.⁶ This point

² *Id.* IV 430 n. 1. This is accepted as true by Moulinié; "De Bonald," P. 1915, p. 29 n. 4.

³ *Not. Biographique,* in Bonald; *OC,* P. 1864, I viii.

⁴ See Ernest Daudet; "Lettres Inédites de Joseph de Maistre," *RDM* 1907, p. 604. See esp. p. 607.

⁵ Bonald; *OC* I xlvii.

⁶ Cf. the Abbé Lantaigne in Anatole France's "L'Orme du Mail," ch. XIII. This as a philosophic formula goes back at

of view precedes his exposition; it is a postulate which he lays down before any argument is begun. But having been laid down, it leaves merely the task of unfolding its implication and articulating its hidden meaning.

The postulate is essentially that of Dante in his "De Monarchia." But whereas Dante could afford to be generous to the inventor of metaphysics, Bonald agrees with Degérando, that the only art which he had neglected to teach was that of discovering the truth.[7] Bonald had no need of going behind Church tradition to authorize his eleatic conception of power. And as he hated to do so, he did not.

If the highest being in the world is one and if those powers which make for unity alone make for righteousness, obviously the real business of the lover of wisdom is to combat both the ideas and the practices of believers in multiplicity. The One alone is good. Hence to reach truth we must synthesize, not analyse as the Idéologues had preached. We must study the Whole, not the parts; society, not the individual; the absolute, not the relative.[8] "Truth," says Bonald, "like men and like society, is a seed which grows in the succession of ages and of men, always ancient in its beginning, always new in its sequential developments."[9] Because men have disre-

---

least to the Pythagoreans. See the *Nichomachean Ethics,* Bk. II ch. vi, ἐσθλοὶ μὲν γὰρ ἁπλῶς παντοδαπῶς δὲ κακοί.

[7] "Recherches Philosophiques," *OC* III 8.

[8] Cf. "De la Politique et de la Morale," *OC* III 794.

[9] "Legislation Primitive," *OC* I 1199.

garded this fundamental of philosophy, they have slipped into the errors of individualism, materialism, atheism.

Truth in the beginning is ancient and in the end is new because it is eternal. It was revealed at a single moment by God, not through continual inspiration, as Bonald feels that Protestants believe, but in the sense that definitely and historically He has revealed Himself to man and that the tradition of that revelation has been handed down in the faith of the synagogue and church.[10] It would seem at first sight as if this contradicted the thesis that truth develops like a seed. And indeed by emphasizing the development of truth much trouble ensued for some of Bonald's readers. Truth develops like a seed, but to a scholastic mind—as to an Aristotelian mind—a seed can develop in only one way, a way determined by the final cause which is the plant. Thus truth could both develop and be eternal.

It is worth noting the striking similarity between the doctrines of Hegel and of Bonald.[11] Both were devel-

[10] " Princ. Const.," *OC* I 17; cf. " Enchiridion " 1623.

[11] See Ed. Quinet; " De la Philosophie et de la Révolution," *RDM* 1831, IV 468. Bonald himself objects to German philosophy which he calls German "rationalism." It errs, he thinks, as French "empiricism" errs, in "wishing to accomplish everything with man alone. The one wishes to compose everything, even the physical world, out of the reason; the other to compose everything, even the moral world, out of sensations. That is, under other names, idealism and materialism. But it must be noted that the German, with his rationalism, is more dependent than the Frenchman on feelings and desires." (" Rech. Philos." *OC* III 25 n. 2).

oped contemporaneously by men interested in not dissimilar societies. Both were defences of monarchy and both firmly asserted that the individual is real only as a member of society. Both saw, moreover, a social meaning to truth, which followers of Hegel have made so much of, and its eternality. The really basic difference between the two men is Hegel's Protestant and Bonald's Catholic background. With the Protestant bent towards self-scrutiny in the search for truth, made philosophical, if you choose, by Kant, Hegel was able to affirm literally the participation, not to say absorption, of every individual in God. To have struck this mystic note would have been impossible for Bonald whose religion needed a God above the world. The tradition which made a kind of mysticism natural for the Protestant made it an abomination for the Catholic. It would have been strange had Bonald done otherwise.

The barriers between men break down, in Bonald's opinion, when we understand that they exist as social creatures. They are then seen to be simply the elements in a greater whole which, in a manner made familiar to us by the Hegelians, gives them their meaning. For that reason Bonald is careful to point out that the life of man in society is neither the result of superimposed force nor of a social contract, as his eighteenth century opponents had taught. It is implied in the laws of nature;[12] it is necessary because it is natural. The life of man becomes what society makes it; for society like a mother receives the germs of talent from nature;

[12] "Princ. Const." *OC* I 47.

she develops them, making her members artists, poets, orators, moralists, scientists.[13] This is not meant as a metaphor. Just as Hegel speaks literally of the Oriental, the Classical, the Germanic societies as literal expressions of the freedom of the despot, of the demos, and of Man, respectively, so Bonald speaks of Jewish, Pagan, and Christian societies as literal expressions of pure theocracy, pure humanism, and the proper balance between the two.[14] But whereas Hegel held that this was a logical development, Bonald thought that the difference was attributable to the wickedness of the Pagans and the Jews and that there had been no development whatsoever. In fact Bonald is much more Augustinian in his philosophy of history than his German contemporary, and, as far as we have seen, reads into its processes no law. Change for him is real, but it is avoidable and is always bad. In the eternal all change disappears and all ages are but one. Since the present always conserves some of the past, as he says in a startling half-anticipation of Bergson,[15] one never really passes out of any epoch into any other.

[13] " Reflect. sur l'hist. de J-B. Bossuet," *OC* III 933.
[14] " Legis. Prim.," *OC* I 1085. Cf. the three ages of power in the hist. of Fr., the personal, the public, and the popular. ("De la Manière d'écrire l'hist." *OC* III 1062.) Bonald's friend, Maistre, duplicates curiously enough Hegel's notion of a necessary evolution through thesis, antithesis, and synthesis, in his "Du Pape," liv. IV, ch. iii, where he says that the schismatic churches are farther from the truth than the Protestant, " for the latter have completed their circle of error, whereas the others have merely begun it and must consequently pass through Calvinism, perhaps even socinianism, before getting back to unity."
[15] " De la manière d'écrire l'hist.," *OC* III 1063.

As the personality of the individual melts into that of society, a process of perfection and not of elimination, so the very ideas by which man thinks are realized in that common social thought which is language. This means on the one hand that there is no truth within the individual, either in mystic contemplation or in Kantian self-analysis; and on the other hand it means that the opposition of one man to the opinion of society will be interpreted not as lofty devotion to insight, but as stubborn pigheadedness. Ideas are without the individual, much as the empiricists had said, but they are not without society. Society is a being in which ideas are innate for the individual to discover. They are interwoven into the very texture of society and social experience reveals them to man when he lives according to the laws of nature.[16]

They are revealed to man in his thinking, and since thinking is impossible without language and language without thought, Bonald treats ideas much as most people would treat words. It is of course the meaning of words and not the sound of which he is thinking. Sounds for him, it must be said to his credit, are no more ideas than images are. Thinking, according to his psychology, is internal speech.

From this follows the celebrated theory of the origin of language, which at the time had profound political and religious consequences.[17] Briefly, since we cannot think without words, we could not have thought of a

[16] "Légis. Prim.," *OC* I 1066.
[17] *Id.* I 1063.

language before having one. Hence we could not have invented it.[18] And since the expressions of one faculty of the soul cannot be employed by another, language could not have been evolved from gestures or inarticulate cries, as the Idéologues believed.[19] The thinking soul imagines, understands, and feels. But to express an image is to make a drawing or a gesture, to reproduce one's experience for the benefit of someone else; to express a feeling—by which Bonald means pleasure or pain—is to laugh or weep, to shudder, to recoil, and the like; to express an idea is to write or speak a word. Thus one speaks his thoughts, says Bonald, but speaks *of* his images and feelings. One cannot laugh an idea nor draw an emotion, although laughter and drawing may excite ideas or emotions and may be excited by them.[20] Contrariwise, animals, who have no intelligence, do not speak, but they have images and feelings for they give vent to cries and make gestures.[21] Language then could not have devolped from the use of the faculties other than thought, nor, since it is required for invention, could it have been invented.

It is interesting to observe, if one may digress for a moment, that for Bonald only those entities are mental which are the private property of individuals, which are a function so to speak of human nature. To him the color *red* could never be mental, though it might affect our minds through our bodies as clear or

[18] " Rech. Philos.," *OC* III 64.
[19] *Id.* 172.
[20] *Id.* 174.
[21] " Sur la pensée de l'homme," *OC* III 426.

muddy, light or dark, agreeable or disagreeable. It is important not to forget this in reading Bonald, for it is what makes him so pre-eminently a scholastic and an opponent of Locke and his disciples, the Condillacists. By focussing psychology upon the effect of the outside world on the individual, they easily focussed the imagination of the public upon the same thing, and it was no long road from sensationalism to complete self-interest. If all was to be sensation, as the hated Idéologues had seemed to say (in their own words " feelings ") the noble world of ideals was to be given up for that of the inner life, and even the inner life was to degenerate into a conglomeration of vulgar colors, sounds, tastes, and the like. This consequence was seen by Bonald and expresses itself throughout his works. In speaking, for instance, of Mme. de Staël, apologist of the pre-consular Revolution and of the Idéologues, he says, " Brought up in the opulence and purple of the Cabinet, given over to the strongest deductions which high society has for women of intelligence, she is much too disposed to see only the brilliant side of men and things, to find happiness in splendor, life in agitation, reason in the successes of the wit."[22] This was, he continues, the outcome of her psychology, individualistic and Protestant.

To return to the theory of language, Bonald was glad to find a mystery at the origin of that which alone could give mankind personality and value. For if it is a mystery, there can be but one explanation of it, the super-

[22] " Observations sur l'ouvrage de Mme. de Staël," *OC* II 608.

natural one. To explain supernaturally seems much less mysterious to some people than to admit one's ignorance, and Bonald relieved his strain by attributing the origin of what he could not explain to the Omnipotent. Language, which with thought forms twin stars revolving one about the other, is created by God, breathed into the first man as a revelation, and passed on by him to his descendants.

If knowledge in its deepest aspects was directly and entirely revealed to the first man, is it not in the traditions of the race that all truth is to be found?[23] That seemed a consequence and the contemporaries and successors of Bonald were not slow to make that consequence explicit. Accordingly when Lamennais began to formulate his doctrine, as we shall see later, it seemed at the time as if he had his strongest support in Bonald. But the theory of Traditionalism was held to deprive men of innate ideas and the Church needed innate ideas. Bonald lived to see Lamennais condemned by Gregory XVI for his Indifferentism and twenty-one years later Pius IX condemned Bonetty for Traditionalism.[24] What Bonald's reaction to this last event would have been we do not know, but his son indignantly repudiated the idea of his father's having founded a heresy.[25] He admitted that his father's language may have seemed

[23] Cf. Bonald's brief statement of the tenets of what Damiron called "the theological school" of philos. in "Princ. Const." *OC* I 6.
[24] "Enchiridion" 1613; 1649.
[25] "M. de Bonald et le Traditionnalisme," *Corresp*. XXXV 288.

to lend support to the doctrine, but said that in reality it did not. For he believed that man was more than *un être enseigné;* in his soul were written the law of God and moral truths, which were awaiting language to make them intelligible. And indeed in the " Recherches Philosophiques " (*OC* III 24), he seemed to say that they were innate within the individual and not merely in society as he had said elsewhere. But he had also said that deaf mutes do not have ideas until they can write; he believed than an idea unspoken was hardly an idea. His son had apparently little effect in convincing people of his father's orthodoxy, for two years after his article appeared, Charles de Rémusat wrote another in which he took for granted what the young nobleman had tried to disprove.[26]

Bonald will always stand with Maistre as joint leader of the Catholic and monarchical counter-revolution. The way had been prepared, however, by the restoration of the cult, due in large measure to the work of Camille Jordan, Royer-Collard, and perhaps Portalis;[27] by the Concordat and its consequences. But Bonald more than anyone else rationalized authority and national solidarity, thus pretty effectively checking the republicans and other political individualists. Napoleon appreciated his value and made advances to him which he made to no one else. As First Consul he had offered to reprint the " Théorie du Pouvoir " at his own expense;[28] as

[26] " Du Traditionalisme," *RDM* IX 51.

[27] Tony Bouillet; " Le Rétablissement du Culte Catholique en 1797," *Corresp.* 1879, LXXX.

[28] Moulinié; " De Bonald " 30.

Emperor he had protected him from the zeal of Fouché; withdrew him from surveillance; offered him the editorship of the *Journal de l'Empire* (formerly the *Journal des Débats*) and a position on the Council of the University.[29] But Bonald refused all these offers. Strange as it may seem, he remained in the Emperor's good graces. When Daunou, the Idéologue, refused a position as Councillor of State, the Emperor thundered, "Don't think that it's because I love you that I offer you this place; it's because I need you."[30] But when Lucien Bonaparte requested Bonald's empty place for one of his friends, the Emperor replied through Fontanes, "This place is reserved for M. de Bonald."[31] Bonald, after waiting two years longer for the return of Louis XVIII, gave in and took his seat, thus earning for himself an undeserved place in the "Dictionnaire des Girouettes." Daunou, an organizer and an analyst, might be necessary, but he was inherently an opponent; his whole philosophy was radically hostile to the imperial régime. Bonald's on the contrary, was philosophic imperialism, and Napoleon knew that to have him as a friend was to have an official apologist, and one of high order who believed in what he excused.

Faguet called Bonald the last of the Scholastics.[32] He

[29] *Id.* 35, 36 n. 3, 37.
[30] Picavet; "Idéologues," 403 n. 1.
[31] Bonald; *OC* I xiv, *Not. Biographique*.
[32] "Politiques et Moralistes du 19ᵉ Siècle," P. 1890, 1er sér., p. 70. B. is not Aristotelian however. We have seen what he thought of Aristotle, who "lowered the human mind by rejecting the theory of innate ideas." ("Rech. Philos." *OC* III

was obviously not the last, but he was—as we have said above—a scholastic in temperament and purpose. Like Saint Thomas, he could hold that members of a state make up one body and the whole community one man.[33] Though he never went to the extremes of Nicholas of Cusa, who made a careful study of the anatomy of the *corpus mysticum* in which the papacy is the soul in the brain, the patriarchate the soul in the ears and eyes, and so on, nevertheless he could have taken over such metaphors without doing violence to his system. Indeed, he probably would have taken them over if he had read widely enough to know them.[34] He would have found in medieval political scientists traditional justification of the Emperor's catechism, for had it not been said by Baldus de Ubaldeis, "The Emperor is lord of the

---

7.) Plato, he felt, though very imperfect in matters of political science, was "endowed with the sublimest qualities of the mind and the happiest gifts of the imagination." (*Ib.*) It is to the neo-Platonic tradition that B.'s scholasticism is allied. To him there is no time in God's world; all proceeds by an emanation from above, sovereignty, power, the values, life itself. He objects to the phrase, "Man is a rational animal," and substitutes for it, "Man is an intelligence served by organs." This intelligence is ultimately distinct from its organs. To Aristotle the absolute gulf between the soul and the body had not occurred, and, although the soul was that for which the body existed, it was all the more closely connected with the body on that account.

[33] "Summ. Theol." II i q. 81, a. 1.

[34] Nowadays scholarship has made wide reading unnecessary. One has only to peruse the notes to Gierke's "Political Theories of the Middle Age," tr. by F. W. Maitland, Camb. 1913. See p. 24.

whole world and God on earth," and by Dietrich of Niem, "To the Emperor is due devotion as to the present and corporeal God"?[35]

Even the more modern parts of Bonald's philosophy are not utterly original. His theory of language, the pride of his bosom, was anticipated.[36] His hated Rousseau had expressed before him the formula, "Speech seems to have been very necessary to have established the usage of speech;"[37] Condillac, in a passage which Rousseau's formula was invented to refute, had linked thought and speech together.[38] As for the divine origin of language, that was almost a commonplace.[39]

[35] *Id.* n. 122 to p. 141.

[36] Cf. Moulinié, 217-226; Damiron; "Essai sur l'hist. de la philos. en Fr. au dix-neuvième siècle," P. 1828, p. 161. Rémusat, in his article on traditionalism mentioned in the text (p. 50), thinks that Vico and Herder also had a hand in it.

Saint-Martin, curiously enough, from Rousseau's premise deduced a non-theological theory. In his famous debate in the Ecole Normale with Garat and in the memoir which he submitted to the *concours* on the influence of signs, he elaborated R.'s idea. He had recourse to a theory that all animals have a gift of expression and that man's is speech. As man has developed, his means of expression has developed. And it will continue to develop until it has reached the point where abstractions and definitions, invariable and regular constructions, will be substituted for the direct impressions made upon us by the vivid world of nature. Then development will be at an end. See Franck; "La Philos. Mystique," ch. iv.

[37] "Discours sur l'inégalité," *OC* Lyon 1796, I 82, esp. p. 88.

[38] "Logic," P. An VI, p. 125.

[39] See Court de Gebelin; "Monde Primitif," P. 1774, II xiii; III 66; Sicard; "Cours d'Instruction d'un Sourd-Muet de Naissance," P. An VIII, xviii; Hugh Blair in the sixth lecture of his "Lectures on Rhetoric," tr. into French in 1783; Harris

Bonald's philosophy is the expression of what is presupposed by Catholic monarchism. From the doctrines suggested above, it is easy to see how an absolute monarchy might be defended or even deduced. As a matter of fact, these doctrines in time come after the ideas they imply and stand, as it were, for formulas abstracted from practice. It is not difficult in a history to rearrange them, so that it looks as if they were Bonald's starting point. But the contrary is the truth. His political theory preceded his epistemology and it was his political theory which was most seductive to his friends. It was the platform of their class. All his life he had lived in a royalist atmosphere. His soul was so inextricably mingled with the soul of the Bourbons that he was unable to tear it loose even to serve their equal in absolutism. There could be no inner struggle for him to make his inclinations fit his ideas; his inclinations were his ideas.[40]

---

in his "Hermes" II 360. Even Mme. De Staël, surely no friend of popes and Catholic tradition, had no difficulty in assigning a divine origin to language. See "Allemagne," Pt. III ch. vii.

[40] The usual points of interest about Bonald, his passion for triads, his views on divorce and free speech, his severity towards wrong-doers, his revival of the idea of trial by God— not very far from that of Ordeal, are out of place here. They can be found in almost every other treatment of Bonald. See Moulinié's excellent study; Mr. Harold Laski's essay in his "Authority in the Modern State, "New Haven, 1919, which seems to me to follow Moulinié fairly closely; Faguet's résumé and appraisal of the whole system in the "Politiques et Moralistes." Jules Simon in "Philosophes et Publicistes Contemporains," *RDM* 1841, XXVII 509 writes feelingly against him, though he appreciates the nobility of his character. See esp. p. 540.

One can say the same of Joseph de Maistre. In his youth a frequenter of the Lyonnais mystics, the Grand Orator of a lodge of Masons,[41] he became a rigid Catholic after the Revolution. Like Bonald he wrote his first book in exile, for he fled from the revolutionary armies when they entered his native Savoy. These two men, who recognized the kinship of their ideas, scarcely wrote a line in contradiction of each other. They took up their pens at the same time to rationalize their hatred of revolution—which was the first appearance of evil in their theology—and to prophesy the return of the Bourbons.

Like Bonald, Joseph de Maistre shrinks from the temporal into the eternal, from the mutable into the unchanging. His philosophy is again that passionate eleatic cry which would have warmed the heart of the vehement Xenophanes. He makes no claim, indeed, that change does not exist; but he is sure that it is evil. Change is a departure from the original perfect pattern; the Greeks were right in putting the Golden Age at the beginning of history; the rest is degeneration.[42] "Man," he says,[43] "is subject to time and nevertheless is by nature a stanger to time. He is at the point where the idea even of eternal happiness, linked with that of time, "tires him and frightens him." Again, prophets who "enjoy the privilege of emerging from time" see the truth, and dreams, in which we have no idea of time

[41] Cogordan; "Joseph de Maistre," P. 1894, p. 17.
[42] "Soirées de Saint-Petersbourg," 9th ed., Lyon et P., 1867, I 98 and 79.
[43] "Soirées," II 273.

(Maistre *loquitur*), are the occasion for revealing to us divine communications."

In so saying, Maistre is at one with the Christian philosophers of history from Saint Augustine to Bossuet. To the Christian time, with its attendant change, can never be productive of good. The good is a judgment pronounced at the dawn of the world on the world as then existing. Change was brought about in human times by man's deliberate disobedience. Had Adam not eaten of the forbidden fruit, man would have lived in a state of permanent perfection, which it would have been folly to modify. Life was then the Platonic idea of life, realized here below, just as man was the image of God. Eden was the terrestrial Paradise, the Kingdom of God on earth. That Kingdom was beyond the reach of time and change. It is the return to it which animates man's moral life.

It is significant that the introduction into the world of evil should have come through disobedience. Bonald and Maistre both see in it the source of everything which is bad. It is better to obey a wicked order than to revolt, they maintain. For even a wicked order is an expression of authority and authority is divine. Cruel as this may seem and be, it is quite in accord with the grand postulate of the system.[45] For above all

---

[44] *Id.* 276.

[45] Loyson is quoted in Damiron, *Op. cit.* 178, as saying that, if Bonald and Maistre were right in their philosophies, " God would have said to man, when He put him in society, ' I am establishing you in a condition which should make you at once both better and happier; I am giving you an absolute master who is responsible to me alone for his conduct to you; but if

THE NEO-CHRISTIANS 87

things, it is authority which conserves, which holds change in restraint, which is most closely analogous to God, the unmoved mover. The mere contemplation of long dynasties, of enduring institutions, is a delight to such minds as these and one can almost feel Maistre's joy as he writes, "No human institution has lasted eighteen centuries," and thus implies the divinity of the Church.[46] Since authority is an opponent of change, it is good; since disobedience is an opponent of authority, it is bad.

Maistre here voices a reaction to the world which is probably elemental. The spectacle of a changing universe has depressed mankind from the days of Heracleitus and before. The poetry of Western Europe is full of these laments, and one can almost generalize and say that not until the eighteenth century did men in any numbers look upon change as a blessing, as an opportunity for creation or progress. Before the doctrine of evolution had seeped down to the mass of the people, change was the destroyer, not the producer, and although there were many men to bewail the permanence and duration of things, there were none to rejoice over their destruction.

The precursors of our contemporaries who rejoice in change were undoubtedly those optimists among philosophers and political scientists who believed in the steady

---

he makes for your ill fortune—I shall hold you guilty for punishing him.'" Maistre's hatred of the Revolution is not stimulated by the slaughter it entailed, for War is divine ("Soirées" II 35) but by the disruption of dynastic continuity.
[46] "Du Pape," Concl. xii.

and infinite perfectibilty of the human species. They were, however, the very men whose teachings were so friendly to the event of all others which Maistre found monstrous, the French Revolution. These men were the Anti-Christians and above all, the Anti-Catholics, of whom Condorcet is as good an example as one could find. Such people saw no solace in the endurance of the *status quo*. The *status quo* to them was but a stage in the great movement toward the realization of perfection. Every year is a step forward; every age is better than the age before. And Condorcet, though he had to poison himself to avoid falling into the hands of the newest and best régime, spent his last days hymning its glories and the greater glories which were to come.

The hatred of change is but one side of Maistre's philosophy. Joined to it is his hatred of diversity. Just as the eternal is the good, so is the one the good; the temporal and the many go hand in hand. In the " Soirées de Saint-Pétersbourg " (II 113), he insists that our sense of numbers and order are proofs of God's existence, so holy is the tie which binds. Or again, " The more one examines the universe, the more one feels driven to believe that evil comes from a certain division which one cannot explain, and that the return to good depends upon a contrary force which pushes us unceasingly towards a certain unity equally inconceivable." Thence he moves on to note the human tendency to unify things " which nature seems to have totally separated." (*Id.* II 190.) The worst thing which he can say about the benighted Greeks is that they were essentially the " esprit de division." [47] He is united as usually with Bonald in defence of medievalism and of all the practical consequences it entails.

The unity of the Middle Ages was an ideal which by the end of the thirteenth century seemed well-nigh realized. Arts and letters, science and philosophy, were to all intents and purposes attuned to the Catholic note. This is to be taken literally, not figuratively. The Church Militant had conquered; it prescribed the very colors to be used in composing stained glass windows;[48] to say nothing of the ultimate axioms of knowledge. It went so far as to say that although kings might wield the temporal sword, they wielded it *ad nutum et patientiam sacerdotis*.[49] There was a divine order, a hierarchy, a system. The world had become a celestial mosaic, in which all deeds and thoughts were symbols whose meaning was the pattern as a whole.

It was that sort of unity which Maistre longed for and which he thought he found exemplified in the absolute monarchy of the old régime. In an absolute monarchy the power is in one hand, in one person; in a republic it is scattered. So in Catholicism, truth is in the Church, expressed by Christ's vicar, the Pope. The Church and the Pope are but one, says Maistre in " du

[47] " Pape " liv. IV, ch. ix. Cf. conclusion to the same work and Lamennais's " Essai sur l'Indifférence," ch. xxv, which cites Saint Augustine's correlation of the beautiful with unity in his Epist. XVIII, *Ad Coelestin*.

[48] Mâle; " L'Art Religieux du XIIIe Siècle en Fr.," 4th ed., P. 1919, esp. 457 ff.

[49] The bull *Unam Sanctam*, " Enchiridion " 469.

Pape" (III, ii). In Protestantism, truth is multiple. The very history of Protestantism, he says (*Id.* IV, iii, iv), is the disintegration of dogma, from the simple and unified enduring pronouncements of the Church, to the complex, various, changing confessions of individuals.

Unity within the national state is not enough for Maistre. Had it been, Napoleon, whom he was forced to admire,[50] would have been almost his ideal, failing only in his lack of respect for the Pope. The power of various states must be unified and of state churches must be destroyed. The stronghold of the French clergy, Gallicanism, he attacked with mighty blows—*Carthago delenda est.* So too, the secular character of kings must be denied. Kings are not merely political personages. The dogma which Machiavelli opposed with such decision is reasserted by Maistre. The King is the subordinate of the Church; the temporal sword is wielded by the spiritual hand. The Pope is called " the natural chief, the most powerful promoter, the great Demiurge of universal civilization." (*Id.* III, ii.) Maistre takes divine right so seriously that he argues from the average length of the reigns of Christian princes to the biological peculiarity of their family stock. It is as different from other stocks, he says (*Id.* III, v), as a tree is from a bush.

Undoubtedly circumstances led Maistre and Bonald to overstate their cases. They reasoned not from love of truth but from hatred of contradiction. There was

[50] Cogordan; *Op. cit.* 68; Daudet, 618; Sainte-Beuve; *CL* XV 72.

no error in their world; there was only sin. Hence they not only disagreed with their opponents; they loathed them; they wished to stamp them out. Bonald always refers to non-catholic philosophies as "philosophies abjectes." Maistre's invective against Voltaire is as revolting as he thinks Voltaire is. "He plunges into the muck, he rolls in it, he laps it up. . . *Paris le couronna; Sodome l'eût banni.*"[51] Their insolence might have been more tolerable had they been more clairvoyant. But what was one to say when Maistre announced in his "Considérations sur la France" (p. 104) that either the Americans would never build the city of Washington; or, if they did, that it would never be called "Washington"; or, if it were, that Congress would never sit there? This was excusable in 1796, but I quote from the edition printed from a copy corrected by him in 1817 and printed in 1866. With such opinions on record, their opponents could afford to laugh at them.[52] Based on the axiom that man is thoroughly bad,[53] that only God's mysterious grace can make him better, their philosophy succeeded only in frightening men from the Church. The one school of thinkers it directly influenced was condemned by the very Church it lived to fortify. One of Maistre's most enthusiastic exponents,

[51] "Soirées" I 243.
[52] See "Considérations," 104. Cf. his prophecy that God was making French the universal language, ("Soirées" I 153) and about the greatness of Lamennais quoted in Maréchal; "Lamennais et Lamartine," P. 1907, p. 127. He had better luck when he prophesied, after the fall of the Decazes ministry, that the royal family would again be driven from France.
[53] "Soirées" I 84, 214.

the Canon Lecigne, admits that he had no following during his lifetime.[54] He attributes this to the lingering of revolutionary habits, although Maistre did not die until 1821. He hesitates to lay the blame for Lamennais on Maistre and attributes no one to the school until the middle of the century when Louis Veuillot rose to a sort of prominence. The others he classifies as followers of Chateaubriand, whom he is right in distinguishing sharply from our two thinkers.

Yet Maistre's Catholic friends read and appreciated his books. The group of "Le Défenseur" was enthusiastic and Maistre received letters of praise from Chateaubriand, Fontanes, Bonald, Lamartine, and Lamennais on the appearance of "Du Pape." Lamartine wrote as follows, pointing out why the warm reception of the work was not more general:

"M. de Bonald and you, Monsieur le Comte, and a few men who follow your footsteps from afar, have founded an imperishable school of high philosophy and Christian politics, which more than any other takes root amid the growing generation. It will bear its fruits and they are judged in advance. . . . You have been surprised that the papers, especially those which ought to adopt your ideas, should have remained silent with regard to you. But that comes from certain prejudices of the country, whose ridiculous gallican pretentions you know so admirably, and from a *mot d'ordre* which people have believed they must religiously observe, and the explanation of which I have given in your behalf to Louis. That has not, however, prevented in any way the rapid circulation of the work."[55]

[54] "Joseph de Maistre," P. 1914, p. 316.
[55] "O. C. de Joseph de Maistre," Lyon 1886, XIV, *Correspondance* 362.

In other words the book was read and believed by all those who had no need of conviction.

It is not until the present day, says Lecigne, in the group of *L'Action Française,* that the voice of Joseph de Maistre was again heard. "If Joseph de Maistre were to return," said his great-grandson, Count Rodolphe de Maistre in 1900, "he would be one of the active members of l'Action Française." His real triumph however would have been the Vatican Council, which declared the primacy of the Pope and his infallibility. "I can see de Maistre," says his admirer, "on the morrow of the Vatican Council. His brow is radiant, all the clouds are scattered, his prophecies are realized. And the look he casts towards the future is from then on as confident as, the evening before, it was troubled and ill at ease." [56]

II

The Christianity of Bonald and Maistre could hardly have moved men to conversion. As men these philosophers were kindly, friendly, even gentle at times, as their letters prove. But as writers they were brilliant and faithful to logic, for the most part, and their words lacked that charm which was known to be necessary if they were to restore Christianity to France. "Persuasive charm," said Fontanes, in his prediction of the Christian apology which was to come, "would perhaps be a greater necessity than victorious logic which subjugates the reason." [57] It was that which the theological

[56] Lecigne; *Op. cit.* 373, 369, 389, 241.
[57] Sainte-Beuve; "Chateaubriand et son Groupe Littéraire," P. 1869, p. 84.

school lacked. They were excellent spokesmen for the Catholics of the old régime who needed no persuasion to admit the truth of their religion. But what could they offer to the gilded youth of Fréron, who had been through the Terror, seen Notre Dame de Paris used as a wine market, and danced in the *bals des victimes?* [58] If they were to be touched, it was not through dogma or even deductive reasoning. They had seen enough of that. It was necessary to break the ground in a more forcible way before the seed was sown. And the instrument alone fitted for such work was sentimentalism. Otherwise Catholicism would remain a sterile doctrine of the classroom, and the passionate denunciation of Church and priest which had been voiced by Voltairean and Rousseauist alike would still whisper dangerously and tempt the young away.

It was this function which Chateaubriand performed. Where he pointed out the beauty of Christianity, the more rational of Catholics would point out its truth. He had not always been so ready to believe. In his younger days, in his " Essai sur les Révolutions " (1797), which he later condemned but could not suppress, had he not expressed himself with the scepticism of a Philosopher? It took the death of his mother to convince him of the error of his ways. " I admit," he said of his conversion in the preface to his " Génie du Christianisme," " that

[58] See Goncourt; " Hist. de la société fr. pendant le Directoire," nouv. ed., P. 1880, p. 140; Ch. Nodier; " Souvenirs de la Révolution et de l'Empire," nouv. ed., P. 1850, I 121. The whole article on the " Réaction Thermodorienne " gives a vivid picture of the social life of the time. I do not know how reliable it is.

I did not yield to a great insight into supernatural things; my conviction came from the heart; I wept and I believed."

It was, then, upon the belief that comes from weeping that the revival of Catholicism was to be founded. The *comédie larmoyante* was to give way to the *religion larmoyante*. " Le Père de Famille " may have produced streaming eyes in 1769 and hisses in 1811, as Mr. Irving Babbitt says;[59] the " Génie du Christianisme " would have produced laughter in 1769 and succeeded in producing contrition in 1802. The same emotions were produced, but by different stimuli; it is an open question which was the more legitimate. It is certain that we cannot close it here, but must be content with noting the change. Chateaubriand and his friends noted it and lost no time in profiting by it. In one of the most eloquent and shallow books in French, he conquered for himself an enduring place in the literature of his country and for Catholicism a place in the hearts of his countrymen. He did not create the return to Catholicism, but he did plead for it in attractive and persuasive language. From then on the movement which had been in progress from the days when Jordan had begun to urge the re-establishment of the cult was stamped with the seal of the world's approval. " Le Génie du Christianisme " was announced year after year and finally made a seasonable appearance in the year of the Concordat. While

[59] " Rousseau and Romanticism," Boston and N. Y., 1919, p. 126.

Napoleon made it legal for one to be a Catholic, Chateaubriand made it fashionable.[60]

The fame of "Atala," which had been published detached from the greater manuscript, was surpassed. Editions were multiplied beyond all precedent. "The book of Citoyen Chateaubriand," said the *Gazette de France* (7 floréal X-27 April 1802), "entitled 'Le Génie du Christianisme' is producing a great sensation. Appearing at the end of a revolution in which the principles of religion and morality were corrupted, in which, under the name of philosophy, an audacious doctrine substituted empty systems for the former beliefs, it is not a matter of surprise that this book should excite the indignation of those who, persisting in their dangerous opinions, find fault with the peace which the government has just offered to the Church, and lacking good reasons, should hurl against the author threadbare sarcasms of which the philosophers of the eighteenth century were so prodigal."[61] Within a year the *Publiciste* (15 floréal XI-5 May 1803) was announcing the

[60] I do not mean to suggest by this that Chateaubriand's conversion was insincere. Whether it was or not is of very little importance for the history of philosophy. Cassagne in his extraordinarily well documented "La Vie Politique de François Chateaubriand," P. 1911 sees in "Le Génie" a well calculated step taken by its author and his circle to further his personal ambitions. The Abbé Bertin, however, has written a learned dissertation, "La sincérité religieuse de Chateaubriand," P. 1899 to sustain the opposite thesis. There is no *a priori* reason why he should not have been sincerely converted and yet lucky enough to have his conversion aid him materially.

[61] Aulard; "P. sous le Consulat," III 3.

second edition dedicated to the First Consul with the "Défense." [62] Three months later the *Observateur* (11 thermidor XI-30 July 1803) said, " New editions of the 'Génie du Christianisme' have just been put on sale. They are this time decorated with the most sumptuous and luxurious typography. . . " [63] And the following winter the *Gazette* heralded several reprints, in 18mo, in octavo, and an abridged edition for children in duodecimo.[64] Ballanche, a printer as well as a philosopher, whose own sentimental book, " Du Sentiment considéré dans ses rapports avec la Littérature et les Arts," was so pathetic a failure, was asked thirty thousand francs by the converted Chauteaubriand for an edition of " le Génie." " And I do not despair of obtaining them," wrote the author to Gueneau.[65] It was as much his personal fortune as that of the Church.

Napoleon, whose own appreciation of Chateaubriand was strengthened by Fontanes's, rewarded him with the ambassadorship to Rome. There he learned that the Vatican too recognized its worth. When he paid his official visit to Pius VII, he was received with tender affection. The Pontiff had a copy of the book by his side, told him that he had read it, and called his " mon fils." [66] In his joy he immediately wrote the news to

[62] *Id*. IV 49.

[63] *Id*. IV 274.

[64] *Id*. IV 699.

[65] " Correspond. Générale de Ch.," pub. by Louis Thomas, P. 1912, I 97.

[66] " Correspond.," letter to Fontanes, 6 July 1803; letter to Joubert, 3 July 1803. Also " Mem. d'Outre-Tombe," II 320.

Napoleon's sister, Mme. Bacciochi, whence it could be accidentally transmitted to the First Consul. "He is in transports of happiness," wrote Fontanes to his friend Joubert.[67] He had thoroughly rehabilitated Catholicism, he might have felt, and left only the Idéologues dissatisfied. The young, whom it was important to capture, were won over without delay. As Sainte-Beuve said, France had a "whole army of parlor Christians." [68]

The argument of "Le Génie du Christianisme" was of the same sort as the argument of Volney's "Ruines" or Condorcet's "Esquisses," founded upon a personal conviction with very little unquestionable evidence. In the past, it runs, Christianity has shown mankind the example of unprecedented courage in the work of missionaries and of unprecedented spirituality in the work of the monastic orders. It rid the world of slavery,[69] it welcomed the weary traveller in its abbeys, it rescued the fallen in soul and body. To the Church the world

[67] Raynal; *Op. cit.* 73.

[68] "Ch. et son Groupe," 330. See the whole fourteenth lecture. Napoleon was a kind of parlor-Christian, too. In the words of Mme. de Staël, "He needed a clergy as chamberlains, titles, decorations, in short he needed all the former caryatides of power." ("Consid. sur la Rév. Fr." ch. vi.) He needed them also, it should be admitted, to help restore order in Fr. and to satisfy what remained of his native religious instincts. Cf. Vandal; "Raisons du Concordat," 516, 597.

[69] Lamennais too was going to teach that Christianity had rid the world of slavery in "Essai sur l'Indifférence," 2d. pt., ch. iii and iv. It was a doctrine to which he clung even in his later days. See "Le Livre du Peuple," xiv. As for the merits of the case, which must particularly interest Americans, see Ferraz; "Hist. de la Philos. Fr.," P. 1880, p. 179.

owes education, letters and the arts; France the civilization of her law and the beneficence of her rulers.

In part true and in part false, "Le Génie du Christianisme" undoubtedly did a valuable service if it aided in clarifying men's minds about the real nature of the Middle Ages. After this book and others of its kind, it could be no longer excusable to use the word "Gothic" as a synonym for "barbarous" and the word "medieval" as a synonym for "ignorant." Were we engaged in writing the history of eighteenth century ideas, we might be able to show that as a matter of fact the regard for the Middle Ages during that period was not so low as writers usually maintain. However it is incontestable that Chateaubriand had a more popular influence than any of his predecessors. Furthermore, by emphasizing the beauty of Christianity, he succeeded in turning men's eyes from what was wicked and inessential in its institutions to what would prove to be its noblest characteristics: its power of inspiration to righteous living and the arts. This was more than Bonald and Maistre could claim for their harsh treatises.

But much better than the argument was the style of "Le Génie." Full of a tender reverence for his subject, Chateaubriand wrote of it in organ tones. The stately dignity of his majestic sentences, hollow, as they seem now, was captivating to the ear habituated to Delille and Fontanes. They warmed hearts chilled by neo-classicism on the one hand and neo-scepticism on the other. Here was no cynicism, no analysis, no ridicule, but genuine nobility of expression. The melancholy which perfumed its pages made its attraction more difficult to resist. And few resisted it. Whatever motive prompted its creation, it satisfied a hunger of the times and no one could say now that he lacked a reason for his beliefs.

A reason was all that was wanted, however shaky it might be. Bit by bit scepticism had gone out of fashion.[70] " Philosophy is losing credit in many minds," wrote Mme. d'Anjou, Louis XVIII's correspondent in Paris (11 July 1800). " Not that the greater part are becoming religious, but that the reign of impiety is drawing to a close. It was a fashion; it has gone out. Today you see more books in defence of religion than in favor of the system of disbelief, and the atheists no longer hold the middle of the road."[71] La Harpe was working on an apology of religion and Mme. de Genlis had announced in August 1801 a " Dictionnaire poétique de la Bible à l'usage des artistes."[72] Ballanche, as we have said, had published his " Du Sentiment " with the appeal to poets and painters to turn to Christianity for their subject matter. " What ! " he cried,[73] " is it not this same religion which enlarged the thoughts of Michelangelo, which guided the sublime brushes of Raphael and of Rubens ? " In vain did Ginguené protest on behalf of the intellectuals that there was no relation between truth and the shedding of tears, in vain did he ridicule Chateaubriand's love for the Middle Ages, the epoch of " la sainte ignorance," in vain did he de-

[70] Gautier; *Op. cit.* 272.
[71] Vandal; *Op. cit.* 503.
[72] Cassagne; *Op. cit.* I 86.
[73] P. 179.

nounce him as anti-revolutionary.[74] The day of Ginguené and his kind was over.

Not only did Chateaubriand give people a kind of sanction for their religion, but he gave them a kind of personal sanction in keeping with the philosophic trend, if aiming at a different goal from that of philosophy. For the authority of tears is the authority of the individual, and the conclusion is irresistible that here Chateaubriand preserved traces of his eighteenth century allegiances. The philosophers of that time had definitely established the mode of self-examination and self-analysis. If all knowledge came from sensation, it came from an individual and not a social source. Chateaubriand continued this tradition. Such procedure certainly was contrary to the ways of the Church. If one is to rely on one's heart for truth, what is to become of authority? Chateaubriand had made a move which would lead to heresy. That is why he incurs the ridicule of such writers as Canon Lecigne. If he was accepted by Pius VII, it was because he was temporarily useful. But a man who criticised Mme. de Staël's " De la Littérature " because its author trusted the outbursts of her heart but half the time, was a man for Popes to shun.[75] He was too interested in developing the individual at the expense, if need be, of society. We have seen how little such an inclination points towards Catholicism as taught by Bonald and Maistre.

[74] *La Décade Philos.*, 30 prairial X (19 June 1802), pp. 537, 549, 552.
[75] Blennerhassett; *Op. cit.* II 422. Cf. " Correspondance " I 23.

It points rather towards the Protestantism of his supposed opponent, Mme. de Staël.

Supposed opponent only. For Mme. de Staël and Chateaubriand had much in common. To be sure they were not always conscious of it. As we have said, Chateaubriand harshly criticised her " De la Littérature " when it appeared, and when " Le Génie " appeared she prophesied that he would cover himself with ridicule.[76] But she had recognized the talent in "Atala "[77] and in the preface to " Delphine " she spoke of the " original, extraordinary, striking imagination of ' le Génie.' "[78] They could praise one another with sincerity, for they were in spite of Chateaubriand's Catholicism, disciples of the one master, Rousseau. Underneath the language of them both is the sentimental tradition.[79]

Rousseau was by no means the soft hearted neurasthenic that certain modern opponents of romanticism would have us believe. The Rousseau of the " Confessions " is supplemented by the Rousseau of the " Contrat Social " and the " Discours sur l'Inégalité." A slight emphasis on one side or the other is all that is needed to show us now the Rousseau of Mr. Irving Babbitt, now the Rousseau of M. Duguit.

Chateaubriand had said in his early " Essai " that had he lived in Rousseau's day, he would have been a disciple, but that he would have asked the master not to

[76] Blennerhassett II 442.
[77] *Id.* 444.
[78] *OC,* ed. Firmin-Didot, P. 1844, I 336.
[79] Cf. Blennerhassett II 424.

publish the news. Mme. de Staël in her earliest published work gave the world her eulogy of the author of "Emile," "Lettres sur les écrits et le caractère de J. J. Rousseau." (1788.) She has no shame in announcing her fresh and youthful enthusiasm for the weary old sentimentalist. To her his weariness is pathetic; his faults are to be laid at other doors than his own; mainly at his wife's who, she thinks, drove him to suicide.[80] He is the one figure, she feels, to whom one can turn for inspiration. It is inspiration which she demands, not precept. Like so many of her contemporaries, she seemed thirsty for enthusiasm. It is as if some instinct had been starved in them.

Mme. de Staël retained the lessons of her master throughout her life under all circumstances. There is scarcely a book from her hands which does not bear his impress. She is not always consistent, as when she slips into admitting that men are naturally "méchants."[81] And of course there are non-Rousseauistic influences at work in her philosophic development. She occasionally shows traces of Ideology, as when she says in her introduction to "De l'influence des passions sur le bonheur"[82] that science begins with complex ideas and in perfecting itself arrives at simple ideas. But her later knowledge of the Germans cures her of any traces of sensationalism.[83]

[80] *Op. cit.* ch. vi., *OC* I 19 n. 1; 22.
[81] Blennerhassett II 417.
[82] *OC* I 112.
[83] "Allemagne," Pt. III, ch. iv.

Knowledge, for Mme. de Staël, seems to be the problem of understanding what is always a bit beyond the reach of the understanding. The few truths which we have to start with do not satisfy man's craving for deeper knowledge. Deeper knowledge, however, for instance knowledge of moral truth, is incompatible with strict precision.[84] Hence man finds himself with no sure guide in those very difficulties which are his most profound concern. This perplexity which is at the heart of every moral decision is no matter to be lightly decided. "The insight of our mind," says the mature Mme. de Staël, "is too uncertain for us to be able to judge the moment when the eternal laws of duty ought to be suspended; or rather, that moment does not exist."[85] We are then trapped between the knowledge that there is a law to cover our case and our innate inability to comprehend it in detail. We know when conscience speaks; we do not know what it says.[86] But we must try to understand it, knowing that we shall fail; we shall find ourselves in the darkness which preceded the creation and not in the light which followed.

This antithesis between our aspirations and our capabilities is never very far from her thought. She admits that she can never keep her feelings and her ideas separate;[87] yet she insists that ideas should never be vague.[88] She does not permit herself to excuse obscurity

[84] "Essai sur les Fictions," intro. remarks, *OC* I 62.
[85] "Allemagne," Pt. III, ch. xiii.
[86] Id. ch. vii.
[87] "De la Littérature," ch. ix, *OC* I 334.
[88] "Allemagne," Pt. III ch. ix.

because she is unable to avoid it. She knows that the passions are the great impetus towards unhappiness; she pleads like a Stoic for mastery over them; but she admits that no one is ever completely master of them.[89] She is a deep believer in the value of religion, as deep as Rousseau; she censures the Institut for its anti-religious bias;[90] but she will not give the ministers of religion rights above those of the rest of mankind.[91] Love, finally, is one of man's greatest blessings, but it is almost never found.[92] The rarest passion is the best.

The springs of action for Mme. de Staël are always non-rational. She reads into "Tom Jones" the lesson that judgments founded upon appearance are false and that natural and involuntary qualities are the highest.[93] Moreover they should be non-rational, for those inner chambers of the soul are the holy of holies where our better nature resides. Because this is true, what she calls "natural morality" is finer than "devotion." Spontaneous unreasoned goodness is better than goodness which is planned. Adapting the familiar lines of Dryden to her purpose, she says:

"He (devotion) raised a mortal to the skies,
"She (natural morality) drew an angel down."[94]

The springs of action, in spite of their non-rational nature, are not utterly irrational and use the reason to

[89] "Passions," concl., *OC* I 172; cf. 170.
[90] "Dix Années d'Exil," ch. ix; *OC* III 265.
[91] "Considérations," ch. ix, *OC* III 265.
[92] "Passions," pref. note to ch. iv, *OC* I 132.
[93] "Fictions," Pt. III, *OC* I 70.
[94] "Passions," sect. ii, *OC* I 160.

give themselves voice. Sentiment in itself is both beauty and truth, but in itself, it is mute.[95] It prompts us to act and we do well to listen, but we need another instrument to articulate its promptings. That instrument is philosophy. "Philosophy," she held in her youth, "is simply the search for truth guided by the reason."[96] The search for truth can be carried on in other ways, one infers; philosophy is the most reasonable way. It is for the individual to accept it or not, and if one admits contradiction in his ideas or supernatural causes in his facts, he will oppose philosophy.

Her notion of philosophy makes the question of its value of interest. Her answer to this question is what is to be expected from a child of the eighteenth century. Philosophy is of no value in itself; its pursuit is useful, for by it one conquers his passions and gains in return the continuous exercise of his active faculties—a good beyond price.[97] Metaphysics, especially idealistic metaphysics, is almost a sure means of developing the moral faculties.[98] As in the Stoics and Spinoza, so in Mme. de

---

[95] "Allemagne," Pt. III ch. v, vii.

[96] "De la Littérature," Pt. II, ch. vi, *OC* I 313. "I never give to the word 'philosophy'... the sense that its detractors have wished to give it in our day, either opposing philosophy to religious ideas, or calling philosophical those systems which are purely sophistic. I mean by philosophy the general knowledge of causes and effects in the moral order or in physical nature, the independence of reason, the exercise of thought, in short in literature those works which depend upon reflection and analysis, and which are not solely the product of the imagination, the heart, or the wit (*l'esprit*)." (*Disc. prélim.,* "De la Littérature," *OC* I 205 n. 1.)

[97] "Passions," sect. III ch. iii, *OC* I 165.

[98] "Allemagne," Pt. III ch. vii.

THE NEO-CHRISTIANS

Staël, the calm which comes only when one is master of the world comes through the exercise of the reason. But in her the reason is not its own excuse for being.

She shows signs in such passages of believing that the soul must and can assent to beliefs that comfort it. She seems, for instance, to prove the truth of immortality by the fact that it is sweet to think of and the falsity of materialism by the revolt of our moral nature against it.[99] This was in 1796, before she knew Kant. After her visits to Germany, such suggestions are more frequent and we find her proving the superiority of Christianity over Pantheism because it answers more satisfactorily the needs of our heart.[100] In a similar spirit she praises Kant for having definitely banished God and morality from metaphysics, since metaphysics is not a science with a specific subject matter but a manner of living.[101]

Since it is a manner of living, one can understand why to her philosophy is an individual affair, like love.[102] All men are not alike; their problems are different; their souls are different; how then could they solve their problems in the same way? Ultimate questions, she believes, have too many sides to permit any one man's answering them all. But when she says things like that, she fails to be as acute strategically as she might be. It would be wiser for her to cling to her anti-intellec-

[99] "Passions," sect. III, ch. iii, *OC* I 165.
[100] "Allemagne," Pt. III ch. vii.
[101] *Id.* Pt. III, ch. vi.
[102] *Id.* Pt. III ch. v.

tualism to the bitter end, to explain philosophy consistently as she explains religions.[103]

There is a fine harmony between her religion and politics and her philosophy. Sure of a natural correlation between truth and individual opinion (reason), she can see nothing but good in encouraging its exercise.[104] Protestantism she feels is based on the right of free inquiry, whereas Catholicism denies this right.[105] To use Bonald's words, Protestantism is based on the authority of evidence; Catholicism upon the evidence of authority. Mme. de Staël would agree and would find as much satisfaction in the situation as Bonald did. "Protestantism and Catholicism," she says,[106] "do not come from there having been popes and a Luther. That is a poor manner of viewing history, to attribute it to chance. Protestantism and Catholicism exist in the human heart; they are moral powers which develop in nations because they exist in each man." But Protestantism alone recognizes this fact and hence will alone receive the support of Mme. de Staël.[107]

This passion for the right of free inquiry is what makes her a liberal in politics. Systems which lose the

[103] *Id.* Pt. IV, ch. iv.
[104] *Id.* Pt. IV, ch. ii.
[105] *Id.*
[106] *Id.* Pt. IV, ch. iv.
[107] It is interesting to note that Mme. de Staël is anxious to point out the charm which Protestantism has for the imagination, in order to counter-balance the kind of apology which Chateaubriand and his group had made for Catholicism. Hence she dwells on the Moravian brotherhood. See "Allemagne," Pt. IV, ch. iii and concluding words.

individual in the state are her abhorrence. The despotic rule of one man like Napoleon, which submerges the individual in his loyalty to a ruler are equally abhorrent. She cares more for the individual than for the nation and her cosmopolitanism makes her notorious. She has no country, as M. Gautier points out.[108] She was born in France—which she passionately loved—of a Genevan father and a Vaudoise mother. Her husband was a Swede. The country of her choice was England; of her birth and friends, France; of her thought, Germany; of her soul, the international society of distinguished men. She had never been a woman of one party, never feeling that one cause—except personal liberty—was worth the loss of free action. During the Directory in Paris, her circle included royalists like Matthieu de Montmorency and Dupont de Nemours and republicans like Daunou, Cabanis, Destutt de Tracy, and Ginguené.[109] With her an individual alone counted and it mattered not what his belief was as long as it included tolerance for others' beliefs.

M. Gautier's thesis that her hatred of Napoleon was in part personal, having arisen from his having wounded her pride may be true. It would indeed be strange if so burning an individualist should not have been sensitive to personal wounds. But, as he too points out, there was between her and the Emperor a difference which could not be reconciled, a difference of philosophy. If ever two souls expressed beliefs from the bottom of their hearts, these two did. The soul of the Emperor

[108] *Op. cit.* 275.
[109] Blennerhassett II 281.

responded to hierarchical order, personal power, authority. He loved the *genres tranchés,* as he told Goethe at Erfurth. He tried to reconstruct in Paris the Augustan Age of Rome. Centralization is the symbol of his rule and he stands in history as one of the last great centralizers on the European continent. Human suffering seems to have counted for as little in his mind as human wills—until the Hundred Days. Then he repented.[110]

There might have been a kindred sentiment with Mme. de Staël as there was for a time with Chateaubriand. But the philosophy of Chateaubriand lacked the one element which saved Mme. de Staël's from becoming egoism. That element was " enthusiasm," which lifts the individual out of himself, transcending his personal needs, and sets him down among his fellows.[111] There

[110] Benj. Constant; "Lettres sur les Cent Jours," 2d letter, first pub. in *La Minerve Française,* 1819, VIII 100.

[111] Blennerhassett III 384. Mme. de Staël seizes upon this terrible deficiency in Napoleon and exhibits it in her "Considérations" (ch. xviii, "De la politique de Bonaparte") to show how it prevented his becoming the real master of the world. (*OC* III 239). Mr. Babbitt too feels that Mme. de Staël has this saving grace. She is never, for instance, so overcome as Chateaubriand by her "uniqueness and wonderfulness," he says (*Op. cit.* 50). I do not subscribe, however, to Mr. Babbitt's interpretation of Chateaubriand as a wilful romantic who took these attitudes because he was romantic. Anyone reading the life of Chateaubriand, torn between personal ambition and a sense of decency, would normally have developed all the quirks of temperament which characterize him. A sympathetic and yet critical study of Chateaubriand, based on modern psychology, and made by someone who is not a fanatic, would clear his case from the docket. There are hopes that the studies now being made by Professor Chinard and his pupils will satisfy this need.

is no such enthusiasm in Chateaubriand, there is none in Napoleon. It is the saving grace of Mme. de Staël. It is what she contributes as her peculiar gift to the movement of French thought which will save the great leaders of French romanticism from the morbidity of their German parallels and make them progressively a force for liberalism and personal independence. Her understanding that the social emotions are the salvation of human beings is present in her early work on Rousseau and is the culmination of her book on Germany. She may have thought that she was learning new lessons from her study of Kant and his followers. In reality she was learning over again the old lessons of her master Rousseau, as translated by German tongues. What she learned from Kant is the dignity of the moral being, the austerity of duty, and the legitimacy of obeying one's conscience. Her study of German philosophy was simply confirmation of what she had always believed, put into words which gave it a novel intellectual sanction.

The two figures of Chateaubriand and Mme. de Staël stand for us in the main as two powerful forces making for a faith in the inner light. Chateaubriand's influence was checked by the heresy which it would necessarily engender in the church he tried to defend. Mme. de Staël's met no such check, and lovers of freedom could look back to her as an outspoken champion of their cause, a champion who had been willing—too willing—to suffer for it. Her epitaph could well be the lines which Benjamin Constant wrote in his journal, *La Minerve Française* (1818, II 109), on the appearance of her

"Considérations sur la Révolution Française." Readers will find in it, he said, "that attachment to liberty, the deep feeling for the dignity of mankind, the respect for morality in politics and great human pursuits, that inexhaustible sensibility which made ths famous woman as admirable for her goodness as for her superior mentality."[112]

III

Developing alongside of Chateaubriand was his contemporary and friend, Pierre-Simon Ballanche. In some ways this fairly obscure figure deserves no special mention in a history of ideas. In his lifetime he was but faintly known. His first book, "Du Sentiment considéré dans ses rapports avec la littérature et les arts," was received, as we have already said, with ridicule when it first appeared. Yet it proposed the same thesis as the "Génie du Christianisme" and appeared earlier. His second major work, "Antigone," published thirteen years later met with a more cordial reception[113] but even it was considered by some critics as an inferior piece of writing and among its friends were to be found some writers who praised for a living. Otherwise the world was lukewarm. To be sure he found biographers during his lifetime. Sainte-Beuve and Loménie each wrote a notice of him, but the former was preparing a course of lectures on Chateaubriand and his group and

---

[112] Cf. Lerminier's tribute in his "De l'Influence de la Philos. etc.," and his criticism of Chateaubriand, p. 295.

[113] Frainnet; *Op. cit.* 52.

could scarcely omit from his studies one who alone shared the intimacy of l'Abbaye-aux-Bois with the author of "René"; the latter was publishing a series of portrait sketches in several volumes which included even Andrew Jackson.[114] Much more significant is the fact that Damiron's first edition of his history of French philosophy, which appeared in 1828, mentions Ballanche merely in an extended footnote to the conclusion (p. 393). By then all of Ballanche's important books had appeared. Perhaps Damiron's neglect is caused by sectarianism. The anonymous philosophical critic of the *Revue des Deux Mondes* (Lerminier?) praises Ballanche highly, apropos of his " Vision d'Hébal " for not imitating the German manner of philosophizing.[115] This little slap at Cousin and his group indicates in what circles Ballanche found favor and may explain why Damiron continued to omit him from his history until its third edition.

Later in 1834 Adolphe Mazure of Poitiers went so far as to say, " M. Ballanche has rivals, he has no masters. M. Cousin has more powerful thought; his speech also, like his looks, troubles and baffles one; it is a torrent which is strong enough to uproot oaks; but if his victory is not sudden, he passes on, he never returns. M. Ballanche on the contrary is a majestic river, which neither passes nor dries up, which charms you with the thousand picturesque incidents which it mirrors, which en-

[114] " Galérie des Contemporains Illustres," par un Homme de Rien, P. 1841.
[115] *RDM* 1831, II 542.

compasses you with its cooling ripples, into which it is a pleasure to descend, so great is the perfect serenity of his soul which reveals itself in his eloquence, appearing as the pure sand under the sparkling surface of a calm sheet of water, constantly gilded by the sun." [116] What fame this proves was not very enduring. The reward of an Academic chair came near the end of his life; he said that it was given him to keep Victor Hugo out of it.[117] By the '80's Jean Vaudon was able to write that Ballanche had almost completely fallen into oblivion.[118] Perhaps the only real influence he had was on a small group of workmen, to whom both Mme. Lenormant— the biographer of Mme. Récamier and of course an authority on the life of Ballanche—and M. Frainnet, his closest student, both refer vaguely. It was a group with Saint-Simonian tendencies which drifted into Fourierism and thence towards Ballanche. Ballanche himself says that he met its leader through Nodier.[119] But little seems to have come of this. M. Frainnet includes Pierre Leroux and Jean Reynaud among the men influenced by him,[129] but his reasoning is by no means conclusive.

If it were for the force of Ballanche's personality or the influence of his ideas, no one would think of includ-

[116] *La Fr. Littéraire* 1834, XI.
[117] Letter to J. J. Ampère in Ampère's " Mélanges d'Hist. littéraire," 2d ed., P. 1876, II 187.
[118] " Ballanche," *Corresp.* 1883, n. s. XCVII 234; Frainnet 338.
[119] Ampère; " Mélanges," II 191.
[120] *Op. cit.* 258.

ing him in a history of French philosophies. He is a sort of backwater in the stream of events. Yet his ideas have a certain interest in themselves. They are a curious compromise between the Catholicism of Bonald and Maistre, leavened with the sentimentalism of Chateaubriand and Mme. de Staël, and the heresy of Lamennais which followed. They are interesting also as a fore-shadowing of modernism, for, as we shall see, Ballanche believed that Catholicism could evolve, that time and change were real and not necessarily evil. For some reason or other he was unable to think his ideas through, or did not choose to. His feelings carried him away from the rigor of Bonald; he was always in danger of heterodoxy, and his life was so closely bound up with members of the Church that this loyal creature could not face the suicide a break would entail. Believing so strongly in the cognitive value of feelings that he headed one of the chapters of his first book, "The study of precepts is not very important," he could not very well forsake them when they prompted him to linger by the side of Mme. Récamier and the group of l'Abbaye-aux-Bois. She and her friends were Catholics, royalists, traditionalists. He too must be of them in spite of incompatibility of many of their ideas. He felt the need of this woman's friendship. He wrote to her in 1815, apropos of his proposed residence in Paris, "I know the nature of my talents; they have no need of a stay in the capital. Their entire existence is comprised of my affections and my feelings. Paris is no more necessary to my talents than to me. It is you and in no wise Paris who are necessary to me."[121] The temperament of Lamennais was tragically different.

There was, to be sure, a certain fund of agreement between Ballanche and Bonald and Maistre. Like all good Churchmen he believed in the fall of man from a state of innocence and happiness to a state of wickedness and misery. With them he was ready to declare that this primitive state was not to be found in savage communities, for they are in a state of degeneration.[122] He thinks that Rousseau on this subject speaks "brilliant absurdities."[123] But, he held, if man has fallen, he can rehabilitate himself, and the law of rehabilitation is woven into the texture of the universe. The dogma of the fall and the law of rehabilitation are one and the same in his mind.[124] With Maistre again he believed that the French Revolution was a mystery arranged by God.[125] He believed that God ordained the death of Louis XVI as vicarious atonement for the sins of France.[126] But that does not imply, according to him, that government should be theocratic. He is gallican not ultramontane.[127] "If Greogory VII could have realized his great designs," he said, "Europe would have become the Orient. The princes of the time

[121] " Souvenirs et correspondance de Mme. Récamier," I 292.
[122] " Essai sur les institutions sociales," *Oeuvres*, P. 1830. II 197; cf. 260.
[123] "Palingénésie Sociale," *Oeuvres* III 51.
[124] *Id.* III 16, 75.
[125] Cf. Frainnet 69.
[126] " Elégie du Duc de Berry." Cf. Maistre's " Eclaircissements sur les sacrifices," ch. iii.
[127] " Reflection diverses," *Oeuvres* III 372

resisted and ought to have resisted." He is furthermore sceptical about the value of the Jesuits, the teachers of Maistre.[128] He even believed in the separation of Church and State. "I was very consular," he said to M. de Loménie, " but not at all imperial; I was glad to see the restoration of the Church, but I was afraid for her sake to see her reborn pompous as before and bound by gratitude to the State. I should have liked her better free to raise herself from her wooden cross without aid. The Consulate and the Church outside the State; there was my ideal in politics and in religion." [129] He wrote a book, " L'Homme sans Nom," depicting the anguish of a regicide's repentance; but his royalism was not that of the old régime; it was that of the Charte.[130] The people are not sovereign, he maintained; their sovereignty is a " senseless dogma." [131] But a government must be plastic enough to adjust itself to the aspirations of society.[132] Otherwise it will be deposed.

These points of disagreement were dangerous and people were aware that they were dangerous. Well might their author have envied his friend, Jourdain, who had the peace and quiet of Holy Orders.[133] There doubts were impossible and calm assured. There friends could not torture one and tyrannize over one's soul. Maistre was especially keensighted when it was a ques-

[128] *Id.* 388.
[129] Loménie; *Op. cit.* 16.
[130] Frainnet 321.
[131] " Le Vieillard et le Jeune Homme," *Oeuvres* II 404.
[132] *Id.* 414.
[133] Frainnet 28

tion of heresy, and though he thanked Ballanche for what was good in his work, the "Essai sur les institutions sociales," he called it a "hybrid" and added, "The sans-culotte awaits you in his camp; I await you in mine."[134] Ballanche may be said to have retorted in his later remark that Maistre's ideas were "dreams of the cave of Trophonius."[135] But he dared not desert the Maistrean camp. His "Ville des Expiations" was considered so little orthodox, that the Comtesse de Hauteville, who owned the manuscript, refused to allow it to be printed.[136] How far Ballanche appreciated his heterodoxy, we have no easy means of determining, though in the case of one detail in his system which seemed suspicious, he was glad to find it anticipated, as he thought, in the Fathers.[137] He would no doubt have been happier had be been sure that he was orthodox.

On the whole Ballanche's difference from Bonald and Maistre rests on his suspicion that time is ultimately real and that history is an actual process which absorbs all institutions, even religious ones. This was never more than a suspicion in his writings, never phrased in metaphysical terms, lying at the back of his reflection, irritating him, mystifying him, and giving to his work that obscurity which usually accompanies mysticism or careless workmanship. In Ballanche's case it was

[134] Sainte-Beuve; "Poètes et Philosophes Modernes de la Fr.," *RDM* 1834, III 703.
[135] "Palin. Soc.," *Oeuvres* III 265.
[136] Frainnet, *Appendix* III 351.
[137] "Palin. Soc.," *Oeuvres* III 60.

not due to careless workmanship. M. Frannet notes the number of trial expressions which occur in the manuscripts now at Lyon.[138] He revised his publications with the greatest pains. His obscurity is the result in part of the comparative novelty of what was central in his thought and in part of his inability or unwillingness to force it to a logical conclusion. If he had carried it to a logical conclusion, he would have been carried along with it into open heresy as Lamennais was.

That change and time are ultimately real was a thought which separated Ballanche from his friends. For Bonald and Maistre they were evil, for Ballanche they are all that permit us to achieve the good. For the former the permanent and the stable are the goal of all life; for the latter, as for Vico from whom he learned so much, the motionless is the brutal.[139] That which elevates man above the beasts is his plasticity, for by it alone is he capable of perfecting himself. His perfectibility—a notion which he inherited from the eighteenth century, *horribile dictu*—was infinite, for its termination was the coincidence of humanity with the condition of Adam, man *in actu* and *in potentia*.[140] " At the end of

---

[138] Frainnet 119.

[139] " Palin. Soc.," *Oeuvres* III 175. Ballanche had studied Vico while in Naples in 1824 with Mme. Récamier (" Souvenirs etc." I 232). For a statement in his published works of his relations to Vico, see " Palin. Soc.," *Oeuvres* III 150. His similarity to Vico was noted during his lifetime by Adolphe Mazure; " Ballanche," *La Fr. Littéraire* 1834, XI 8.

[140] " Vision d'Hébal," P. 1831, pp. 31, 36. Cf. " Ville des Expiations—La Charité Chrétienne," *La Fr. Littéraire* 1834, XII 6 and 1833, V 238.

the world," he said, "the world of substances will perish, the world of essences will continue to exist as before the phenomenal creation." The similarity between this theory and that of Plotinus, whom Ballanche does not seem to have known, is obvious. In Plotinus too the idea of man descends to earth, solely to rehabilitate itself by ascending to heaven. It encounters evil voluntarily for its own perfection. But in Plotinus there was an individual idea for each man; whereas in Ballanche, as in the Neo-Platonists after Plotinus, there is one idea for the race. This was needed for Christian dogma, such as vicarious atonement and inherited guilt. The realization of this idea, which Ballanche calls "rehabilitation," is the process of history.

This is the first of his potential heresies. In his eyes all men are called to rehabilitation, the bad as well as the good. If they have not time enough in this life, they will be born again, but sooner or later they will achieve that state which the first man enjoyed in the earthly paradise. This was his second potential heresy. In vain did he call upon Origen in support of his views; the Church did not believe in metempsychosis and could not. Origen himself had been condemned for the belief as early as 543 and along with him anyone who happened to agree with him.[141] Similarly the Priscillian belief that human souls descended to earth because of sins committed in a heavenly pre-existence was anathematized at the Council of Braga in 561.[142] The Church has never retracted on these points and Ballanche would have had

---

[141] "Enchiridion" 203.
[142] *Id.* 236.

no defence if he had been called to account. Fortunately for him, he was a layman.

From his second potential heresy followed his third, that there was no eternal Hell.[143] How could there be if men were to be given an infinite series of chances to atone for the evils which they committed in life? Life, he believed, was Hell enough.[144] To extend it unimproved is irreconcilable with the goodness of God. He had every hope that the theologians would some day see the matter with his eyes.[145] For the Church to see it through his eyes, however, would be to reject the dogma of the Church's immutability. But on this question Ballanche entertains the fourth potential heresy: the growth of religion.

Being made for a temporal creature, Man, religion is subject to temporal laws; its truths are released like a news-story, like the " Génie du Christianisme " in fact, only when the public is ready for them. Thus God manifested the doctrine of immortality to the Christians and not to the Jews, for they were too carnal to understand it. But if the Jews lacked complete knowledge, was it not possible that they shared what they had with other primitive peoples? Was it not likely in fact that they were but one of several repositories of divine truth? It was, indeed, and no people had been without its share.[146] " Truth necessary to the human race has always been and always will be in the human race."

[143] " Orphée," *Oeuvres* IV 393, 404.
[144] *Id.*
[145] " Palin. Soc.," *Oeuvres* III 319.
[146] *Id.* 150, 335; " Orphée," *Oeuvres* IV 419.

But Christianity itself, is it not at least free from change? One can almost feel the anxious heart-beats of Mme. Récamier as she listened for the answer to this question. The answer was definite if veiled. Christianity was but a symbol, a collection of symbols, to be interpreted not by the stupid literalness of the reason, but by the sympathy of the heart—one hears the voices of Chateaubriand and Mme. de Staël.[147] But at least there is a body of men who alone have the power and authority to interpret them, the priests? No, says the terrible meek, Ballanche, not so. "My son, we are Christians, but we know and we avow that Christianity has produced a sort of paganism which enlightened spirits put farthest from their thoughts. Pure Christianity, true Christianity is for the people of to-day what initiation was for the people of olden times. The unbelievers of to-day have refused to initiate themselves; the true initiation is ever within."[148] There was no mistaking this final heresy. It was personal interpretation; it was what Bonald and Maistre called Protestantism.

This heresy was inevitable. For Ballanche like Chateaubriand was a Christian from sentiment and not from

[147] This is but an extension of his earlier theory that art should also be interpreted by the heart, as expounded in his "Du Sentiment," p. 7. Later in the same work, p. 46, he demonstrates how much surer a guide the feelings are than the reason. "In vain is man convinced by the reason; if he is not persuaded by feeling, a good thought will never become a good deed" (p. 48). He quotes Adam Smith in defence of this theory (p. 245).

[148] "Ville," *La Fr. Littéraire* 1833, V 241.

reason. His feelings alone carried him along; he appreciated the beauty of Christianity much more than its truth. Like Chateaubriand, he believed in its civilizing force, a help for the weak, an enlightenment for the ignorant, above all an inspiration for the arts, replacing paganism. But he did not see in it an apology for authority and a substitute for the intellectual autonomy of the individual. This man who spent his whole life at the beck and call of another, taught a philosophy in which the basis of all knowledge was in the individual alone.

The individualism was softened and the heresy toned down in the setting of traditionalism. Like Bonald and Maistre and the earlier Lamennais, he believed in the divine origin of language and the sacredness of institutions.[149] But he never went to the extent of Lamennais in making tradition the sole organ of truth. As was to be expected, tradition became in his hands, like religion itself, a growing developing thing, instead of a fixed thing, *semper eadem*. He became one of the pioneers in a movement towards realizing the optimistic faith of those believers in progress who had been preaching since the seventeenth century. To him Maistre was a backward-looker, an *archéophile*. " This great man,"

[149] " Instit. Soc.," *Oeuvres* II 199. For an excellent account of the differences between him and Bonald and Maistre, see Barchou; " Essai d'une formule génèrale de l'humanité d'après les idées de M. Ballanche," *RDM* 1831, II 424. Cf. Ferraz; *Op. cit.* 275. Barchou calls B. a mediator between Maistre and Rousseau, between " divine right and the sovereignty of the people " (p. 425).

he said,[150] "this noble theosopher . . . had ears for the voice of by-gone centuries alone; his soul was in sympathy only with the society of olden times. He knew not how to distinguish the cry of the future so perfectly articulated; he had no glimpse of new destinies; the people could not understand him, for he had ceased to speak their language." He himself was a *néophile*. Yet he seemed to be defending the same creed as Maistre. Was he not nearer the camp of the sans-culottes than anyone suspected?

As he preached to his group of laborers his simple faith in brotherly love, he probably achieved more than at any other time the goal which life had in store for him, but which he rejected. The undercurrents of his soul have never been sounded, but one cannot resist the impression that he wilfully prevented himself from completely expressing his thoughts because of the social tragedy which would ensue. True to his friend of friends, he was untrue to himself, and what joy he gave to her and the narrow circle which moved about her, was more than balanced by the sorrow of his own inner life. Again, as in Chateaubriand, the romantic melancholy which colored his utterance was no pose assumed for the fun of being romantic; it was the natural outgrowth of a definite seed.

It remained for Lamennais to bring out of this seed all of its possibilities.

[150] *Oeuvres* III 265.

IV

The heresies of Ballanche were heresies in root. The heresies of Lamennais were heresies in flower. The former started from assumptions which were contrary to the teachings of the Church. The latter started from assumptions which seemed to him and to his group to be the inner essence of Church dogma. He took the dogma seriously and treated it logically. The others knew where to stop.

By Ballanche's time the counter-revolution had gone through its youth and maturity and was showing a startling incapacity for settling down in its old age. The help it had received from Bonald and Maistre had been welcome enough and was salutary. But there was a grain of unwholesome matter there. That grain was the theory of tradition. The help it had received from Chateaubriand was downright noxious. Like a strong stimulant it had set the movement on its feet, but it did not provide the necessary nutriment to keep it there. On the contrary it engendered the dangerous habit engendered by all stimulants of relying on it as a permanent rather than a temporary aid. Add to this the well-meant help of Ballanche and you will see why Lamennais's brand of Christianity went the way of the wicked. A movement which had begun in orthodoxy ended in heresy. One of the strongest supporters of the Church found himself cast adrift for his pains. Perhaps it was just as well that Ballanche confined his activities to l'Abbaye-aux-Bois.

The traditional way of treating Lamennais is to divide his career into two parts, the first of which is orthodox and ultramontane, the second heterodox and anarchistic. There is a certain justice in this, for everyone knows the contrast between the brilliant beginning of his life under the ægis of the Church and the wretched end. Everyone knows that the Abbé Félicité de la Mennais was the most intense spokesman for the supremacy of the Pope in all matters, temporal as well as spiritual,[151] that Leo XII received him with as affectionate tenderness as Pius VII had shown to Chateaubriand, that there was even talk of giving him the red hat.[152] And everyone knows that F. Lamennais, author of "Une Voix de Prison" and "Le Livre du Peuple" went to his grave having specified that his body be presented to no church for funeral rites. He had become an anarchist and an internationalist.

Why should the tradition not be respected?

Because Lamennais was but developing the logical implications of his original point of view, taking his traditionalism and his ultramontanism seriously. He was determined that nothing should stand in the way of realizing their entire consequences. He himself was far from believing in a complete break with the past. He recognized his mistakes, his grave mistakes,[153] his haste in

[151] Cf. my apparently exaggerated statement with Ferraz (*Op. cit.* 268) which holds that before Lamennais the ultramontane party was "not yet constituted and had not even the shadow of existence."

[152] Spuller; "Lamennais," P. 1892, p. 123.

[153] See preface to the collection of articles from *Le Mémorial Catholique* and *L'Avenir*, *OC*, P. 1836-1837, X vi.

combating for Rome, for instance,[154] and his extreme ultramontanism,[155] but never his fundamental point of view.[156] That point of view was that the sole test of certitude lay not in the reason of the individual, but in the reason of the race. This he contrasted first with rationalistic individualism, which teaches that the individual's reason is eminently fitted to perceive the truth without aid. He thought that this would destroy truth's unity, since there is so much disagreement between individuals. He contrasted it second with a mysticism like Pascal's. His emphasis upon a social basis of intellectual values colors all of his thinking, gives it its fundamental unity, and produces its growth. "If we are not mistaken," he said in 1838,[157] "each of our works marks some progress made along the road on which we are marching to-day." It is that progress which we shall try to show here, for it seems to us the legitimate conclusion of the Catholic movement begun by Bonald and Maistre and propelled by Chateaubriand.

The first of Lamennais's works was his "Essai sur l'indifférence en matière de religion." Taking his inspiration from Bonald and Maistre, he preached that religion was vitally necessary to society and that society was vitally necessary to man. Without his social relations man would be reduced to a mere point, a nothing.[158] This is the germ of his later theory of solidarity. With-

[154] *OC* X xvi.
[155] *OC* X liii.
[156] *OC* X viii and xi.
[157] *OC* X lxi.
[158] "Essai," *OC* II v.

out its religious leaven, society would be dead, an inert mass. For the aim of society is civilization. Civilization comes only in order, for in order alone is there rest.[159] But where shall we find a force which orders, which unifies, which harmonizes? Only in the force which draws individuals to God. For that alone is a force which is truly social in the sense that it is overindividual. Such forces as that of the social contract, the doctrine of which is "absurd, deadly, degrading,"[160] rest upon the ultimate rights of the individual, which means disintegration of the social organism. Such a doctrine is Protestant, not Catholic, which is enough to condemn it.[161] For by shifting the emphasis from the group to the individual, it destroys society.[162] Society then simply exists at the arbitrary coincidence of individual desires. But that, of course, is the ruination of society and with society gone, what becomes of the individual? He, too, is ultimately lost.

It is to be noticed that when Lamennais speaks of society, he is not thinking of France. He is not like Maistre who scorned the medieval realism of those who assert that Mankind exists. "I see Frenchmen, Italians, Germans," said Maistre, "I do not see Man." Lamennais was more consistent than Maistre, or more naïf, perhaps both, and to him the problem of life was the problem of the relation of Man and God. Hence

[159] *Id. OC* I 275.
[160] *Id. OC* I 281.
[161] *Id. OC* I 4, 32, 294.
[162] *Id. OC* I 287.

the immediate social order had no inherent merit in his eyes, except insofar as it furthered the plans of God. To his predecessors, it was a realization of the plans of God. In his zeal Lamennais applauded the revolt of the Poles against the schismatic Tzar, and then wondered why the Pope censured him for approving of revolution. So too he lampooned the weak-kneed monarchy which dared to compromise with Revolution, which dallied with Gallicanism and other worldly movements. To him the legitimate dynasty was restored not for political but for religious ends, to bring France back to the Christian life. But there is no evidence that he was ever in secret correspondence with Louis XVIII and his nobility was of too recent a date to prompt him to jealousy of his family's prerogatives.

The religion which above all others unites men in society, says Lamennais,[162a] and thus perfects them, is Catholicism. Catholicism alone is real religion; the schismatic and protestant sects are imitations, so to speak. Quoting Maistre's "Du Pape," he tries to show that Protestantism, by appealing to individual interpretation, makes the Scriptures no single body of doctrine and hence disintegrates authority. Where then is its unifying power? No, Catholicism alone focusses the acts of men on a goal which is beyond men, bends their wills to a power which is above their wills, draws their hearts to a love which is outside their hearts. It is a religion, one might say, of humanity, not a sect of individual men.

[162a] *Id.*, pref. to 2d pt., *OC* II xix.

Its substantiation will be found not in the reason of any one man, but in the reason of the race as a whole. Which is better, asks Lamennais,[163] to say, "I believe in myself," or, "I believe in mankind"? In the case of conflict between my ideas and those of man as a whole, which ought to prevail? Even the Pagans believed in the *consensus gentium*. Before that the individual reason must give way. "Common consent, *sensus communis,* is for us the seal of truth; there is no other."[164] This anti-rationalism holds good even in science.[165]

The impotency of the reason was a doctrine which, one might think, would have served the Church in good stead. It permitted a belief in miracles and unsubstantiated dogma; it subordinated man before a higher power. But the Church has never been willing to admit it as a principle and Lamennais was going to find his defence of faith, which was meant to be a help to the Church, thrown back at him with repulsion and indignation.

The reason of the race must give itself voice and it was not difficult for Lamennais, with Bonald and Maistre behind him, to hear that voice in tradition. Tradition, however, must be shown to be homogeneous, and since Lamennais means religious tradition above all, his next step was to show the harmony between all religions.[166] He even goes so far as to say,[167]

---

[163] "Essai," avertissement to 4th ed., *OC* II lxxxii.
[164] "Essai," *OC* II 21.
[165] *Id. OC* II 25 n. 1.
[166] *Id.,* ch. xxiii and xxiv, *OC* II 32-139.
[167] *OC* III 138.

"We should now be able to observe how idolatry by subjecting man to his senses, fixing his mind on material objects, arrests the development of his intelligence and forms an invincible obstacle to the perfecting of society. But these considerations would lead us too far afield. It is enough to have shown that all which is universal in idolatry is true, and founded on a tradition which goes back to the origins of mankind; that insofar as idolatry is false, it lacks and always has lacked essential characters of true religion, unity, perpetuity, holiness."

Non-Catholic religions are true only insofar as they agree with Catholicism, for it was understood, as we have said, that "Catholicism" was equivalent to "religion." But this equivalence could never be demonstrated either by the reason or by the feelings; it will be revealed only by submission to authority, which is the testimony of God Himself, "reason universal, immutable, infinite."[168] Its proof, though Lamennais does not say so in so many words, would be its refutation. Refuse credence to authority and sectarianism sets in. With sectarianism comes individualism; with individualism, anarchy; with anarchy, the death of society; with the death of society, the annihilation of the individual. In other words, authority on religious matters is a social need, the satisfaction of which is justified in the perfection of the individual.[169] This authority is to be found lodged in the Catholic Church alone.[170]

[168] "Essai," *OC* II 193.
[169] *Id. OC* II 195.
[170] *Id. OC* II 203.

But that charges the Church with the development of humanity and the perfection of the godlike in man. It was not a charge which the Church was willing or able, unfortunately, to undertake. Lamennais, however, did not understand this. He thought that since Popes were God on earth, or what amounted to the same thing, they could do anything they chose. Their sovereignty, their right to exact obedience, was simply their independence, their self-dependence.[171] What God wanted, it seemed obvious, was that Man, His image, should be kept in line with the divine pattern after which he was made. How was it possible that Popes should wish otherwise? To him, in those early days, the idea that Popes are human with no clearer vision than their psychophysical organism provides would have been horrible. They are Christ's vicars; they are the ruling power in the Church Invisible as well as in the Church Visible. With their peculiar supernatural means of acquiring peculiar supernatural information, there was only one possible course of action open to them, the fulfillment of God's will. When Lamennais found that they were not fulfilling it—as he understood it—only two courses of action were open to him: either to conclude that he misunderstood God's will, or that they did. To have followed the former course would have been to be a good priest. To have followed the latter was to be very human. But for Lamennais it was more. It was to do what philosophers and Protestants had

[171] Pref. to articles from *L'Avenir*, OC X lvi.

been doing: to rely on the reason rather than on tradition.[172]

Lamennais was ultramontane to such a degree that he was more Catholic than the Pope. But the mountains beyond which his ruler lived were not of this earth and the Pope could not understand such ultramontanism.

After a period of years stretching from 1808, when his "Reflexions sur l'état de l'église en France pendant le dix-huitième siècle et sur sa situation actuelle" was seized by the Imperial censor, to 1830, he devoted his life to the warm defence and elucidation of this doctrine and to its propagation among the young men of France. At his home in Brittany he began the work of that society which included among its members Rohrsbacher, Gerbet, Montalembert, Lacordaire, and later Maurice de Guérin. Bit by bit his thought matured that Catholicism was the one force needed to bind men into that salutary unity which was brotherly love and in-

[172] See the conclusion to his "Défense de l'Essai sur l'Indifférence;" "In order that one may sharply conceive how our first principles differ from that of philosophy, we shall reduce both to their simplest expression.

"First principle from which we start: *That which all men believe to be true is true.*

"First principle of philosophy: *That which the reason of each man perceives clearly and distinctly is true.*" (L.'s italics)

Yet he said later in his own defense, "We had obeyed our conscience when we spoke, and they were offended by it." ("Affaires de Rome," concl., *OC* XII 276). Tradition might have shown him that obedience to conscience is no excuse for disobedience to Popes.

dividual perfection. To him the Church was still as persecuted as it had been under Napoleon or under the Directory. "We ask," he said in 1829, while Charles X was still on the throne,[173] "we ask for the Catholic Church the liberty promised by the Charte to all religions, the liberty which is enjoyed by Protestants and Jews, and which would be enjoyed by the votaries of Mohammed and of Buddha if there were any in France. . . . We ask for liberty of conscience, liberty of the press, liberty of education, which is what the Belgian Catholics ask for, like us oppressed by a persecuting government. . . . It is not a question here of political quarrels, of systems of administration, it is a question of that which one cannot without crime steal from any man whatsoever, and it is time that Catholics know whether it is intended to put them beyond the law common to all and to reduce them to a state of slavery, the equal of which has never existed in the world." All this indignation and extravagance was over the ordinances of 1828. The *Globe,* the philosophic paper of the time which we shall meet again in our studies, joined the Catholics in their protests. The Church, thought Lamennais, by submitting to the articles of 1682, was submitting to claims put upon it by a non-religious power; it was debasing its sovereignty before a force which in the nature of things was baser than it. Only a stronger force could save it and saved it must be in

[173] Pref. to "Des Progrès de la Rév. et de la Guerre contre l'Eglise," *OC* IX viii.

spite of itself. *L'Avenir* and " l'Agence génerale pour la défense de la liberté religieuse " were the result.[174]

That religion existed for the sake of humanity had been one of the earliest thoughts of Lamennais. That its truths were substantiated by the common reason of humanity alone was coeval. Why then was it unnatural that he should have defended the cause of the Church—which to him was alone truly religious—simultaneously with that of the People? The cause of God and Liberty were one and inseparable. He said in 1836-1837, looking back on these events, that the only end which *L'Avenir* entertained was the double purpose of preserving Catholicism from the evils which menaced it and, by uniting it to liberty, to prepare for liberty's enduring and peaceful triumph.[175] Christianity was for him " the highest expression of truth and love." He felt authorized to develop truth by educating human intelligence and love by improving the condition of mankind.

The doctrines of *L'Avenir* were briefly summed up as follows in the issue of December 7, 1830.[176] They in-

[174] *L'Agence* existed for the following end:

1. The annulment of every act against liberty of the clergy, by suits in courts, propaganda, etc.

2. The support of every establishment of instruction against all acts prejudicial to liberty of teaching.

3. The maintenance of the right of association for prayer, study, charity, etc.

4. The unification of local organizations into larger associations to repel all acts of " tyranny hostile to religious liberty." (" Affaires de Rome," *OC* XII 74.)

[175] See *OC* X lxxx and xcii.

[176] *OC* X 196; cf. " Affaires," *OC* XII 26.

cluded first, an absolute belief in the unity of the Church—thus excluding Gallicanism; second, a conviction that legitimacy of rule is based on justice or moral law, which excluded the dynastic principle.[177] But a government which violates its charters is not a just government, whereas a government which violates its charters in the opinion of a Bonald and a Maistre is simply freeing itself from a repressive and illegitimate burden. These two points of doctrine were enough to cause trouble. For however ultramontane the Pope might conceivably be, the bishops of France were largely Gallican. To them Lamennais and his sheet could be merely trouble-makers. Again liberty of conscience in France meant liberty of conscience for the minority, because the minority did not happen to have consciences which told them that they owed allegiance to what the hair-raising phrase of the time called " a foreign sovereign." But this was precisely what the conscience of the Mennaisians commanded.

The specific platform of *L'Avenir* contained the following planks: (1) total separation of Church and State—involving in Lamennais's mind the suppression of the ecclesiastical budget; (2) freedom of instruction—involving the repudiation of the "monopole universitaire"; (3) freedom of the press; (4) freedom of association; (5) extension of the suffrage; (6) decentralization—the permission for the communes and

[177] Curiously enough this is not unlike Benjamin Constant's theory of sovereignty, which was being formulated at about the same time. See Duguit; "The Law and the State," *Harv. Law R.*, Nov. 1917, XXXI 111.

provinces to organize their own administration, in other words, political regionalism.[178] One need not read another word to see why Gregory XVI, a Pharaoh who knew not Joseph, would condemn these planks and order the platform demolished. But when one considers that in the "Affaires de Rome"[179] Lamennais said that *L'Avenir* was urging the Papacy to recognize that nothing was stationary in the world and that the time had come for kings to go and for the people to rule themselves, one can see why the Pope trembled with horror. The interests of Gregory were as temporal as they were spiritual. The Papal States had need of French and Austrian armies if they were to be kept in order. Furthermore the Church was constructed on monarchical principles and could not tolerate this emphasis on freedom, liberty, rights. To be sure, freedom of conscience was a thing which might have been condoned, but why should Protestants and Jews enjoy it to breed more Protestants and Jews? No, even freedom of conscience would do the Church no good; she wanted and needed special privileges. This idealism, she thought, was all very well, but it would not do in a practical world. Sometimes it is necessary to compromise.

Lamennais could not understand compromise. This man who proved so brilliantly the inefficacy of the reason could not but act as if the law of contradiction guided our lives as well as our syllogisms. The encyclical "Mirari Vos" decided the death penalty for the "Agence" and for *L'Avenir*. It called the belief in liberty of

[178] *OC* X 199.
[179] *OC* XII 26.

conscience an "absurd and erroneous opinion" which flowed from "this stinking fount of indifferentism" (ex hoc putidissimo *indifferentismi* fonte) and wonders at the "supreme impudence" of some who think that any good could come to religion from that source.[180] It called liberty of the press "detestable and impossible to execrate sufficiently." "We shudder with horror (perhorrescimus), venerable brothers, to see with what monstrous doctrines, or rather with portentous errors we are crushed," wrote the Pope, and noted again the impudence of those who think that the one good book which might result from freedom of the press would atone for the host of bad ones which would inevitably ensue.[181] He looked back to the time when bad books were burned and to the creation of the Index with approval.[182] He pointed to the testimony of Saint Augustine (*In Psalm. CXXIV*, n. 7), of Saint Eucherius (*Apud Ruinart. Act. SS:MM. de SS. Murit. et Soc.* n. 4), of Tertullian (*Apolog.* cap. XXXVII) to prove that good Christians submit even to bad rulers. That removed the plank of the separation of Church and State, which was constructed by "lovers of a most shameless freedom."[183] Lamennais and his followers

[180] *OC* XII 336; "Enchiridion" 1613.
[181] *OC* XII 338; "Enchiridion" 1614.
[182] *OC* XII 340.
[183] *OC* XII 348; "Enchiridion" 1615. Cardinal Pacca, transmitting the encyclical to L., said that what displeased His Holiness the most was that the editors of *L'Avenir* had been presumptuous enough to settle points in public which it was the prerogative of Rome to settle; that they had taught civil and political liberty (the word "civil" in italics); that any

saw the impossibility of going on, and on the tenth of September 1832 signed their submission to the Church. The Pope signified his joy in a letter to the Archbishop of Toulouse the following May, but added that he was disturbed by certain rumors in the air.[184] These rumors, which Lamennais said were a trap set by his enemies who hoped he would be tempted into breaking his silence,[185] he interpreted as the news that "L'Agence" was about to begin again or had not ceased to exist. He wrote to Gregory to that effect. As Gregory had not been so specific as Lamennais, he could note with sorrow the testimony of a guilty conscience, and in October he expressed his grief to the Bishop of Rennes, basing his direct charges of Lamennais's faithlessness on a letter supposed to have been published by him in the *Journal de la Haye* three months before the letter to the Archbishop of Toulouse had been composed. This letter, said the Pope, was next to the last straw. But Lamennais said that he looked for it in the *Journal de la Haye* and failed to find it.[186] The last straw was the "Polish Pilgrim," a book *plenum temeritatis ac malitiae,* which showed conclusively that Lamennais's submission was not sincere.[187] The only gesture left for Lamennais to

---

Catholic should have taught liberty of worship and of the press. But the worst (*ce qui a mis le comble à l'amertume du Saint-Père*) was proposing to unite Catholics with liberals (*OC* XII 131). L. held that "Christianity and liberty, inseparably united in their common root, are the necessary conditions of one another" (Pref., *OC* X lxiii).

[184] *OC* XII 358.
[185] *OC* XII 137.
[186] *OC* XII 368 n. 1.
[187] *OC* XII 368.

make was the signature of his complete submission to the doctrines of the Pope's encyclical "Mirari Vos."

This was done [188] for the sake of peace, for Lamennais said that he appreciated his having signed the opinion that the Pope was God. The "bowels of paternal charity" were dilated for the repentant priest.[189] But within a half year an encyclical had been sent forth condemning a work which Lamennais said had been written a year earlier than its publication,[190] the "Paroles d'un Croyant." In this book, said the Pope, "by an impious misuse of the Word of God, the people are corrupted into breaking the chains of the whole public order, into weakening authority (of Church and State), into exciting, encouraging, and strengthening sedition in the realm, tumults and rebellions; this book therefor, which contains propositions respectively false, full of calumny, rash, leading to anarchy, contrary to the Word of God, impious, scandalous, erroneous, already condemned by the Church, in the case of the Waldenses, Wicliffites, Hussites, and other heretics of that kind, do we reprove, condemn, and wish and decree that it shall be held as reproved and condemned in perpetuity."[191]

The "Paroles d'un Croyant" were Lamennais's definite break with the Church. In it he held to every main

[188] *OC* VII 147, 166 n. 1.
[189] *OC* XII 378.
[190] *OC* XII 172.
[191] "Singulari Nos," *OC* XII 394; "Enchiridion" 1617, in part. L. in excuse of "Les Paroles" said in a letter to the Archbishop of Paris that it was a work of "philosophy, science, and politics only, not of religion." (*OC* XII 172).

doctrine of his earlier days but one—the authority of the Pope. It was a manifesto of one who believed that there was and should be no intermediary between God and His people. Humanity was still the darling of religion; religion was still Christianity; Christianity was still Catholicism—minus the hierarchy. This book was the forerunner of " Le Livre du Peûple " (1837), " Amschaspands et Darvands " (1843) and " Une Voix de Prison." There is a community of ideas in all three and we shall take them up together.

True religion is one, he held, exactly as he had held in the " Essai sur l'indifférence." It must not however be confused with the form it assumes, for the form is multiple and, as Ballanche had pointed out, it came into being and passed away. But truer religion, which is Christianity, is the bond between God and Man and is eternal. It alone of all the *soi disant* religions has progressively abolished slavery—this was written in 1837—and serfdom, and encouraged the spread of gentleness of manners and laws and of equity, hitherto unknown. In a word, to it are to be traced all the benefits which we enjoy above the Ancients and above the non-Christian peoples. If ills are mingled with these goods, it is not because of their inherent presence in religion, but because of the misinterpretation which men have made of religion.[192]

Lamennais here is obviously contradicting his traditionalism. In his last work, the " Esquisse de Philosophie," he still maintained that universal reason is more

[192] " Livre du Peuple " xiv.

reliable than individual, but surely if Christianity can be misinterpreted in its sectarian manifestations, tradition can be wrong. As in his own life he had acted as an individualist and a rationalist, so in his book he includes certain statements which are perhaps involuntary admission of the truths of individualism and rationalism. Thus he talks like Rousseau in the "Livre du Peuple,"[193] when he says that human ills come from the vices of society, which has been turned from its natural end by the selfishness of a few. And again, when he says that Nature by herself is decent, implying that the touch of Man makes her corrupt. The plants, for instance, do not steal one another's sap nor poison one another's perfume.[194] The dove is faithful to its mate and unlike man does not break its marriage vows.[195] The eagle, the chamois, the insect on the grass, the bird, all are free; only the poor are hounded.[196] "Qui me l'eût dit, ô mon Dieu, que je pleurerois d'être homme!" But society, he had said, is the vessel of truth, and it is next to impossible to reconcile this with his harsh criticism of society as it exists.

Society, as it should exist, is more easily understood. The eighteenth century is present in his belief that man-

[193] *viii*, ed. Garnier, P. 1864. Cf. Morley's "Rousseau," Lond. 1886, II 228; Gibson; "The Abbé de Lamennais and the Liberal Catholic Movement in Fr.," Lond. 1896, p. 55. Their similarity was remarked by Damiron in 1828—before Lamennais's break with the Church, *Op. cit.* 131. Lamartine noticed a similarity between their styles in 1818, after reading the "Essai"—see Maréchal; "L. and Lamartine," p. 60.
[194] "Livre" xi 136.
[195] *Id.* xii 140.
[196] "Voix de Prison" xv 207.

kind has certain rights. The right to life is inalienable;[197] it is the right of every man to develop himself according to the laws of his being. The right to liberty is equally inalienable[198] and is implied in the right to life. For to develop is to choose and to choose wisely is to choose without human compulsion. But it is not to choose without law or divine compulsion, and man is *never* free from his real master, God.[199] The Christian theocratic element now appears. Lamennais speaks like a Calvinist as he emphasizes the correlation of duties and rights. Rights are individual things; they center about the self; but Lamennais has not forgotten his old teaching that men isolated from one another vanish into thin air. The moral instrument for lifting men out of themselves and binding them to one another, is duty. Rights have as an aim the good of the individual; duties the good of all. And since society is nobler to his mind than the individuals who compose it, though it exists for their sake, duties are—if anything—more noble than rights. For in doing one's duty, one achieves one's rights.[200] From this there follow just two commandments, which Lamennais thinks contain the substance of justice and charity, (a) respect the life, liberty, and property of others; (b) help others to conserve and develop their lives, liberty, and property.[201] Victor Cousin, the philosophic apologist of the Bourgeois Mon-

[197] "Livre" v 114.
[198] *Id.* 116.
[199] *Id.* 117.
[200] *Id.*, "Au lecteur," 93; iv 111; ix 130.
[201] *Id.* xi 139.

archy, was preaching about the same thing as this anarchist in his little tract, " Justice et Charité."

This ethics is essentially theocratic. It is because God made Man in His own image that Man must be free. Liberty is the heart and soul of Christianity, he holds— the motto of *L'Avenir* was " Dieu et liberté "—and in the famous section of the " Paroles d'un Croyant " where the seven crowned men plot the enslavement of the human race, he makes the leader cry, " Cursed be Christ, who has brought Liberty upon earth." [202] To rid themselves of liberty, they decide to abolish religion, science, and thought; to strengthen national boundaries, local pride, fear, and luxury which produces cowardice. Liberty is the gift of God, servitude of Satan. It is the only way of serving God, of uniting man into a community of loyal and religious service.[203] This constant harping upon the delights of liberty and its necessity for the existence of true religion was enough to upset Rome, no matter what other tune accompanied it.

But liberty would be useless without solidarity, for liberty alone might make the strong triumph over the weak. Accordingly God has commanded brotherly love.[204] All men are equal before Him, although their physical and mental abilities are not equal. Lamennais insists that superiority of gifts is no excuse for domination; there is no divine right of rule.[205] Every man is morally autonomous;[206] there is no sympathy ex-

---

[202] *OC* XI 48.
[203] " Paroles " xix, xxxix, xl.
[204] *Id.* vii; " Livre " xi.
[205] " Livre " vii 122.
[206] *Id.* 123.

pressed for non-moral considerations of man. Man as an economic being, however, does not enjoy equality and perhaps cannot. Lamennais suggests that social instability destroys the equality of fortune and, as an amelioration of present social evil, suggests the "abolition of the laws of privilege and monopoly; the diffusion of capital which is multiplied by credit, or the rendering of the instruments of production accessible to all." [207] The affiliations of this theory are obvious.

Solidarity, which is the "fraternity" of the Revolutionists, moves mountains, is alone of sufficient strength to exterminate the evils which man encounters on his journey through life.[208] Such solidarity is recognized to be international, for as the bonds of the family are transcended by social duty, so are those of the state. "Votre patrie," cries Lamennais,[209] "c'est le ciel." Thus the exile is no worse off than anyone else.[210] God in His justice has united men into families, and families into nations, and all nations are sisters. "He who divides nations from nations, divides what God has joined; he is doing the work of Satan." This solidarity of peoples, or internationalism, is simply again a recognition that life is an affair between Man and God, which, as we have tried to make clear, was Lamennais's idea in his most Catholic days. It is the most extreme form of ultramontanism. It is absolute theocracy.

[207] "Livre" xvi 164.
[208] "Paroles" vii; "Livre" 94, vi 119.
[209] "Paroles" xviii, *OC* XI 67.
[210] *Id.* xli; but see "Livre" xiii.

If national barriers are to break down, the duties of an individual to his political superior are minimized. Lamennais becomes, consistently enough, anti-militaristic, for military duty is duty to two idols, Fidelity and Honor, which Cæsar uses to draw men away from God.[211] Similarly he urges rebellion, without hate but with grim determination.[212] He is, in fact, an anarchist as much as he is anything definite. The people, he maintains,[213] do not need to be led; they are capable of self-leadership; they are not the herd to which they have been compared; they are intelligent human beings of unequal gifts but of equal importance in the eyes of God. Lamennais's love of the poor is equalled only by his hatred of their rulers. He has written nobly of their lot and of their beauty of soul. The obvious relation between their poverty and that of Jesus has seldom failed to move men of a Franciscan turn of mind and Lamennais is at his best when he is praying for them.[214] They are the weak and the oppressed and it is for them that the heart of God is beating; they are His chosen.[215] They are the laborers, the fishermen, the soldiers, the artists, the scientists, the mass of society, and they are held in the hands of the privileged few.[216] They have become their property; and the few who own them, own them because they have broken the bonds

---

[211] " Paroles " xxxv; *OC* XI 134.

[212] *Id.* xii, *OC* XI 44; xxxvi, *OC* XI 137; " Livre," " Au Lecteur " 95.

[213] " Paroles " xxii, *OC* XI 84; " Livre " vii.

[214] " Voix " iii.

[215] " Paroles xxvii, *OC* XI 102.

[216] " Livre " ii.

of fraternity, have forsaken duty for rights, society for self.[217]

Thus was the doctrine of ultramontanism inverted into anarchism. The one premise always present in Lamennais's thought is the social criterion of values, based upon the feeling that society is somehow finer and more significant than the individuals who compose it. Therein he is at one with Bonald and Maistre and in their doctrine of traditionalism he sees but another instance of his premise. Had Ballanche carried through his ideas, it must now be apparent how harmonious they would have been with Lamennais's. What Lamennais showed at any rate was that Protestantism, or the doctrine of individual interpretation (which was synonymous with Protestantism in Catholic circles) was not the sole enemy of papal authority. The same result could be attained more directly by starting from Catholicism itself.

V

Traditionalism in itself was not condemned until 1855 in a decretal against Bonetty, a priest.[218] But as early as 1840, Gregory XVI had induced the Abbé Bautain to subscribe to a denial of what amounted to the same thing.[219] Its condemnation, a half century later than its beginnings in the neo-Christians, marks the end of that peculiar movement among Catholic philosophers which arose from considerations upon the

[217] *Id.* i.
[218] " Enchiridion " 1649.
[219] *Id.* 1622.

French Revolution. It served its purpose, when it arose, in justifying men's fidelity to the Church, and, even in the forms in which it was condemned, appeared as an instrument to raise her above all else in life. When the Church developed to the point where she asserted her own supremacy, she outlawed those of her children who dared assert it for her. Surely the Vatican Council said little more than an enunciation of Mennaisianism, with the inefficacy of the reason left out. Surely the doctrines of Bautain and Bonetty give men over to the Church more fully than the doctrine of Maistre did. Where both Lamennais and Bautain preached the inefficacy of the individual reason, they preached full submission to the authority of the Church. When Pius IX was declared to be infallible *cum ex cathedra loquitur,* he was declared to be exactly what they had said his predecessors were. Here was an infallible power condemning doctrines which supported its infallibility.

But these doctrines admitted much that anti-Catholics were happy to see admitted, in short that the Church taught truths which were contrary to reason. With the growth of natural science in the nineteenth century, it would hardly have been profitable to admit any such doctrine as that. Bautain, to be sure, tried to demonstrate that even natural science accepts truths on faith, but there were plenty of Catholic scientists to dispute that and to defend the rights of free inquiry and free polemic in their own interests. The Church had need of a stout defence both of the efficacy of faith and of reason, and wished the faithful to believe that faith could be the result of reason, preceded by reason, and in no wise contradictory to reason. If it seemed to be contradictory to reason, so much the worse for the reasoner. Reason should choose postulates whose implications would not conflict with the dogmas of the Church. It was very simple. "For who knows not or cannot not know that all faith should be given to God when He speaks, and that nought is more compatible with reason itself than to acquiesce and to hold firmly to those things which have been revealed by God, who neither errs nor causes error."[220] The Vatican Council explained the matter once and for all.[221]

Novelty in Catholic philosophy was tried in vain. Nothing contributed by the Traditionalists was accepted by the Church except their aid. They had, it is true, done much to raise the prestige of Rome, weakened as it seemed by the atheism of the Revolution, by the despotism of Napoleon, by the Gallicanism of the Restoration. But such enthusiasm as it raised was sentimental, and could in the long run do only harm. The Church had lived long enough to know the value of quietly waiting. If Catholic philosophers were dutiful children of the Church, they would submit. If not, they must pay the penalty.

If Traditionalism was not influential in molding the policies of the Church, it was only a little more influential in molding the character of French culture. Its adherents were opposed to the new movement in literature

[220] Pius IX's encycl., "Qui pluribus," "Enchiridion" 1639.
[221] "Const. Dogmat. de fide cathol." cap. 3 and 4; "Enchiridion" 1789.

and in science. It is true that in certain literary circles it was not without effect. M. Maréchal has shown what it did for the young Victor Hugo and for Lamartine. But it achieved its results through Lamennais and the liberalism which was the final philosophy of both poets was hardly an achievement of which the Church would have been proud. Lamennais's personal influence was great, even before he left the Church. But the literature which his disciples published was impressive only in the case of the Mennaisian Lamartine. Maurice de Guérin may be added to Lamartine. But with the exception of his journal, there is hardly a trace of his contact with the Mennaisian philosophy.

The art of the neo-Christian tradition which flows from Chateaubriand seems at first sight to be a much more authentic instance of the christianizing of literature. Chateaubriand himself said that after the publication of "René," "A whole family of René poets and René prose-writers began to swarm. One heard only woe-begone and unstrung phrases. They talked of nothing but winds and storms, in uncouth words tossed into the clouds and the night. There was not a ninny fresh from high-school who did not dream of being the most unhappy of men; not a baby of sixteen years who had not drained life dry, who was not tormented by his genius, who, in the depths of his thoughts, was not given over to the *waves of his passions,* who did not beat his pale and disheveled brow, and astound his stupefied fellows with a sorrow whose name was unknown to him and to them as well."[222] This is simply Chateau-

---

[222] "Mém. d'Outre-Tombe" II 262.

briand's own testimony to a fad which he created. But it was a fad insofar as it affected the art of literature and not religion. It made for romantic melancholy and not for Christian piety. In that field grew nothing of importance sown by Chateaubriand.

One of the aims of " Le Génie du Christianisme "[223] as of Ballanche's " Du Sentiment,"[224] had been to show painters that there were subjects in Christian legend as worthy of delineation as those taken from pagan antiquity. This was of course a challenge to David and his school, whose aim had been to go back to what Winckelmann had told them was classic serenity, which meant a drawing of the human figure as if it were made of marble, with little or no feeling for color. But Chateaubriand's aim was not to affect an innovation in æsthetic method; it was simply to furnish a new subject matter. He himself was a Davidian and would probably have thought it inconceivable that the Davidians should be dethroned.[225]

His aim of furnishing a new subject matter at least would seem to have been achieved. During the Revolution religious subjects had all but disappeared from exhibitions.[226] But after the Restoration they reappear. One hundred and ninety religious compositions only were shown from 1791 to 1812 in the Salon.[227] The lists

[223] 3d pt., liv. i, ch. 3; liv. ii, ch. 3.
[224] P. 179.
[225] See Rosenthal; "La Peinture Romantique," P. 1900, p. 39 n. 8.
[226] Rosenthal 40.
[227] *Id.* 40 n. 4.

we have of the paintings in the Salons of 1817, 1819, 1822, 1824, 1827, while showing a steady growth towards romantic predominance, still show a surprising number of such titles as " Saint Etienne prêchant l'Evangile " (Abel de Pujol, 1817), " l'Annonciation " (Lordon, 1817), " Mort de Saint Louis " (Ary Sheffer, 1817), " Martyre de Saint Cyr " (Heim, 1819), " Ecce Homo " (Rougel, 1819), " La Samaritaine " (De Boistremond, 1822), " Descente de la Croix " (Delaroche, 1822), " David et Saul " (Gros, 1822). *La Minerve Française* (VII 263) was delighted to ridicule this, and Jouy enjoyed himself thoroughly reporting the Salon of 1819, with its pictures of " saints, monks, powers, riches," everything " except *la patrie*." One is tempted to say that this is surely a realization of Chateaubriand's dream, but as a matter of cold fact, there was an economic reason behind it. The Revolution had stripped the churches of their paintings and it was desirable to replace them. Very few of the great painters of the time were affected. They continued to choose their subjects from Homer—Prudhon's " Andromaque " (1817); from the tragedians—Guérin's " Clytemnestre " (1817); from Apuleius—David's "L'Amour et Psyche" (1817); from Ariosto—Ingre's " Roger délivrant Angélique " (1819); from European history—Horace Vernet's " Bataille de la Navas de Tolosa " (1817); Gros's " L'Embarquement de la Duchesse d'Angoulême " (1819); Ary Sheffer's " Les Bourgeois de Calais " (1819).[223] In a majority of cases the religious paintings

[223] For a list of all exhibits, see Rosenthal, *App.* I.

seem to have been ordered by churches. Jouy says that Paris gossip attributes their appearance to orders from the Minister of the Interior. But though the *Minerve* is biassed in such matters, it is true that out of the pictures taken from Christian history exhibited in the Salons from 1817 to 1827, about fifty per cent now hang in French churches.

A real change was being introduced into the French artistic consciousness at this time, but neo-Christianity was but a contributing cause. The Catholicism of the Sentimentalists, Chateaubriand's group, was, as we have said, not much different in essence from the Protestantism of Mme. de Staël. It came from Rousseau and found its fullest expression in French romanticism. Romanticism had an historical interest, a nationalistic interest, an ethical interest, which were fed by Chateaubriand. But it was not his Catholicism which fed them. It was the mystic strain in his character, which made him and Ballanche and Lamennais so different from the rationalistic Bonald and Maistre. The latter took the weapons of the Rationalists to defend the Church. The former turned from rationalism, as Rousseau did, and pronounced their creed because of the stimulus of their feelings. The Voltairean method proved of more lasting value than the Rousseauistic, and those who used it stayed within the Church. As for the others, as long as they dealt in artistic trifles, no harm was done. When they interfered in religious apologetics, however, it was necessary to call a halt. The Church was not Romantic.

CHAPTER FOUR

The Introduction of Foreign Thinkers

By the time of Laromiguière and Royer-Collard, that is near the end of the Empire, philosophy was on its way to becoming primarily an academic interest. During the Revolution it had passed from the salon to the tribune; during the Consulat and Empire it had become the accomplishment of amateurs; but now that it was once more given a place in the educational system of the country, it was to be treated with seriousness. It could no longer be ridiculed as the passion of reformers and revolutionists. Its enemies must now attack it as the instrument of heresy.

But insofar as it was represented in the university, it was, it must be confessed, a singularly unproductive subject. Laromiguière could talk persuasively and could both charm and enlighten auditors who had little knowledge of their teacher's predecessors. But there was nothing more to be mined from the vein of Ideology; all that had been there was worked out and unless one were willing to spend his life in constant recasting of old metal, it was hardly likely that one would stay in that field. The members of the school at Auteuil were too self-satisfied to be adventurous; they were as sectarian as the Catholics. Had they been more open-minded, they would have discovered in their group the struggling

Maine de Biran; they would have attempted the solution of the problem of activity instead of leaving it to their enemies, and the history of philosophy at this point would have revealed an almost unique instance of coöperative instead of competitive development. The progress of French philosophy, insofar as it depended on strictly metaphysical interests, was to depend largely on the various solutions given to this very problem. That the Idéologues did not fully appreciate its importance is sufficient evidence that their real place is in the eighteenth century.

If Ideology was sterile, Catholicism, as we have said, was not to prove much more fertile. By its very nature it was bound to be what old age had made Ideology, exposition rather than discovery. But there was little stimulation in exposition. If one was to find new sources of inspiration, then, one must look beyond France. It had been done before. Voltaire had gone to Newton, Condillac to Locke; England had proved the great foster-mother of French genius whenever French genius had had need of sustenance. It was not a novelty in French intellectual history that the colleague of Laromiguière should turn to Scotland for his inspiration and find it in the work of Thomas Reid.

Thomas Reid is perhaps one of the last men whom one would imagine as a possible stimulus to a French thinker. No one could call him a great writer, nor a very original philosopher. There is so little brilliance in the expression of his ideas that it is sometimes difficult to find them. He was the acme of staid sobriety. But he had a certain shrewdness in his comprehension of philosophy which was invaluable and which revealed a soul made to resist the charm of novelty. He was a challenge to innovation and, though the power of his philosophy rested to a certain extent on a question-begging epithet, it was seldom attacked at its weakest point. Hence he seemed a reliable and conservative writer, not so conservative as to be reactionary, but conservative enough to be safe. He was after all the man who could help the youth of 1812 to self-understanding without despair. And that was what their teachers felt was needed.

If one believes that a certain fatality governs the rise and fall of thinkers and ideas, the case of Thomas Reid's popularity in France might be to the point. His " Inquiry into the Human Mind " had been published in a French translation at Amsterdam twenty-one years before the States General met.[1] It seems to have attracted no attention. It did not even appear in Grimm's " Correspondence " (1753-1793) where everything of any importance appeared. The French public, however, had been made acquainted with the notion of " common sense " from the works of Claude Buffier, and indeed the Jesuit's English translator accused " the Transtweedian philosopher " of direct plagiarism.[2] But their acquaintance with Reid and his leading idea did not

[1] " Recherches sur l'Entendement Humain d'après les Principes du Sens Commun," Amsterdam 1768.
[2] See the preface to " First Truths or the Origin of Our Opinions Explained," tr. from the French of Père Buffier, Lond. 1780

produce noticeable results and it is fair to say that he did not come into his own in France as an intellectual power until the time of Royer-Collard.[3]

Royer-Collard is better known as a jurist than as a philosopher. It is as the work of a jurist that his teaching is best understood. He showed the same respect for tradition and precedent in his philosophy, as he did in his theory of sovereignty and in his speeches in defense of freedom of worship. He gathered from his legal experience a respect for unwritten and uncodified custom. He felt the common notions of the Stoics in his daily work. Moreover, his legal experience was supplemented by his personal character and habits. In contrast to Laromiguière, who had been illuminated by the brilliance of the eighteenth century, Royer-Collard received his light from the restrained glow of the seventeenth. He had no love of sceptics and sensationalists; he preferred the apologists. His reading was Pascal, Corneille, Bossuet, Milton—in English we are told.[4] His life was as disciplined as his reading. His end in teaching was to give to his pupils the same calm pleasure which he himself enjoyed and in the two and one-half years during which he was Professor of the History of Philosophy (1812-1814) he seems to have had a certain success.

When he entered the Faculté des Lettres, there was little beyond his political position to give him prestige.[5]

[3] Cf. Janet; "Victor Cousin et son Oeuvre," P. 1885, p. 5.
[4] Franck's *Dictionnaire*, art. "Royer-Collard."
[5] Cf. Spuller; "Royer-Collard," P. 1895, p. 76; Damiron; *Op. cit.* 508.

He had no reputation as a philosopher, had up to that time founded no school and followed no master. Though Taine's story that his subject was Reid because he found one day a copy of the " Inquiry " on the Quais is too good to be true,[6] yet it is doubtful whether he had ever seriously considered the problems of philosophy as a dominating interest in life before his position obliged him to.

His very limitations kept him within the covers of Reid. Had he had a philosophy of his own to promulgate, he would obviously have spent his time on that. But that, it must not be forgotten, would have been highly undesirable during the last years of the Empire when Philosophy was suspect. Reid was just the man to be the philosopher of the " Doctrinaires."

During the first year of Royer-Collard's teaching, Reid was cautiously presented to the class in extracts from the " Inquiry."[7] Bit by bit his philosophy was made more precise and the second year was utilized for the substantiation and elucidation of the professor's own ideas. Reid showed Royer-Collard that knowledge was more than Condillacian sensations and less than innate ideas. It was founded not in atomic and unrelated bits of psychical stuff, but in judgments upon a real world. Thus the fundamental postulate of Hume—as Reid understood it—and of Condillac and the Idéologues—as Royer-Collard understood it—was denied. It was a denial based upon the general experience of mankind, as witnessed, for example, in speech.

[6] " Philos. Classiques," P. Nouv. ed. 21.
[7] Spuller; *Op. cit.* 80.

The attack upon sensationalism was a movement towards the right wing of the philosophic parliament. The proof through an appeal to the *consensus gentium*, though shared by Lamennais, was a democratic gesture. But for Thomas Reid, such things as traditionalism and ideology naturally did not exist. He was amply content to overthrow the doctrine of David Hume, which he thought not only sceptical, but dangerouly sceptical. For Royer-Collard Hume did not exist.[8] For him the devil to be exorcised was Condillac. Reid's philosophy was a printed charm apt not only to exorcise devils but to make saints.

Thus a middle course—later to be pursued by Cousin —between sensationalism and Catholicism was charted. It was that middle course which everyone had looked for in vain till then. Its importance was highly practical and only slightly theoretical. For during the Empire, as before and later, a man's philosophy meant his politics.[9] Royer-Collard had a very simple and homely explanation of why men pursue philosophy and why

[8] See his list of "all those who have introduced into philos. science some truth or delivered it from some error," in which neither Hume nor Kant figure. "Discours" of 1811, p. 12; ed. Schimberg, 5.

[9] Cf. Spuller; *Op. cit.* 81: "En cultivant la philos., le grave professeur ne savait s'abstraire ni de ses croyances relig. et morales, ni de ses préoccupations politiques. . . . R-C. ne pouvait pas trouver la vérité philos., puisqu'il cherchait tout autre chose, c'est-à-dire, une direction pour l'âme des hommes aussi bien que des sociétés." I do not agree with Oscar de la Vallée, "M. R.-C. et la démocratie française," (*R. Contemporaine,* 1862, II 450) when he seems to put the philosophical R-C. above political strategy.

they should continue to: philosophy is the satisfaction of curiosity about the causes of facts " observed within and without man"; it is the "source of the liveliest pleasures of the intelligence."[10] But he feared that the teaching of philosophy might have more than a hedonistic effect. It might lead men from belief in a limited monarchy either towards absolutism or republicanism. He was teaching this moderate doctrine, it must be recalled, under the eye of Napoleon, for whom he had not the warmest affection, and though his doctrine seems mild enough now to cause no shock to the most sensitive nervous system, in its own day it was not so characterless.

It may not be superfluous to summarize briefly what Royer-Collard taught in the second year of his professorship. Nothing is left of his first year.

His philosophy, a study of the origin of ideas, is based upon a distinction between sensation and perception. Sensation, for Royer-Collard, as for some of his philosophical opponents for that matter, is what would be called nowadays "affection" by some psychologists, that is the agreeableness or disagreeableness of an experience, pleasure or pain in Royer-Collard's terminology.[11] But sensation is a subjective phenomenon; it does not exist apart from psychical beings; it is "in us." Apart from sensation, however, there is an

[10] We use the text of Schimberg, "Les Frag. Philos. de R-C.," P. 1913. This is, as far as possible, a chronological arrangement of Jouffroy's text, originally published in his translation of Reid.

[11] Schimberg 21.

existent which is not in us and is revealed to us by the sensation. That sensation is not discovered by reasoning; it is discovered by some unknown process. "Nature is our sole guide."[12] "Each of our sensations is a natural sign, which without any forecast and as by a sort of enchantment suggests to us the sudden conception of some external existence, and not only the conception of this existence but the invincible persuasion of its reality."[13] The knowledge of this other existent is perception. Had Royer-Collard been interested in investigating this "unknown process," he might have been an epistemologist of importance.

Having insisted upon Reid's distinction between sensation and perception, Royer-Collard then points out the danger of ignoring it. If perception and sensation are both sensation, i. e., subjective, the external world does not exist.[14] This result, which had been accepted with equanimity by other philosophers, fills Royer-Collard with apprehension. "Here we are then come to this point, where the physical and mental worlds crumbling together leave sensation to reign in solitude above the abyss of nothingness."[15] He refuses to accept this seemingly absurd conclusion and does not mention the possibility of an Absolute Mind even to confute it. In the second place, if perception and sensation are both subjective, morality loses its foundation. For morality is founded on the sentiment of joy at the sight

[12] *Id.* 22.
[13] *Ib.*
[14] *Id.* 27.
[15] *Id.* 40.

of good and of horror at the sight of evil.[16] If there is nothing real but sentiments, good and evil are both relative and the morality of Epicurus, which has only to be cited to be disproved, is the result.[17] For the opinion of mankind is against it as it is against subjectivism.

The agnostic element in the process by which we posit an external world is duplicated in Royer-Collard's notion of what the external world is like. We know that it has the fundamental primary qualities of extension and solidity [18] which are "modified" in various ways, so as to give us the the ideas of divisibility, figure, mobility, etc. As for the secondary qualities, we know merely that they exist and that they are "the unknown causes of certain sensations." [19] That is sufficient to establish their independence of humanity in the opinion of Royer-Collard.

But so far the human mind is simply a mass of unrelated perceptions and sensations. Royer-Collard next moves on to explain how they become related. The power of relating is found in the human mind itself; it is the principle of causality.[20] Curiously enough, the principle of causality reduces to much the same thing as Hume's habitual experiencing of two events in succession, though Royer-Collard does not seem aware of this and indeed thinks that he is far

[16] *Id.* 28.
[17] *Id.* 29.
[18] *Id.* 44.
[19] *Id.* 42.
[20] *Id.* 51.

removed from Hume.[21] For our notion of causality comes not from sensory experience but from our consciousness of will.[22] Yet, it will be observed, and Royer-Collard observed it too,[23] it is one thing to perceive a causal process; it is another to perceive the necessity of the connection involved. Has Royer-Collard gone so far beyond Hume as he thinks?

The principle of causality is fortified by the principle of induction. It rests upon two judgments, the stability and the generality of the laws which govern the universe.[24] It too comes not from experience but from " our nature itself."[25] Here again he steps into a kind of Humism of whose implications he is not entirely aware. The question which he should have asked, and indeed he may have asked it—we have merely fragments of his lectures—is, "Why does human nature posit the principles of causality and induction?" Maine de Biran asked that question and answered it to his own satisfaction. But, as we have seen, Royer-Collard objected to some of Maine de Biran's pet theories, such as the perception of sensations without a perception of the Ego. He preferred a more legalistic solution of such problems. He preferred to base the validity of his two main principles on "common sense" for that seemed to require no further substantiation. Here was an autonomous something.

[21] *Id.* 59.
[22] *Id.* 60.
[23] *Id.* 62.
[24] *Id.* 63.
[25] *Id.* 64.

These doctrines and the manner in which they are founded, together with the doctrines of absolute space and time, are sufficient to place Royer-Collard in the history of philosophy. They show that he was neither an innovator of ideas nor a brilliant expositor. He has the importance of an historical fact. The doctrines which he imported from Scotland were to be of great influence in his day. His pupil, Cousin, undoubtedly found in the theory of common-sense an inspiration of eclecticism and in the Reidian theory of knowledge an inspiration of his spiritualism. Cousin's contemporary and pupil, Jouffroy, the translator of Reid, was a more orthodox devotee of common-sense and, though dimmed by Cousin's glory, he was not without a following of his own. Royer-Collard therefore can be said to have propelled the "new philosophy," as it was called, into the current of nineteenth century thought. For it makes little difference to the history of ideas whether a man is profound or superficial. A man's influence depends more often than not on his eloquence. That may have been the secret of Royer-Collard's.[26]

II

The influence of Reid and the Scottish School acted through Jouffroy and was weakened by the introduction into France or German thought. The two main German philosophers who were made known to the French public during the first half of the nineteenth century were Kant and Schelling. Such thinkers as

[26] Cf. Spuller; *Op. cit.* 84.

Herder, Lessing, Goethe, Schiller, the Schlegels, Novalis, the German romanticists in general, had a literary rather than a philosophic influence. Fichte, curiously enough, attained no popularity at all. That German philosophy should have reached the position it had is in large part the work of one man, Victor Cousin, although it must not be forgotten that if one man is able to initiate a movement, it is because other men have prepared the way.

Kant was known in France as early as the Revolution. At that time, when interest was largely directed towards social affairs, he was looked upon by the public at large as a revolutionist. Cabanis, for instance, who acted as correspondent for Garat's journal, "Le Conservateur"—not to be confused with François de Neufchâteau's—writes (2 September 1797) that the representatives of the new Batavian Republic are "penetrated with the principles of the philosophy of Kant,"[27] as if that made them better republicans. Again, he writes from Hamburg (3 October 1797) that "the strongest works in favor of liberty come from the pupils of Kant. The enthusiasm for the cause and for the philosopher seem inseparable in many minds."[28] This, adds the writer justly, is not said as the result of blind admiration for Kant on his part, for it concludes a letter in which "the new Leibniz" is harshly criticised for his vagueness and obscurity, although it does not pass over "his lively enthusiasm

[27] *Le Conservateur*, no. 2 (16 fructidor V), p. 10.
[28] *Id.* no. 50, p. 397.

for virtue, his great love of man, his energetic feeling for liberty."

A classic anecdote,[29] which would endear Kant to the Revolutionists, is given in the *Clef du Cabinet* (14 brumaire VII).[30] Kant therein is praised for his having practised what he preached. It would appear, according to this anecdote, that Frederick William II, to whom Kant's principles had been denounced as hostile to the Prussian form of government, ordered him to retract or be deprived of his chair. Kant is said to have replied—I cite only the anecdote, not the facts—"The King can dispose of my lot, but he cannot oblige me to deny my conscience and my inmost convictions." Whereupon the King relented. The *Journal des Défenseurs de la Patrie* (16 ventôse VIII—6 March 1800) quotes the Austrian general, Starray, to the effect that Kantianism had corrupted the students of Heidelberg: they were not sufficiently deferential to him and his staff.[31] So the *Moniteur* (11 ventôse III—1 March 1795) speaks of him even at that early date as the prophet of a new political order. "The philosophy of Kant," says its German correspondent, "has numerous disciples in and out of the universities. It is looked upon as full of new conceptions regarding the nature

[29] Repeated in Villers, " Not. littéraire sur M. Emmanuel Kant et sur l'état de la métaphysique en Allemagne au moment ou ce philos. a commencé à y faire sensation," in François de Neufchâteau's *Conservateur*, P. An VIII, II 31, an early version of the introduction to his book on Kant.

[30] Aulard; " P. éndant la Réaction Thermidorienne et sous le Directoire," P. 1902, V 193.

[31] Aulard; " P. sous le Consulat," I 194.

of the understanding of the human mind and capable of giving a new spurt to philosophy, which appears to be devoting its meditations to the liberty of peoples." [32] On the 13 nivôse IV (3 January 1796) there appeared in its pages a long—three and one half column—article on Kant's "Project of Perpetual Peace." Herein Kant is contrasted with the counter-revolutionary French. He is a philosopher "who professes with generosity a republicanism not of France but of the entire world." He has just "supported with the weight of his name the cause of republican constitutions." The reporter, naturally enough, italizes Kant's words, "If it should occur that a powerful and enlightened people should be enabled to form a republic, this republic, which by its nature ought to be inclined towards perpetual peace, will be a center for federal association for other states, which will be attached to it in order to assure the freedom of the states in conformity with the idea of the rights of peoples and of extending little by little the common bond." [33] The feeling that Kant was friendly to Republican ideals seems to have lingered on in the popular French mind. M. Mathiez's book on Théophilanthropie cites an "Almanach de la Franc-Maçonnerie" published in Angers in 1886 which puts Kant along with Buddha and Zoroaster as one of the martyrs and benefactors of humanity.[34]

As the popular opinion of philosophy in general declined, Kant's reputation suffered with his French con-

[32] *Moniteur,* reprint, XXIII 561.
[33] *Moniteur* XXVII 100.
[34] " Le Théophilanthropie etc." 610 n.

frères. The philosophers themselves, according to a report of the Prefect of Police (26 October 1801) complained bitterly of their new position in society and feared that public hatred would be drawn to them.[35] It was at this time that Napoleon linked Kant's name with Cagliostro's and " all the dreamers of Germany." [36] It was then that the *Journal des Défenseurs de la Patrie* in the very article quoted above says that Kant's reputation " is dying before his eyes." Three years later the *Gazette de France* (31 December 1803) laughs him to scorn, sarcastically predicting that since doctrines change with each century, Kantianism may very well be the doctrine of the Nineteenth.[37] Some of this new feeling against Kant may have been political in origin and not merely a part of the general change in the public esteem of philosophy. For Siéyès, who was about to propose a new constitution for the Convention after the fall of Robespierre, wrote to Kant for advice. Kant declined to answer. But a letter, " Antwortschreiben an dem Abt Siéyès " (tr. from the Latin, Bâle 1797), railing at the Revolution and all its works, was published as his.[38]

So much for the popular regard for Kant. The interest of the French philosophical public in him was shown as early as October 1794, when Müller, an Alsatian, in a letter to his friend Grégoire, announced that he would try his hand at a sketch of the critical

[35] Aulard; " P. sous le Consulat," II 590.
[36] " Opinions de Napoléon etc." 223.
[37] Aulard; " P. sous le Consulat," IV 607.
[38] See Barni; " Kant et la Rév. Fr.," *R. de P.*, 1856, XXX 505.

philosophy.[39] This sketch does not seem to have been published. Another of Grégoire's friend, Blessig, wrote him in 1796 that the papers were reporting a similar project of Siéyès. In that year there appeared both a translation of the "Project of Perpetual Peace" and Imhoff's translation of "The Sentiment of the Beautiful and the Sublime." The *Publiciste* of the 7th of Pluviôse, Year VII (26 January 1799) announced that a French writer was at work on a translation of the first critique, "a work which has a great reputation in Germany."[40] Meanwhile François de Neufchâteau had been running a series of articles in his *Spectateur du Nord,* written by Charles Villers and "Ph. Huldiger"[41] which he later published in the second volume of *Le Conservateur* (1800). It is interesting also that Cuvier in his "Leçons d'Anatomie" (An VIII, I 6) cites him offhand as a proponent of the theory that the whole of the living organism determines the parts, as if there were not a doubt about the prestige of such a citation. By 1804 Schweighauser, writing on "The Present State of Philosophy in Germany," can say, "The works of Kant are too well known for me to give a detailed account of them here."[42]

[39] See Gazier; "Frag. de lettres inédites rélatives à la philos. de Kt. (1794-1810)," *R. Philos.* 1888, p. 58; Picavet; "Critique de la Raison Pratique," P. 1888, Intro.

[40] Aulard: "P. pendant la Réaction Thermidorienne," V 340.

[41] He was Tranchant de Laverne, an *officier de dragons* (d. 1815) according to Quérard. Picavet, in his introduction to the "Critique of Practical Reason" (vii, n. 4) thinks that he was a friend of Grégoire.

[42] "Mélanges de Littérature et de Philos.," P. 1804, I 191.

Such interest as that noted above centered in the main about Kant as a moralist. According to Blessig the need in France was for a *clear* report on Kant's philosophy as a whole, lest there should occur there what had occurred already in Germany, " that a great number of feeble and light-headed people believe that they have found in Kant merely the patriarch of scepticism and even of atheism. It would be necessary," he went on, " as I see it, to preface the work with an introduction terse as far as the principles go, and intelligible as to style; and I believe that it would be well to append a synopsis of the work which Kant gave out two years ago on the Christian religion." [43]

Viller in his early articles shares the same interest. In fact, he says,[44] those who know Kant as a metaphysician know only a part of him. He is stronger as a destructive critic than as a system builder.[45] Hence there are presented not his metaphysical works but his " Idea of what a Universal History might be in the view of a Cosmopolitan " (*Idee zu einer allgemeinen Geschichte in Weltbürgerlicher Absicht; Berl. Monatsch.*, Nov. 1784), and his " Theory of Pure Moral Religion," (*Theorie der Reiner moralischen Religion,* Riga 1796)—in accordance with Blessig's desire? The application of Kant's cosmopolitanism to the revolutionary movement in France, which like modern sovietism pretended to be a means of international salvation, was too obvious to be overlooked. Villers could not

[43] Gazier; *Op. cit.* 59.
[44] François de Neufchâteau's *Conservateur* II 31.
[45] *Id.* 51.

but relate Kant's opinion that our forebears have been working for our happiness and we for our descendants to certain contemporary beliefs in France.[46] Again Kant's faith in a union of nations, harking back as he said to the Abbé de Saint-Pierre and Rousseau, is echoed by Villers, who believes that men are not far from enjoying the happiness that such a union will surely entail.[47] Kant, he believes, was a prophet who foresaw the political troubles of the times just as he foresaw the discovery of Uranus.[48] Indeed Villers's attitude towards Kant is that of an apostle rather than of an expositor. Kant is to him the one person who could help the world in those troubled days. It was this religious devotion which led him to abuse the French public later on for not accepting his master with the same zeal. So "Huldiger" also writes of Kant. Kant is to produce "a revolution in the human mind, advance knowledge, rectify acquired knowledge, assure the progress of future knowledge, etc., etc."[49] Such enthusiasm, if it did nothing more, was bound to call attention to Kantianism.

When the nineteenth century opened, the essays of *Le Conservateur* seem to have awakened most sympathy in Lyons. For the Lyonnais were traditional mystics. Kant's reputation as a student of moral and religious problems and the devout manner in which his opinions were discussed, were such as would not endear

[46] *Op. cit.* II 65.
[47] *Id.* 75.
[48] *Id.* 78. Cf. p. 82 and the translator's concluding notes.
[49] *Conservateur* II 210.

him to men of a sceptical turn of mind, although later he was to become known in France principally as a sceptic. "The Kantian philosophy proves victoriously the immateriality (and hence the indestructibility) of the soul, since it demonstrates that matter can provide nothing for the ideas of the reason," wrote "Huldiger"[50] "From the principle of the existence of the soul," he continued, "is easily deduced that of freedom, as from the necessity in which the reason finds itself to discover an absolute cause which links together in an absolute whole the diverse parts of this vast universe, is deduced the idea of God. By these very principles, this new philosophy destroys materialism forever." How strange this will seem to the modern reader as a judgment on Kantianism. Yet, stranger still, a reader of *Le Conservateur* would find Kant proved an opponent of idealism, dogmatism, and scepticism.

Even the immature Ballanche in Lyons expressed the astonishment that all readers of Kant or of his expositors expressed at the general ignorance of his works.[51] Ballanche went so far as to say that what he called "sentiment" in that early work of his is the basis of Kant's system of philosophy.[52] It is this remark which convinces the historian of French ideas that Ballanche's Kant is the Kant of Villers and "Huldiger." For what he calls "sentiment" is "the moral power which judges by instinct and without deliberation that which conforms to the laws of our nature, considered

[50] *Id.* II 223.
[51] "Du Sentiment," 28.
[52] *Id.* 29.

under the aspect of our *animality,* our *personality,* our *spirituality*. Sentiment never separates these three aspects; it apperceives them in an indivisible instant. The first establishes the empire of physical sensibility or sensations; the second, that of individuality or conscience; the third, that of our intellectual faculties, or of our soul." [53] In " Huldiger's " translation of the " Theory of Pure Moral Religion," the basis of human nature are given as animality, humanity, and personality.[54] Animality in this article is that which accounts for our self-preservation, the propagation of the species, and gregariousness. Humanity is the basis of our sympathy for others. Personality is the basis for morality. The parallel is not absolute but sufficiently close to suggest the historical relationship between the two writers, especially when it is supported by other details.

Another Lyonnais to be interested in Kant was Ampère, as we have already seen. He and Stapfer were responsible for introducing Kant to Maine de Biran. Ampère uses the Kantian terminology as if it were second nature. Stapfer had been a Kantian while a professor in Berne (1791-1798) and knew the critical philosophy probably better than most of his friends in Paris.[55] But besides these two men whose conversation and correspondence helped to spread Kantanianism, there were in the early years of the nineteenth

[53] *Id.* 12.
[54] *Conservateur* II 95.
[55] Luginbuehl; "Philippe Albert Stapfer," Fr. tr., P. 1888, p. 46.

century the works of the Dutch poet, P. Kinker, translated by le Fèvre, Charles Villers, Degérando, not to mention the Polish mathematician and philosopher, J. Hoene-Wronsky.[56]

Kinker's book, "Essai d'une Exposition Succincte de la Critique de la Raison Pure" (Amsterdam 1801),

---

[56] A former artillery officer in the army of Kosciusko. After a sojourn in Germany and in the Polish Legion of Marseille, he lived in poverty in Paris. According to Michaud's "Biographie Universelle," "His works concern transcendental philos. and mathematics of the highest order; he looked upon himself at once as a Messiah and as a new Newton; he announced that he had discovered the general and rigorous solution of equations of all degrees, the creation of a definitive theory of numbers, the general solution of the mechanical construction of matter in its three states of solidity, liquidity, and aeroform fluidity."

In 1893 he published a small book, the first volume of a projected set of eight, "La Philos. Critique découverte par Kant," Marseille et P., An XI. "The object of this work," said the announcement on the first page, "is the exposition first of the complete system of the critical philosophy as it was given by Kt.; second, of everything which has been done to date in Germany as a consequence of the discoveries of this great man." As a matter of fact Wronsky is interested in his own theory of what he calls the "last foundation" of the critical philosophy and, whatever he may have written on this subject elsewhere, this work does not show what the foundation in question was. Later he gave a course on transcendental philosophy of which the program was published in 1811. In it he tried to deduce all science from the principles of transcendentalism, just as he had—so he maintained—deduced the principles of mathematics. Though this course was protected by Fontanes, according to the printed program, the lecturer had no influence on his contemporaries. J. Dickstein, however, (R. Philos. 1888, p. 416) gives him greater importance than I do.

as its French title goes, is prefaced by the usual remarks about French sloth in acquiring a knowledge of Kant. Nothing has been published to speak of, says le Fèvre, " which would arouse the suspicion that the French take the slightest interest in a new science, the first effect of which will be to end baneful dissensions, the only result of which .... is scepticism and a contempt for all philosophy." [57] The main interest of this book is the review which it inspired Destutt de Tracy to write and to read before the second class of the Institut (7 floréal X).

The interpretation of the leading Ideologist of Kant's doctrine is clearly expressed in this memoir. His knowledge of Kant—like that of most of his contemporaries in France who had read Kant—was derived from Born's Latin version of his writings and not from the German originals.[58] His main objections to the critical philosophy indicate what he understood it to be. They are, for instance, (1) that sensibility is not passive since no perception is produced unless an impression excites activity; (2) sensibility receives other impressions than those *extra corpus,* for it receives internal sensations and past sensations;[59] (3) it is not necessary to have a general idea in order to make a judgment, to " pronounce that a thing is good to us, that a savor is sweet to our taste, by reporting them to the general ideas of *goodness* and *sweetness* "; (4) that Kant does

[57] *Op. cit.* i.
[58] Destutt de Tracy; " De la métaphysique de Kt.," *Mem. de l'Inst: Sci. Mor. et Pol.* IV 551.
[59] *Ib.*

not *prove* that there are two kinds of knowledge, one from our inherent faculties, one from experience, "the result of the application of these faculties to objects."[60]

As one reads Destutt one sees that curiously enough what bothers his mind in Kantianism is the feeling that perhaps it is a disguised Neo-Platonism. The Idéologues were always puzzled by the problem of general ideas which they believed to arise from "single perceptions" and from "sensations."[61] That general ideas have any reality apart from that of their origin was to them inadmissible. One sees their horror of abstractions appearing in their pupil, Stendhal, who repudiates with mockery the notion that there is such a thing as "ideal beauty." He says that he is opposed to the "idées vides" of Plato, Kant, and their school (*sic*).

That Kant was to be viewed with suspicion was also the opinion of the last of the Idéologues, Laromiguière. But his criticism was somewhat different from that of his predecessors. In a letter to his friend and pupil, Saphary, written as late as 15 May 1826, he speaks of the passage on Kant in the new edition of his "Leçons" which "will surprise those who know this author only by reputation."[62] Laromiguière in his edition of 1815-1818 had not mentioned Kant among the philosophers who had contributed to the progress of their subject,[63] nor had Royer-Collard in his opening

[60] *Id.* 561.
[61] *Id.* 578.
[62] Picavet; "Les Idéologues," Appendix, 604. Cf. letter of 13 Apr. 1827, *Id.* 606.
[63] "Leçons" II Intro.

lecture of the course of 1811. In the account of which he writes to Saphary, Kant is dismissed as a disguised sensationalist and sceptic, since he admits the impossibility of knowing objects outside of space and time. As space and time belong exclusively to sensibility, all objects which are known must be known through the senses. Hence, when we believe certain truths which by their nature cannot be known through the senses, we cannot believe them with right and justice. Kant thus becomes a sceptic, as Blessig had feared years before. His error was to limit " human sensibility " to " sensible perceptions." What he should have understood was that there are sentiments of inner psychical states, sentiments of relation, sentiments of moral values.[64] In other words Laromiguière tries to solve one of the problems which had interested Rousseau, long before Kant, the problem of relational judgments, much in the manner of some of our contemporary realists, by the positing of such knowledge among the elementary facts of cognitive experience. For his term " sentiment," as he uses it here, one has only to substitute " immediate experience "—or the term of William James, " feeling." The problem then becomes one of fact. Do we have immediate experiences of terms in relation? Happily we are not required to discuss the question here.

Charles Villers's book was much more influential in introducing Kant to the French than Kinker's was. Villers seems to have been one of those sectarians upon

[64] *Id*. 6th ed., P. 1844, II 126.

whom Tracy comments so disdainfully in his review of Kinker. " People profess the philosophic doctrine of Kant as they profess the theological doctrine of Jesus, Mohammed, or Brahma." [65] To Villers the critical philosophy with the new chemistry were " the two major tendencies of our age, the two most remarkable steps which our generation has climbed and from which it will never again descend." [66] It is this marvel which has been ignored in France. The works which have so far been translated of Kant are as representative of him as the " Essai sur le goût " and " Le Temple de Cnide " are representative of Montesquieu.[67] His doctrine has been banned by many governments; one of his pupils has lost his chair on the charge of atheism; never was a man so misunderstood.[68] " It will be believed with difficulty some day, when the literary history of the nineteenth century is written, that of two enlightened nations, living side by side, separated only by a river, one should have ignored with such constancy for twenty years what was occurring in the other." [69] " For about twenty years," he says later,[70] " a new philosophy which is of interest to all human science and to morality, which occupies the attention, either favorably or unfavorably, of all savants and thinking men, from Koenigsberg to Stuttgard, from Copenhagen

[65] P. 547.
[66] " Philos. de Kt.," Metz 1801, p. x.
[67] *Id.* xix.
[68] *Id.* xxvi n.
[69] *Id.* lvii.
[70] *Id.* lx.

to Salzburg, this philosophy is still unknown to the French, and there has not been found one man who has undertaken to study it and to make it known to his country." On the basis of this exaggerated estimate of the need for his book, Villers proposes to give an introduction to the critical philosophy.

Naturally this tone of exaggeration moved the French public to hostility. The French had their own philosophical problems to solve; there was no urgent reason to cross the Rhine in search of others. Their patience was exhausted. As Degérando had taken upon himself the task of demolishing the "Génie du Christianisme," so Ginguené in the *Décade* undertook the destruction of the "La Philosophie de Kant." "I warn [readers]," he said,[71] "that the book commences at page 251 and ends at page 262." Within a few month the *Décade*[72] counted the slain, saying, "Within two weeks the *pétard* was forgotten by the public and the philosophers of Paris were neither wonderstruck by it, nor frightened, nor irritated. . . . A great thing had been announced to them and they saw only a little one; they wished to know a foreign philosopher, worthy of respect and too little known, and they were grossly abused, literary France was insulted, and they were taught nothing."

In spite of his apostolic tone and his wretched style, Villers gave an account of Kant's philosophy which was not only much the best thing that had as yet

[71] *Décade*, 30 fruct. IX (17 Sept. 1801).
[72] *Décade*, 20 brumaire X (11 Nov. 1801).

appeared on the subject, but was in itself worthy of serious consideration. He displayed not only a knowledge of Kant, but, what was rarer, of Kant's antecedents; his correlation of Kant's unknown things-in-themselves and subjective space and time with Maupertuis's reflections on the same matter are of interest to historians even to-day.[73]

The most important result of Viller's book would seem to be its effect on Mme. de Staël. This woman to whom philosophy was a guide to life, fell in love with the most technical and least winsome of philosophers upon reading it. She immediately made the acquaintance of its author and incorporated what she learned from him in "De l'Allemagne," of whose influence it seems almost supererogatory to speak.

To Mme. de Staël, Kant was father not only of a different philosophy, but of a new philosophy.[74] Less poetic than Platonism, less religious than occasionalism, it is more genuinely moral than either, one gathers, for it heightens "moral dignity, establishing all that is beautiful in the heart upon a strongly reasoned theory." She admits the obscurity of the Kantian metaphysics, which is the foundation in question, but compares Kant to the Israelites who had as their guide a pillar of fire by night and a pillar of cloud by day.

Mme. de Staël is above all attracted by the practical effects of Kant's doctrine and by the prophet's moral enthusiasm, just as Cabanis was. "Metaphysics," she

[73] Villers; Appendix to *Op. cit.* Cf. Maupertuis, "Fourth Letter," *Oeuvres,* Lyon 1756, II 196.
[74] "Allemagne," ch. 6, Pt. III, 428.

said,[75] "social institutions, the sciences, all should be appreciated in accordance with the moral perfection of man: it is the touchstone which is given the ignorant as well as the man of learning." One cannot but sympathize with her. Moral dignity was exactly what was lacking at this time. The stern devotion to duty, even in a bad cause, would have been a refreshing novelty. No one seemed firm in the strength of his spirit except those who, like Mme. de Staël, had been exiled. Opportunism was the reigning philosophy of life as the *Dictionnaire des Girouettes*[76] tried to make clear. The Empire had been founded by opportunism and had been kept alive by it. It built up reputations and terminated great careers. If ever there was a day in which eternal principles were openly made temporal, it was the day when Mme. de Staël's book appeared. Much hostility and fun were directed against it, to be sure.[77] It deserved a great deal of what it received, for there is not a line in it from cover to cover which displays the slightest sense of humor.

The treatment of Kant which received the most cordial attention from philosophers, was that of Degérando in his "Histoire Comparée des Systèmes de Philosophie" (P. 1804). Dégerando, like Villers, deplores the sort of barrier which existed between French and German men of letters, but in a manner much more fitting to the task of eliminating it.[78] He discusses Kant's

[75] *Id.* Pt. III, ch. 1.
[76] p. 175.
[77] Blennerhassett; *Op. cit.* III 515.
[78] *Op. cit.* I 439 n. 1.

aims, his methods, his results. He finds Kant's aim to be the construction of a *via media* between scepticism and dogmatism, rationalism and empiricism, idealism and materialism.[79] The first aim gives rise to the problem, "How is knowledge possible?"[80] The second, "What is the law in virtue of which we form a chain of observed phenomena?"[81] The third, "What is the criterion of *a priori* and *a posteriori* knowledge.[82] Degérando then takes up each of these problems in turn and gives what he thinks is Kant's solution. The rest of his exposition is concerned with synthetic and analytic judgments,[83] the reason,[84] matter and form,[85] space and time,[86] the categories,[87] etc. Hence, as his exposition was interlarded with quotations, readers of it were bound to derive from it not only a concise idea of what Kant was teaching, but also an acquaintance with the Kantian terminology.

Degérando is by no means overcome with the majesty and originality of Kant's thought. He admits its success[88] but attributes it not only to the vast range of its details, its order, its severity;[89] but also to its satisfying of man's weakness for the mysterious and difficult. The new philosophy was surrounded by a haze of glory; to be a disciple was to have been initiated into some Eleu-

[79] *Id.* II 180.
[80] *Id.* II 182.
[81] *Id.* II 183.
[82] *Id.* II 184.
[83] *Id.* II 200.
[84] *Id.* II 202.
[85] *Id.* II 205.
[86] *Id.* II 208.
[87] *Id.* II 212.
[88] *Id.* II 247.
[89] *Ib.*

sinian rite until then unknown.[90] It is this sectarianism which embitters Kantians and their opponents.[91] The sole positive result seems to be the number of philosophical systems it has begotten.[92]

After the publication of Degérando's history, information was available both on Kant's life and ethics, and also on his metaphysics. It was then that the philosophers began to read and study him not only in synopses of his work but in the original. The Lyonnais group had already begun studying him, as we have seen; the circle of Joubert, which included Bonald, Fontanes, Mme. de Krudener, Chateaubriand,[93] was soon to be introduced to him, for their host was deep in the Latin translation and was finding little there but emptiness;[94] the group at Auteuil, to which Degérando belonged, had given him fairly serious attention. Biran's philosophic club, whose members included the elder Ampère, Stapfer, Royer-Collard, and the young Victor Cousin, was to be the most successful patron of the critical philosophy of the times.

In spite of its influence, Kant cannot be said to have played a large part in the philosophy of the early nineteenth century in France. Some years later, when Victor Cousin came to the fore, students were to receive an impetus to study him more closely. Cousin's

[90] *Id.* II 249.
[91] *Id.* II 266.
[92] *Id.* II 269.
[93] Raynal; "Correspondants de J. Joubert," 124.
[94] "Pensées de J. Joubert," 4th ed., P. 1864, II 62.

interest in Kant was not so profound as it might seem at first sight. His deeper interest was in Schelling and Hegel with both of whom he was able to maintain a lasting friendship.[95] From both he absorbed certain doctrines. But he did inspire the first complete and scholarly translation of Kant's critiques, that of Jules Barni, who devoted both his intellectual life and a good part of his income to this work.[96]

Whether the feeling that Kant was a revolutionist persisted; or whether the notion that he was a religious sceptic held sway, the Restoration did not feel that warmth for him which it felt for his successors in Germany. Yet in the second half of the nineteenth century; one of the leading philosophical schools claimed, with more or less reason, direct descent from Koenigsberg, and readers of so non-academic a book as Barrès's "Les Déracinés" will recall how strong a hold Kantianism developed upon the philosophic teaching of French professors.

III

One may, I think, say with confidence that the works of Schelling were known to only a very limited group before the time of Cousin. It is true that Degérando had included him in his history and that Ancillon in

[95] See his correspondence with them in Barthélemy-Saint-Hilaire; "M. Victor Cousin, Sa Vie et sa Correspondance," P. 1895.

[96] See Dide; "Jules Barni, Sa Vie et ses Oeuvres," P. 1891, p. 56.

1809 had spoken of him in the normal manner as one of the followers and opponents of Kant, contrasting him as a "naturalist" with Fichte, the "transcendentalist"[97] But the account covers merely a few pages. Mme. de Staël writes of Schelling and Fichte in much the same way.[98] Random notices in the public press do not seem to occur with the abundance one might expect. For Schelling was at that time a great figure in Germany, whose only rival was the more youthful Hegel. His philosophy of nature was, moreover, the type of thinking which ought to have appealed both to the growing romanticists and to those strange figures like Hoene-Wronski, Baudreville, Allix, Azaïs,[99] who read a moral significance into the natural order in a manner like that of some of the medieval symbolists or of the

[97] "Mélanges de Littérature et de Philos.," P. 1809, II 134, 142.

[98] "Allemagne," Pt. III, ch. 7.

[99] J. B. P. Baudreville, author of "Mes Conjectures sur le Feu, Considérés dans l'Univers et dans l'Homme Physique et Moral," Strasbourg, 1808. This book represented God as the active and Matter as the passive elements in the universe. Fire was God's agent in carrying out His will. Baudreville, who was an artillery officer under Napoleon, made much of the use of heat in producing chemical changes and physical movement and in maintaining life. He was inspired largely by the discoveries of Lavoisier, Laplace, Galvani, and even by Mesmer. He was typical of a kind of philosopher during the Empire and the Restoration.

A good account of J-A-F. Allix's "Théorie de l'Univers," P. 1818, is given in the *Minerve* II 57. For Azaïs, see our Appendix.

neo-platonists, and who had their followings here and there in France.

The notices of Schelling and of Fichte, too, which appear before the time of Cousin are extraordinarily hostile. They remind one of Napoleon's remarks about philosophers in general. Even the *Mélanges de Littérature, d'Histoire, et de Philosophie* whose purpose was to introduce foreign ideas to Frenchmen,[100] cannot mention the post-Kantians without ridicule. Perhaps the fairest article on them is that of Schweighauser, the classical student, on "The Present State of Philosophy in Germany." But he, too, feels that both Fichte and Schelling are much less worthy of serious consideration than Kant. For the rest, the magazine vents its scorn upon the new schools in its literary notices. "The secrets of nature," it says in one of these notices,[101] "are being revealed more and more to the happy disciples of Fichte and Schelling. In a book *on the nature of things*, published at Leipzig, M. J. J. Wagner was sufficiently inspired to explain and demonstrate *a priori* the phenomena of physics and chemistry, which *wretched observers* are constrained to determine by experiment, etc." Or again, Treviranus, author of a book which attempts to derive natural science and medicine from philosophy, is said to be distinguished from "the new school of Schelling," "by his study of facts and his respect for experience."[102] Mesmel's essay on logic is

[100] See Prospectus, I 1804 and Degérando's article, "Des Communications littér. et philos. entre les nations de l'Europe."
[101] III 1804 p. xv.
[102] *Id.* xvi.

said to have been praised for its poetic style. "We shall remark in passing that one of the discoveries of this new school is that *logic is in no way a part of philosophy* as we had been simple enough to believe. This is a painful loss to philosophy, but one must believe that these gentlemen have their reasons for condemning it."[103] These examples will suffice to justify our opinion.

But if the editors of the *Mélanges* were hostile to the post-Kantians, the reason for their hostility may be found in the presence of Villers among them. He seemed to feel that his worship of Kant involved the persecution of all other sects. The name of Kant thus finds respect whenever it appears. There is, of course, an article on his death.[104] There is an account of his "Conjectures on the beginning of human history."[105] There is a reprint of Jaesch's appeal to Kant's correspondents to forward their letters for publication.[106] There is a long article by Schweighauser epitomizing Kant's physical geography.[107] There is finally a free translation of a treatise of Kant on theodicy.[108] And yet with all this respect for Kant and ridicule for his successors, the *Mélanges* does not find it beneath its dignity to speak of the very inferior Azaïs's "Essai sur le Monde" as a "very singular and very systematic

[103] *Id.* xl.
[104] *Id.* 389.
[105] *Id.* 1805, VII 363.
[106] *Id.* 1806, IX ix.
[107] *Id.* 1806, XI 334.
[108] *Id.* 1807, XV 90.

work, but written with a clearness rarely found in productions of this kind."[109]

In 1817 the *Mélanges* found a sort of successor in the *Archives philosophiques, politiques, et littéraires*. This paper was directed by Royer-Collard, Guizot, Cousin, and their group. It had much the same goal as that of the *Mélanges* except that it spent more space on topics which were purely French. It was more conscious of the subterranean agitation in Europe than the *Mélanges* had been ten years before. "Whoever will observe attentively the present state of the world," it said in its prospectus,[110] " will be necessarily led to recognize in it a great character; a new spirit which is stirring the bulk of Europe in all directions, philosophy as well as politics, moral doctrines as well as literary systems, opinions as well as facts; everything is moved to follow a direction different from that of earlier times." Where it will end, no man can say. In order to follow it, the editors felt that they must know foreign letters and philosophy.

The philosophical interests seem to have been in the hands of Cousin—perhaps under the guidance of Royer-Collard. Cousin gives to Schelling and Fichte the respect with which we are accustomed to see them treated to-day. He wonders at the omission of Schelling from the French translation of Buhle's "History of Modern Philosophy"[111] and hopes to make it good himself. But this hope was never realized in the

[109] *Id.* 1806, XI lxx.
[110] *Archives* I 4.
[111] P. 1817, I 49.

Archives and Cousin used what space he had for the development of his own ideas on Locke, Reid, and Kant,[112] on his distinction between spontaneity and reflection,[113] which was supposed to be a refutation of Fichte, by the way, on real and ideal beauty,[114] on Descartes's proof of his own existence,[115] and on *programmes de cours* of his own and of Jouffroy.[116] He was not yet prepared to treat the post-Kantians as men deserving extended notice.

The successor to the *Archives* may be said to have been the *Globe* (1824-1831). It too prided itself on its catholic interests at a time when all the peoples of Europe were united towards a common goal.[117] It was proud of its range and disclaimed any idea of anglicising or germanizing France by the propagation of English or German literatures. It was on the whole in favor of romanticism as against classicism; it was profoundly liberal in its politics; it was eclectic in its philosophy. Yet one looks in vain in its pages for an article on Schelling or Hegel and finds but two small biographical articles on Fichte, one on his youth and one on his death, both of which were lifted from the *Nouvelle Revue Germanique*.[118] Purely anecdotal, these articles mention their subject's philosophy merely in

---

[112] *Id.* I 200.
[113] *Id.* 1817, II 330.
[114] *Id.* 1818, III, opening essay.
[115] *Id.* III 316.
[116] *Id.* III 436; IV 86.
[117] See Prospectus.
[118] 1829, I 345; *le Globe*, 30 Sept. 1824, VII 615; 10 Oct. 1829, VII 639.

passing, as if it were either without interest to the French reader, or too well known to require elucidation.

Cousins personal introduction to Schelling came about on his visit to Germany in 1818. His entry into Germany the preceding year had not brought him face to face with him. As they were two kindred spirits, "enthusiastic and expansive," as Paul Janet put it,[119] they quickly reached an understanding.

Cousin never admitted in public the effect which Schelling had had upon his thought. He was above all a professor and a politician, the leader of a school; his business in life was to expand and criticise other men's ideas and to keep his own intact. He must pretend that his interest in Schelling was similar to his interest in Plato and Aristotle. Schelling was simply another philosopher. He wrote to his friend Kehl, in 1817, "I should be still younger than my age if I were going to muddle our nascent school of spiritualism by throwing it roughly into the premature study of foreign doctrines of which it is not easy to grasp firmly the merits and the defects and to measure the exact import. No, let us leave the new French philosophy to develop naturally by its own virtue, by the power of its own method, that psychological method, so disdained in Germany and which is, in my eyes, the one source of all true light, etc., etc."[120] Yet later, in 1866[121] Cousin admitted borrowing from both Hegel and Schelling,

[119] "Victor Cousin et son Oeuvre," P. 1885, p. 181.
[120] Barthélemy-Saint-Hilaire; "M. Victor Cousin, Sa Vie et sa Correspondance," P. 1895, I 74.
[121] "Frag. Philos." V lxiv, lxvi.

and in an unpublished fragment on Hegel, he speaks of Shelling's system—without denoting which one he is referring to—as "the true system."[122]

It would never have done to make such admissions openly while still a professor. Let some younger man, who had no pretensions to leadership, be the French Schellingian. "Mon jeune ami, M. Ravaisson,"[123] who was then in Germany, seems to have been selected as the likeliest candidate. The first work of the great German to be translated into French was to be his judgment on the philosophy of M. Cousin. It was Schelling's preface to the German translation of Cousin's preface to his "Fragments Philosophiques." It appeared as "Jugement de M. de Schelling sur la philosophie de M. Cousin,"[124] but was translated not by Ravaisson but by Wilm. It broke a silence on the part of Schelling of twenty years. It was not until eight years later that one of his complete works, "System des Transcendentalen Idealismus" was translated. What occasioned this delay is not utterly clear. Schelling was not entirely satisfied with Cousin's opinion of him nor of Cousin's neutrality in the Schelling-Hegel quarrel.[125] Was Cousin deliberately holding back? Did he feel that a revelation of Schelling's own writings to the French public would be a danger to eclecticism?

[122] Barthélemy-Saint-Hilaire; *Op. cit.* III 54.
[123] C.'s letter to Schelling, 26 June 1835 in Barthélemy-Saint-Hilaire; *Op. cit.* III 92.
[124] Strasbourg et P., 1835.
[125] See his letter of 27 Nov. 1828, Barthélemy-Saint-Hilaire; *Op. cit.* I 257 and C.'s answer, *Id.* 268.

Was he hesitant about having Schelling translated unless Hegel were too? Or was he unable to interest possible translators, he who had no trouble when other philosophers were concerned?

The interest of the French public in Schelling had already been aroused. In 1833 the *Revue des Deux Mondes,* always friendly to trans-rhenan culture, published a long article by Barchou-Penhoën[126] the interpreter of Ballanche and Fichte, which gave a detailed exposition of both Schelling's philosophy of nature and of his philosophy of history. He went into the details of Schelling's system, the dualism of opposing forces, of chemical combinations, of organic substances, of sex. He spoke of Schelling's conception—later utilized by Bergson—of the summation and continuance of the past in any present moment of life. He contrasted the philosophy of nature with materialism, pointing out that whereas the materialist made life the product of infra-vital existence, the Schellingian made life the producer of infra-vital existence, again in a measure anticipating a Bergsonian doctrine of importance. He did not overlook the essential unity of the vital principle, which corresponded interestingly enough with Cousin's God, who at times became a highly personalized Jehovah, and at times the world itself.

Schelling had also, to some extent, been presented to the scientific public. The long and detailed "History of Natural Sciences," which was begun by Cuvier and completed by his friend, T. Magdeleine de Saint-Agy,

[126] *RDM* 1833, I 337.

devotes a whole section to the philosophy of nature, deriving Schelling's system from Goethe's ideas of transformationism on the one hand and on the other from Kielmaier's formula of the law of recapitulation. He speaks briefly of the Schellingian theory of polarity and develops its consequences with some fretfulness over Schelling's metaphors, but on the whole with restraint.[127]

Schelling's philosophy of nature was charming in its apparently scientific solution of oppositions which science makes no attempt to solve. The conquests in chemistry and electricity were catching the popular imagination in a way which anticipates the contemporary fascination of psychology. The publishers' announcements had many an item of popular interpretations of science. Schelling was bound to be *à la mode*, for his facts were no more difficult to understand than those of a hundred disreputable philosophers in France and they were interpreted in the light of a philosophical theory which was more respectable, which was almost sacred. Men like Azaïs and Baudreville were beyond the pale; Schelling was a professor and a member of a number of learned societies. He was also a foreigner.

His philosophy of history was constructed to please the French of the day more than the philosophy of nature. In the second part of his article, Barchou-Penhöen discussed that element of Schellingianism.[128] The opposition in natural forces was here shown to be mirrored in the contrast between determined nature

[127] V 313-331.
[128] *RDM* 1833, II 163.

and free history—compare Bergson's determined matter and free life. But since there is in human history a mingling of material and vital principles, history is seen to be a synthesis of necessity and freedom. But is this real freedom, freedom that is wanted by revolutionists? It is exactly the kind of freedom which General Cavaignac offered them through the medium of Cousin's little tract, "Justice and Charity." Just as Cousin emphasized the correlation of rights and duties,[129] so Schelling emphasized the correlation of necessity and freedom. It was of course the Kantian doctrine of freedom within the limits of duty, but it was presented in an unfamiliar manner.

The appearance of a synthesis realizing itself here on earth was another point to win the hearts of Frenchmen. It invested the idea of progress with new authority, the authority of natural science. The precision of historical periods, the periods of fatality, of nature, of providence, in which God will appear to man, was exactly what was demanded of a kind of thinking little given to precision. Comte was satisfying the same need with his positivism. Barchou-Penhöen's readers were living under Louis-Philippe. Was he not a synthesis himself—in 1833—of monarchy and democracy? He, the King, was the incarnation of that strange principle of liberty which is identical with and yet different from necessity.

This feeling of satisfaction with Schelling is well expressed by M. A. Lèbre, writing ten years later in

[129] "Justice et Charité," P. 1848, p. 22.

an article called, "La Crise Actuelle de la Philosophie Allemande"[130] "This philosophy," he said, "satisfied the most opposed needs, the good sense which makes us believe in an external world, the reason which rediscovers itself throughout the universe, the sympathy which attracts us towards nature and makes us love in her a sister associated to our destiny. All the sciences took a new spurt. They no longer remained isolated, like the scattered stones of a building whose plan is lost, their nobility was heightened, for all had for their goal the august science of God. It was one's life whose secret was found in nature, it was one's history which was duplicated in the annals of humanity. All was coördinated in a magnificent harmony." What Mme. de Staël had admired in the German philosophers was their examination of self-consciousness.[131] What the readers of the romantic period admired was the adjustment of self-consciousness to the natural order, for that was far more the *mal de siècle* for which they sought a cure than ignorance of the self.[132]

[130] *RDM* n. s., 1843, I 7.

[131] "Allemagne," Pt. III, ch. 7, after the account of Fichte and Schelling.

[132] If one reads the first chapter of the "Confessions d'un Enfant du Siècle," he will see how to Musset, at any rate, the problem in life was to find a *pou sto*. See, for instance, the passage, "Ce fut comme une dénégation de toutes choses du ciel et de la terre, qu'on peut nommer désenchantement, ou, si l'on veut, *désespérance;* comme si l'humanité en lethargie avait été crue morte par ceux qui lui tâtaient le pouls. De même que ce soldat à qui l'on demanda jadis: A quoi crois-tu? et qui le premier répondit: A moi; ainsi la jeunesse de France, entendant cette question, répondit la première: A rien."

The introduction of Schelling into French thought may be said to be strictly due to Ancillon and Mme. de Staël. It was vaguely encouraged by Cousin. The first important writer, however, upon whom Schelling had an influence was Ravaisson, who belongs properly to the second half of the century.

CHAPTER FIVE

THE RISE OF ECLECTICISM

The name of Victor Cousin is almost synonymous with the name of philosophy in France after the Restoration, for he ruled the philosophic milieu with a relentless vigor. He took over the chair of Royer-Collard when he was but twenty-three years old and held at the same time the direction of philosophy at the Ecole Normale. This task might easily have awed and inhibited a person of more years, for the duties of his position involved political as well as philosophical sagacity. But its importance was an inspiration to this youth. He plunged into philosophical instruction like a swimmer into a stream, sped through it easily and deftly, avoiding treacherous currents with the dexterity of one who is divinely guided. He laid out a course which ought to have proved a safeguard to his fellow adventurers and indeed it did, as long as they followed him. But unfortunately the river in which he swam was not left to the control of nature. It had been dammed at its broadest part by men who wished to use its power for their own ends, and the young enthusiast, after a race of five years, found himself swept over a precipitate cascade. Left for dead, he spent a certain time in repose, and soon was back in the stream as lively as ever.

Cousin seems to have seen his goal from the very start. It was no more a purely philosophic goal than that of the Idéologues or the Traditionalists. It was a political goal.[1] His task was to found a philosophy which would be non-Catholic and non-atheist, which would provide for liberalism but not for republicanism. It was to be a philosophy of the *media via,* neither extreme right nor extreme left. He was, he said later,[2] a believer in the principles of the French Revolution. Yet he thought that they could be best safe-guarded in a constitutional monarchy. One might imagine that this compromise philosophy would have done very well after the excesses of the Emperor. But the Restoration was not interested in compromises. It was interested in more autocracy, provided it was legitimate autocracy. Cousin therefore was not officially appreciated until the reign of political compromise. He was eminently fitted to give philosophical expression to the rule of Louis-Philippe. Who can doubt that he accomplished that much at least?

His first duty was to rid himself and his audience of the Sensationalism of the eighteenth century, which

[1] His opponents saw this early in his career. See Lerminier; "Lettres Philos. à un Berlinois," Lettre III, *RDM,* 1832, XI 744. After Cousin's arrest, says L., he saw the futility of Hegelianism. "Il saisit sur-le-champ combien le changement était capital; ce ne sera plus un philosophe opposant, révolutionnaire, inquiétant pour les puissances, mais un sage dominant tous les partis, tous les systèmes, et, par son inépuisable impartialité, pouvant donner des garanties au pouvoir le plus ombrageux." Cf. P. Leroux; "Réfutation de l'Eclectisme," P. 1839, *passim.*

[2] "Fragments Philos.," 5th ed., P. 1886, III 2.

THE RISE OF ECLECTICISM

he trickily called, after Villers perhaps,[3] "sensualism." "We finally chose," he said,[4] "the eighteenth century because, while recognizing what there was of true and noble even in the desires and tendencies of the century from which we are emerging, we propose firmly to combat and break the tradition of materialism and atheism, of the blind hatred of Christianity, of revolutionary violence and servility, which it handed on to us and which at the beginning of the Restoration still weighed upon our minds and souls with a deadly weight and was an obstacle both to the establishment of liberty and of true philosophy." This course was given in the winter of 1818-1819. Five years earlier, as we have mentioned in a preceding chapter, Victor Cousin had sustained the thesis in the Faculty of Letters that Condillac had gathered together all the knowledge of Bacon, Descartes, Malebranche, and Locke about philosophic method and had amplified it, and that analysis is the proper method of philosophy.[5] His advance was rapid. In three years he had forgotten Ideology and Condillacism. In due season he was able to cry to the youth of the land, in his preface to "The True, the Beautiful, and the Good,"[6] "If you love freedom and your country, flee from that which has proved their ruin. Far from you be that gloomy philosophy which preaches materialism

[3] "Philos. de Kant," p. 154.
[4] "La Philos. Sensualiste," pref. to 3d ed., dated 1855, P. 1856, ii.
[5] "De Methodo, etc.," esp. the theses, p. 19.
[6] I use the edition of 1884, p. v. Hereafter *VBB*.

and atheism as doctrines destined to regenerate the world; they kill, true enough, but they do not regenerate." This was a far cry from his dissertation. But what Cousin hated in sensationalism was its pragmatic import. It could not satisfy man's most imperious need, the need of "fixed immutable principles ... wherein the spirit rests with limitless confidence."[7] Parmenides had no better defence of idealism to offer Socrates.

It is in the development of this point of view that Cousin's spirit of compromise makes itself evident. He does not grapple with the problem of whether the spirit's need of rest is a criterion of the truth of those doctrines which satisfy it. He is content to assert it. But the need engenders a whole metaphysics. For the possibility of those fixed principles, he continued, lies in the existence of a fixed immutable subject of experience which perceives the sameness and the difference of the objects which affect it.[8] The subject, which like Condillac's statue, is merely a compound of sensations, could never act upon the sensations which it experiences. It would not have experiences; it would be experiences. This would result in the intolerable scepticism of Hume. And since Cousin felt that the intolerable was the false, the philosophy of the Idéologues is false. He did not deny the existence of the body, or the need of having a body, if ever the mind is to perform its functions properly. Indeed he praises the sensationalists for their perspicacity in

[7] *VFB* 19.
[8] *VBB* 43.

seeing this.[9] But he did deny that the sense-organs are more than instruments for the soul—which is not different from what Bonald had said.

It might appear that such a doctrine would lead to mysticism. But here Cousin compromises. Mysticism is "pusillanimously sceptical" about the reason. It seeks too much when it demands an intuitive vision of God.[10] It corrupts feeling by exaggerating its power;[11] it is based upon an incomplete account of human nature.[12] This last objection is the only one which can be tested by fact. One looks in vain for any extended substantiation of it in Cousin. He preferred to give deeper reasons why mysticism should be spurned. It leads to quietism, which is little different in the long run from the tolerance of evil and crime.[13]

In this insistence upon the practical effects of a doctrine as a means of refuting it, Cousin showed again his political interests. Mysticism in his mind seems to have been as much associated with the new social sects appearing in France, Saint-Simonism, for instance, and Fourierism, as with the philosophy of Boehme and Saint Theresa. Their programs of reform were not based upon the need of a strong middle class but upon sentiments such as brotherly love. The development of Saint-Simon's ideas through Father Enfantin would be sufficient to indicate the

[9] *VBB* 435.
[10] *VBB* 105.
[11] *VBB* 111.
[12] *VBB* 113.
[13] *VBB* 116.

alliance of mysticism with social cults which, in germ in Cousin's early years, was plainly alarming. Would there not be a danger to constitutional monarchy in a purely spiritual life? Might the danger not be especially grave for his young auditors?

It is also possible that in Cousin's mind mysticism simply meant " anti-rationalism." In spite of the rationalistic Bonald and Maistre, rationalism was accused of leading to atheism and was at times confused even with sensationalism. For the words were now used to mean a reliance upon the reason as distinguished from, say, faith—and now as the derivation of all reality from Reason. The sensationalists were often rationalists in the first sense. Hence philosophy as contrasted with religion was anathema to the religious party. But Cousin staunchly held out for the free right of inquiry and believed that this right was invested in the reason. Therefore his attacks on mysticism were as often as not attacks on the Traditionalists. He did not combat them openly, since during the Restoration they were associated with the government. But he could more subtly indicate their weak points. When he said, for instance, that just as one must not make the reason a purely personal affair, so one must not with Malebranche confuse it with God,[14] did he really think that anyone in 1817 was going to Malebranche for guidance in philosophy? The danger was rather in fleeing to the bosom of Lamennais.

[14] *VBB* 101.

In his own eyes, Cousin was an empiricist of the most pronounced type.[15] He believed in following the method of observation, as any experimentalist would, and not in laying down general ideas from which deductions might be drawn. That method, like his pragmatism, was not further substantiated. But his empiricism was limited. If the empirical school would pretend that there is nothing beyond experience, he would leave it.[16] There are certain general principles which the mind possesses—the principles of "substance" and of "causalty"—knowledge of which is preceded by observation but not explained by it.[17] This, said Cousin, was the extent of his agreement with Kant. These general principles are revealed by the mind's self-scrutiny, as they were in both Maine de Biran and, alas, in Schelling.

Since it is of high importance to understand them, the first task of the philosopher is a study of the Ego, a study which Cousin thought began with Descartes.[18] This task developed into what Cousin called "the psychological method," well expounded by his pupil, Jouffroy.[19] But Jouffroy believed that direct observation revealed the Ego in its nudity,[20] whereas Cousin held

[15] "Premiers Essais," 3d ed., P. 1855, p. 151. Hereafter *PE*. Cf. *VBB* 20.
[16] *VBB* 13.
[17] *VBB* 14.
[18] *PE* x.
[19] "De l'organization des sciences philosophiques," and "De la légitimité de la distinction de la psychologie et de la physiologie," in "Nouveaux Mélanges Philos.," P. 1842, pp. 206, 223.
[20] "Nouv. Mél." 236.

that the Ego retreated from observation, leaving only its phenomenal states to be observed.[21] One might have thought that this disagreement would have led the founder of the method to doubt its efficacy. The contrary was true, for Cousin with good nature held that the study of the Ego was made not for the primary Cartesian purpose of proving its existence, but of describing its properties.[22] As was fitting, Cousin found by his inner scrutiny that it turned out to be not the passive receptor, supposed by him to be believed in by the Idéologues, but an active force.[23] Hence the dictum, "Nothing is in the intellect which was not previously in the senses," is untrue. Only in so far as the mind is active, does it know anything, even that it is passive.[24] The sensation, of course, is something done to the mind; but the knowledge of it is something done to the sensation.

The very word "act" meant to Cousin a voluntary act, and its use led him to a voluntarism as pronounced as Maine de Biran's. But if it were to be developed, as Fichte had developed his, it would lead to an egoism more exaggerated than that of the sensationalists —which, as a matter of fact, was not exaggerated at all except in the accounts of their opponents. It would tend to make the Ego not only the creator of knowledge but also of the world as Cousin foresaw in his early article, "Du Clair et de l'obscur dans les con-

[21] Cf. Ravaisson; "La Philos. en Fr." 25.
[22] "Sur le vrai sens du *cogito, ergo sum*," in *Archives Philos.*, 1818, III 316. Cf. Jouffroy; "Mélanges Philos.," P. 1833, p. 244.
[23] *PE* 178. Cf. Plotinus; "Enneads" IV vi 2; VI i 20.
[24] *PE* 179.

naissances humaines," [25] an article intended to be a refutation of Fichte based on Fichte's premises. Happily, like a number of other philosophers, he knew where he was going before he started out and was careful that his analysis of the human mind provide a defence against any solipsistic difficulties. Accordingly it discovered for him two other faculties to counter-balance the unpleasant traits of the will. They are the sensibility—which is passive and hence entails an external world—and knowledge, by which man conceives principles which are different from the impressions of the senses, or the resolutions of the will.[26] This analysis, it must be confessed, leaves one dazed by its banality; it seems little more than the traditional sensation, will, and reason of the Aristotelian tradition and hardly likely to prove convincing to sensationalists or their friends. Cousin nowhere, so far as I have been able to discover, tried to prove the unanalysable character of will or reason, except in the assertion that will is active and sensation passive. He, moreover, found the scheme anything but banal, and went so far as to say in 1853—and to repeat as late as 1860, " This classification of the human faculties, which would be sought for in vain before our course, is our work, and with the exception of a few differences more nominal than real, is to-day generally adopted and is the basis of the psychology of our time." [27] The very fact of its banality may have been its charm. It was a return to

[25] *Archives Philos.*, 1817, II 330; *PE* 250.
[26] *VBB* 32.
[27] *VBB* 32 n. 1.

old ways of thinking, involved no mental contortions, and maintained a dignified impartiality to all parts of the human mind.

There lay behind this theory of the human faculties another theory of which Cousin was equally proud. This was the theory of spontaneity and reflection.[28] Spontaneity and reflection are two forms of human freedom. Reflection is the free movement of the intellect about a problem which needs resolution. Reflection is practically synonymous with premeditation and deliberation. But reflection is by its nature retroactive. It does not create; it manipulates its old possessions. Spontaneity, on the other hand, is the performance of knowledge itself; a free act, impossible to describe accurately, for language is the medium of reflection. Cousin later said that what he meant by "spontaneity" was what Leibniz meant by the force inherent in the monads.[29] But whereas Leibniz believed that this force was the essence of the universe, the fundamental being of things, Cousin, interestingly enough, thought that it is only one of the two fundamental aspects of the world. Spontaneity is incomplete without reflection. It is incomplete because it is dumb. But similarly reflection is incomplete without spontaneity, for without it, it would lack stuff upon which to work. It would be, one might say, little if anything more than a form of man's passivity.

Correlated with spontaneity and reflection are the concepts of "cause" and "substance," which form

[28] See *PE* 250.
[29] *PE* 256 n.

another reciprocally related pair of terms. "The search for their nature, their origin, and certitude, is the entire body of philosophy."[30] It is useless to try to reduce one to the other, for as soon as one is stated, the other is presupposed. Now this kind of dialectic is familiar enough to readers of post-Kantian German philosophies. It was not unfamiliar to the French. Schweighauser had been sarcastic at its expense as early as 1804 in his article, "Sir l'état actuel de la philosophie en Allemagne."[31] It was clearly in the Schellingian vein, the vein in which all positive and negative forces were found running together in a kind of synthesis. There was no acknowledgment on Cousin's part that he had borrowed the notion from Schelling, and in fact in 1817 he was but studying German.[32] But he had read Degérando, and his friend, Dubois,[33] says that his knowledge of Fichte, and presumably of all the post-Kantians, came first through Buhle and Degérando. Yet Cousin was always chary about acknowledging his debt to foreign thinkers and over-generous in attributing what he taught to the inspiration of respectable Frenchmen. The point must be insisted upon for it was of peculiar importance to the literature, if not to the philosophy, of the age. If Cousin had been freer to develop philosophic ideas with no thought for political conse-

[30] *PE* 256.
[31] *Mélanges* I 199.
[32] Barthélemy-Saint-Hilaire; *Op. cit.* I 67.
[33] "Cousin, Jouffroy, Damiron," P. 1902, p. 52.

quences, it is not unlikely that he would have made much of this sort of dialectic.

As it was, he used it when necessary. He used it in the little tract, "Justice et Charité," to which we have already referred and shall refer again later, and he used it in his doctrine of eclecticism. The doctrine of eclecticism would seem to have two logical roots, the Reidian doctrine of common-sense and the Kantian doctrine of the transcendental unity of apperception. In both cases truth is the possession of something over-individual. The influence of Reid made truth the possession of Society—in the manner of Lamennais; of Kant, the possession of God. But historically its root is Reid. For truth, in Cousin's early years, was a synthesis of past truths which in themselves are fragmentary. As early as December, 1816, in his *discours d'ouverture,* he announced a study of Locke, Reid, and Kant which he hoped would result in a synthesis of their truths. Linked with this idea— which he later said was merely a method of studying the history of philosophy—was a philosophic doctrine itself, spiritualism.[34] He said[35] that his philosophy was called ' spiritualism " because " its character is to subordinate the senses to the spirit and to tend— by all the means which the reason admits—to elevate and ennoble mankind. It teaches the spirituality of the soul, the freedom and responsibility of human actions, moral obligation, disinterested virtue, the dig-

[34] "Lettres inédites de V. C. à Ernest Bersot," Versaille, 1897, p. 17.
[35] *VBB* 35.

nity of justice, the beauty of charity; and beyond the limits of the world, it shows a God, author and pattern of humanity, who, after having made man for an excellent end, will not abandon him to the mysterious unfolding of destiny. This philosophy is the natural ally of all good causes." But spiritualism, as opposed to the materialism of the Idéologues, existed in the philosophy of Royer-Collard.

The Kantian influence made itself felt later on. Cousin was as impartial as anyone well can be in his historical courses. He almost duplicated the lack of favoritism which he had shown towards the mental faculties. But, to be sure, that "deplorable philosophy," "the root of the country's misery," sensationalism, could hardly be looked upon with so paternal an eye. It spread scepticism and materialism from man to man and destroyed the foundations of true liberty.[36] With it excepted, he tried to absorb all that was true in the past.[37] He believed that each philosophy, like each faculty, had its contribution to make to human knowledge. Later he grouped them under the names of sensualism, idealism, scepticism, and mysticism, arranged in order of increasing truth. If one were to believe in a philosophy fused out of these elements, could one not be theistic and yet not ultramontane, liberal and not republican? Was one not able still to remain in the middle of the road? This, as Cousin said himself, was not "blind syncretism,"

[36] *PE* ix.
[37] *PE* xvi.

but a fitting together of fragments into a whole.[38] But it was a whole which the pattern-maker determined beforehand and made up of fragments selected with deliberation and intent.

II

Eclecticism stood politically for constitutional monarchy. This put its leader mid-way between the absolutists and the republicans. In this he followed the politics of his master, Royer-Collard. Flattered, as his friend Dubois believed,[39] by his oratorical success and by the society of Villemain and his group, Cousin came to adopt their political beliefs as a whole. He was their philosophical spokesman on the *Archives* and his philosophy was the philosophy of its successor, the *Globe*. Cousin himself found the earliest expression of his constitutionalism in his youthful lecture, " On the true principle of morality," given in his course of 1817, wherein he had called the granting of the Charte the gift of true liberty to France.[40] During the Second Empire, he invited his readers' attention to what he had said in 1828.[41] Then he had depicted the state of the pre-revolutionary monarchy, the indolence and corruption of the Court. Invoking the principle of Hegelian dialectic, without mentioning Hegel, he demonstrated that such a condition could lead only to its

---

[38] *VBB* II, 14. Cf. " Frag. Philos.," V 299; and pref. to 1st ed., 1826, p. xxxiii.
[39] *Op. cit.* xxii.
[40] *PE* 285; " Philos. Sensualiste," 3d ed. P. 1856, p. 342.
[41] " Philos. Sensualiste " 343.

opposite, the Terror. "The Charte," he went on,[42] "has emerged from the two systems, which now have had their day, absolute monarchy and democracy." He may be said never to have compromised on this issue, which was in itself a compromise.

Naturally this attitude won him the hatred, as he knew, of both reactionaries and republicans.[43] The reactionaries, who were the Church party attacked him on the grounds of anti-nationalism and anti-Catholicism.

The charge of anti-nationalism was concurred in by nationalists who were not necessarily Catholic and absolutists. Thus Quinet called eclecticism an attempt to live under the same roof with the enemy.[44] Secretan called it simply an "elegant and free reproduction of Hegel's theology and philosophy of history."[45] It soon

[42] *Id.* appendix II, p. 344. Cf. the undiluted version in "Intro. à l'hist. de la philos.," nouv. ed., P. 1841, p. 428.

[43] Cf. Sainte-Beuve; *CL* VI 152 ("De la retraite de MM. Villemain et Cousin). "Les rigoureux observateurs de la nature humaine lui ont reproché de maintenir orgueilleusement certains dogmes qu'une philosophie hardie se croyait en droit de contester, de ne tenir aucun compte de l'homme physique et naturel dans les opérations de l'esprit, de se soucier moins d'être un vrai philosophe . . . que de vouloir fonder une grande école de philosophie . . . et d'aller jusqu'à faire ensuite de cette philosophie une doctrine d'Etat, ayant cours et influence. Il en est résulté que sa grande et ambitieuse tentative, qui mécontentait et inquiétait les hommes religieux et le Clergé, ne satisfaisait point d'ailleurs les savants et le petit nombre des libres philosophes; elle avait contre elle les croyants, et n' avait pour elle les physiologistes. Mais ce n'est point ceux-ci qui l'ont le plus nui."

[44] "De la révolution et de la philos.," *RDM* 1831, IV 469.

[45] "La Philos. de V. C.," P. 1868, p. 37.

became a tradition to speak of eclecticism as a foreign plant in French soil.[46]

Cousin, appreciating the gravity of such a charge in France, naturally enough denied it flatly. He was at pains to ally himself with Royer-Collard, to Royer-Collard's distaste, says Sainte-Beuve,[47] Maine de Biran, and Descartes. He felt the sting of the chauvinistic lash. "It is not patriotism," he writes,[48] "it is the profound feeling for truth and justice which makes us place all philosophy . . . under the invocation of Descartes's name." And again, in a preface dated 1855, "We did not give the new philosophy foreign guides, were they even the sage Reid or the profound and virtuous philosopher of Koenigsberg; we placed it early under the invocation of Descartes."[49]

As a matter of fact, when he took his chair he placed it under the invocation of Royer-Collard, his immediate superior. His one thought, he said,[50] on filling the chair of his master, was to extend his teaching. That was doubtless Royer-Collard's one thought too. He stayed content with the Scottish philosophy until he happened to re-read Descartes's "Meditations" and suddenly saw the full significance of the famous *cogito ergo sum*. The full significance seems to have been that a "scientific" point of departure

[46] E. g., Gunn; "Modern Fr. Philos.," Lond. and N. Y., 1923, p. 319.
[47] *CL* VIII 298.
[48] *VBB* 2.
[49] *PE* ix; cf. *PE* 227 n. 1.
[50] *Id.* ix, 198.

THE RISE OF ECLECTICISM

was necessary for philosophy and that it was to be found in personal existence.[51] We have seen already that even in Germany in 1817, he refused to admit that the Germans could influence French doctrines.[52] Yet when he resumed his chair in 1828, he did not hesitate to laud the Schellingian philosophy of nature and to indicate the advance which France might make by inspiring herself to some extent by its ideas, just as Germany might not lose through a study of eclecticism.[53] This was not his final judgment.

His final judgment came when he revised his "Premiers Essais." Then he calmly announced, "There is eclecticism, the thing and the word, in a lesson of December, 1816, before we could have found it in the Alexandrian school, which was then but little known to us, or in a deeper study of the doctrine of Leibniz, above all before we had the least idea that there was then in Germany systems from which we should one day be accused of having filched it. We borrowed eclecticism from no one. It was born spontaneously in our mind from the sight of the striking conflicts and hidden harmonies of the three great schools of the eighteenth century. . . . Eclecticism is then a doctrine *toute française* and which belongs to us."[54]

[51] "Sur le vrai sens du *cogito, ergo sum*," Archives III 322; cf. *PE* 31.

[52] Letter to Kehl, 15 Nov. 1817, in Barthélemy-Saint-Hilaire; *Op. cit.* I 74.

[53] "Intro. à l'hist. de la philos.," 420.

[54] *PE* 227 n. Cf. Baudrillart; "Philos. et publicistes contemporains," *RDM* 1850, p. 58.

As a matter of fact, there is almost no Descartes in Cousin; there is more Schelling than he was willing to admit; and what he took from Royer-Collard, Royer-Collard took from Reid. If we wish to be charitable we may attribute the Schellingian elements to a developed Biranism. For Cousin had high praise for Biran from his first acquaintance with him. In his "Discours d'Ouverture" of 1816, for instance, he had utilized his account of the origins of the idea of casualty and substance.[55] It may be possible that study of these ideas gave rise to his theory of spontaneity and reflection, cause and substance, and their interrelations. Cousin was always so sketchy in the presentation of his ideas that it is next to impossible to trace them with certainty to their source.

The accusation of anti-Catholicism rested largely on Cousin's defence of the teaching of philosophy in the university and of the particular pet ideas of constitutional monarchy, free speech, a free press, and freedom of worship.[56] Freedom of worship finally meant in 1830, the disestablishment of the Church. A free press and free speech had already been denounced by

[55] *PE* 19.
[56] "Intro. à l'hist. de la philos.," 431. After the death of Jouffroy, the Catholics found another weapon to use against C. in the famous passage on J.'s religious doubts. Damiron tells of their reaction to it in the preface to his edition of J.'s posthumous "Cours d'Esthétique," P. 1843. But not all Catholics were hostile. The Abbé J. Cognat, for instance, in the *Ami de la Religion*, no. 5684, 3 Dec. 1853, on the occasion of the 2d edition of *VBB* was highly complimentary, saying that the only thing which Cousin lacked—to make him really great, one gathers—was faith (p. 547).

THE RISE OF ECLECTICISM 215

the Pope in the encyclical *Mirari Vos*. The teaching of philosophy meant irreligion, atheism, pantheism, and a host of other abominations. Cousin could plead, but in vain, that his philosophy was simply non-religious, that it had nothing to say about religion. The Abbé Bautain was there to reply, "One must be either a Christian or an anti-Christian philosopher. The mixed position, which the philosophy of to-day is trying to assume, is not tenable. There is no golden mean for eternal truths. . . . If philosophy is not the daughter and we shall dare say the handmaid of religion, she is its enemy."[57] A similar attack was brought against Cousin as late as 1851 by Roux-Lavergne in his "Monsieur Cousin et Ses Doctrines" (Bruxelles 1851). But in this he is depicted as the successor of the Philosophers of the Revolution, as one who used "the most talent, zeal, and ability" in the service of the "detestable cause" of "suppressing the authority of religion in order to substitute in its place the impotence of human opinions" (p. 111). Such charges were natural enough. For after all, both philosophers and clergymen talked of God, the soul, morality. With the same subject matter, there was little to distinguish the two disciplines in the mind of the Catholic party. Cousin went on record, in the series of speeches made in the Chambre des Pairs, April-May 1844,[58] as saying that philosophy taught among other things, "the

[57] "Résumé des Conférences philos. faites au Cercle Catholique," *Corresp.* 1843, III 37. Cf. Forcade; "Quelques mots sur la philos. officielle," *Corresp.* 1843, IV 401, 405.
[58] "Défense de l'université et de la philos.," P. 1844, p. 67.

spirituality of the soul, the freedom of man, the law of duty, the distinction of virtue and vice, of merit and demerit, divine providence, and its immortal promises inscribed in our most intimate needs, in its justice and its goodness." But was this not a religious doctrine? Why then had he said, "The University is in no way the Church's enemy; it is her friend, it is her ally; but after all, it is not the Church."[59] If it be admitted, as the Catholics had insisted, that the University was not the Church, then it should perhaps be concluded that it has no right to meddle with the Church's affairs. If it be admitted that its province is to sanction the philosophical teaching of the Church's doctrine, then it should perhaps be concluded that the University is the Church.

The real question—which was more or less avoided by Victor Cousin—was the question of where theological and moral problems belonged. Cousin attempted a compromise on this question as he had on practically every other. The law of June 28, 1833[60] which called forth a book on moral and religious instruction for Catholic primary schools, normal schools, and examining committees, probably from the hand of Cousin himself, provided that among other things moral and religious instruction should be given the pupils.[61] But

[59] "Discours—Chambre des Pairs—26 déc. 1838 . . . sur la renaissance de la domination ecclésiastique," P. 1839, p. 19.

[60] Duvergier XXXIII 234.

[61] The book to which I refer is "Livre d'instruction morale et relig. à l'usage des écoles primaires catholiques, élémentaires et supérieures, des écoles normales et des commissions d'examen," 2d ed., P. 1834. This work—listed under the name of C. in the

the parents of the children were to have the power of deciding whether their children were to share in these lessons or not. This provision, said the optimistic reporter of the law, Rénouard, could offend no one, for

---

author-catalogue of the Bibliothèque Nationale—consists of a series of excerpts from the OT and NT, followed by a catechism.

Rénouard, reporting the law, said (Duvergier XXXIII 235 n. 1), "Charger les instituteurs primaires d'un enseignement relig., ce n'est pas contrarier l'enseignement dogmatique du ministre du culte, ni envahir sur les exercises relig. d'aucune nature. L'instruction relig., qui se completera dans les exercises de piété propre à chaque culte ou à chaque communion, repose d'abord sur des notions générales dont aucun scrupule ne peut s'offenser, et sans lesquelles, dans les temples comme hors des temples, il n'y aurait aucune langue raisonnable à parler à des enfans."

To judge from C.'s famous report "Sur l'état de l'instruction publique dans quelques pays de l'Allemagne et particulièrement en Prusse," P. 1833, his decision to have religious instruction in the schools was largely formed from his tour of inspection of the schools of Germany. "The more I think of all this, *M. le Ministre,* the more I examine the schools here, the more I converse with the directors of the normal school and the councilors of the ministry, the more I am persuaded that we must at any cost have an understanding with the clergy for the instruction of the people, and make a special carefully thought out branch of instruction out of religious teaching in our *écoles normales primaires*" (p. 395). He ends on this lofty note, "Celui qui vous parle ainsi est un philosophe, autrefois mal vu et même persecuté par le sacerdoce: mais ce philosophe a le coeur au-dessus de ses propres insultes, et il connaît trop l'humanité et l'histoire pour ne pas regarder la religion comme une puissance indestructible, le christianisme bien enseigné comme un moyen de civilisation pour le peuple, et un soutien necessaire pour les individus auxquels la société impose de pénibles et humbles fonctions sans aucun avenir de fortune, sans aucune consolation d'amour-propre" (p. 396).

It was this report which was circulated gratuitously in the United States, esp. in N. Y. and Mass.

there are certain general religious ideas which belong to all. The direction of worship, the actual performance of ritual, belong to the various clergies; morals and religious history belong to the laity as well as to the clergy. But to-day it seems obvious—and how much more obvious it ought to have seemed then—that there was a wall at this point which the Catholics would have to leap if they were going to live in agreement with the government. How could they, to whom such notions were utterly repugnant, have been expected to come sailing over this wall with happy smiles when they had spent about 1800 years in building it. Were they to be reduced to the empty office of masters of ceremonies?

Cousin must be done the justice of admitting that his main desire seems to have been a philosophical renaissance in the interests of French civilization. That he should have his troubles with the Church was natural. To smooth them there existed no well-defined principle which one could pronounce without fear of ruin. A philosopher must make the best of things and so arrange his life as to have a minimum of annoyance. He expounded his programme to his young friend Bersot, then in Bordeaux, who was having his difficulties with the clergy. First, he said, give your course with that psychological severity which will set aside any irritating question; next avoid all arguments about philosophy, and enclose yourself inflexibly in the profession of a sincere respect for religion; third, mix in nothing . . . *laissez tout faire* and work in silence;

THE RISE OF ECLECTICISM

fourth, work and think of your theses.[62] This was a programme which might have worked if the clergy had not had a real quarrel with philosophy, and if they had been content to see their prerogatives usurped by men who professed a sincere respect for religion. As they were determined to have their own way at any cost, the programme was not to prove especially effective. Furthermore Cousin was hardly the man to *laisser tout faire et travailler en silence* himself. He was trying to further a cause and a cause of compromise where none was possible. Yet he never appreciated the impossibility. As late as 1863 when his philosophy was petrifying in classrooms and when kings who knew not Joseph were coming into power, he urged Bersot to show the world that there was room between M. Veuillot and M. Littré.[63] That room was supposedly occupied by the philosophy of Cousin.

The ultra-liberals hated Cousin as much as the reactionaries. Just as the government of Charles X denounced him to the Prussian Ambassador in Paris and thus may have caused his famous arrest [64] so the Jacobins denounced him before the people. It will not be

---

[62] " Lettres inédites " 6.

[63] *Id.* 14. Later the room grew more cramped. In 1863, when he heard that Bersot was going to print a review of Renan's "Life of Jesus," he protested violently on the grounds that it was an anti-religious book. He then admitted that his own philosophy " confesses its impotence to replace religion among human kind. . . . The philosophy of Renan has neither these scruples nor these embarrassments, etc., etc." The whole letter is a plea not to rob humanity of its relig. See p. 15.

[64] See Bréville; " L'Arrestation de Victor Cousin en Allemagne—1824-1825," P. 1910, esp. 17.

forgotten how Sénécal in "L'Education Sentimentale" "execrated M. Cousin even more than the Jesuits for eclecticism taught one to draw certitude from the reason, developed egoism, and destroyed solidarity."[65] But the less extravagant liberals than those of fiction felt the same contempt for him. Lerminier, for instance, in his "Lettres Philosophiques à un Berlinois," denied that Cousin was a philosopher at all.[66] He was rather, said Lerminier, an *erudito*. Leroux, who had been fairly closely associated with him on the *Globe,* did not find a good word to say for him.[67] Comte called him a "fameux sophiste."[68] Chateaubriand, whose opinion, we admit, is not authoritative but interesting nevertheless, admired his style but preferred the philosophical ability of a Père Ventura.[69] Sainte-Beuve could scarcely mention him without a shudder.

At the root of the dislike for Cousin among liberals is beyond doubt his spirit of compromise. But the special cause may be seen in his political philosophy as expressed in the tract, "Justice et Charité," of which mention has already been made. This was one of that series of *petits traités* produced by the Académie des Sciences Morales et Politiques in July, 1848, at the request of General Cavaignac. This Academy, which as the Second Class of the Institut had been suppressed by Napoleon, had now become so docile as to

[65] See ed. définitive (Charpentier), P. 1909, Pt. II, ch. vi, 321.
[66] *RDM* 1832, XI 736, esp. 750.
[67] "Refutation de l'eclectisme," P. 1839.
[68] "Cours de Philos. Positive," P. 1908, III 408.
[69] Letter to Mme. Récamier, 16 Dec. 1828; in "Souvenirs et Corresp. de Mme. R.," II 284.

accept with zeal the request of the *chef du pouvoir exécutif* that it " join in the defense of social principles attacked by publications of all kinds. Persuaded that it is not enough to establish material order by force if one does not also establish mental order by the help of true ideas, he regards it as necessary to pacify the public mind while enlightening it." [70] The Academy agreed with General Cavaignac and replied that it had already begun to oppose the popular theories with the principles " upon which are founded the rights of property, the well-being of families, the liberties of peoples, the progress of the world," and that each member of the Academy " would congratulate himself that in helping the Academy to fulfill its mission, he was serving together with the eternal cause of truth, the most pressing interests of the country." [71]

[70] Report of the Séance of 17 July 1848, reprinted in " Justice et Charité," P. 1848. The *petits traités* were compôsed of the following books:
Cousin; "Justice et Charité."
Troplong; " De la Propriété d' après le Code Civil."
Hippolyte Passy; " Des Causes de l'Inégalité des Richesses."
Ch. Dupin; " Bien-être et Concorde des Classes du Peuple Français."
Thiers; " Du Droit de Propriété."
Mignet; " Vie de Franklin."
Barthélemy-Saint-Hilaire; " De la Vraie Démocratie."
Villerme; " Des Associations Ouvrières."
Portalis; " L'Homme et la Société, ou Essai sur les Droits et les Devoirs Respectifs de l'Homme et de la Société."
Blanqui; " Des Classes Ouvrières en Fr., pendant l'année 1848."
Damiron; " De la Providence."
Lelut; " De la Santé du Peuple."
[71] " Just. et Ch." 8.

Cousin's share in this labor of love had a destructive as well as a constructive side. The destructive side was the demolition of the theory of human equality [72] and of such doctrines as the right of every man to work [73] or to aid. It will easily be seen at what social theories this blow—which turned out to be not even a gentle tap when delivered—was aimed.

The constructive side of Cousin's tract was of a nature to appeal to employers who knew but little of human psychology. It placed the foundation of all moral and political systems on the twins, justice and charity, each of which would be insufficient if alone.[74] Justice consists in seeing that natural rights are preserved.[75] But natural rights are limited. They consist largely in "liberty" which is the only thing in which all men are equal. The first of all liberties is the search for truth [76] the second is religion, in so far as it does not debase human dignity.[77] The third seems to be the right to property, which is sacred "because it represents the right to oneself (*le droit de la personne elle-même*)." "We are the first piece of property we own." [78] Surely such a social philosophy hurled at the men of 1848 was hardly likely to pacify them. The revolution was being fought neither for academic freedom, nor religious liberty, nor property holdings.

[72] *Id.* 24.
[73] *Id.* 41.
[74] *Id.* 17.
[75] *Id.* 38.
[76] *Id.* 26.
[77] *Id.*
[78] *Id.* 27.

Cousin simply refused to grapple with a problem and fight it out. Perhaps he was unable to.

His discussion of charity is as thin as that of justice. Though he has been maintaining that every right has a correlative duty and *vice versa*,[79] he now maintains that the duty of being charitable has not the correlative right of exacting charity.[80] The state, he goes on to say, ought to aid the unemployed *in a certain measure,* by giving them employment, for instance, on public works. But it is false that the workman has the right to work, for only those things are rights which one can assure by force.[81] What the state owes to its citizens, in fine, are (1) aid and protection for the preservation and development of their physical life —as in infant asylums; (2) aid for their intellectual life; (3) aid for their moral life; (4) correction and punishment of criminals.[82] Did Cousin honestly think

---

[79] This was surprisingly *vieux jeu* in 1848. Dupont de Nemours eighty years before in another little tract—directed against and not in favor of the government then in power— used exactly the same *clichés,* such as the reciprocity of rights and duties. See his *éloge* of Quesnay: " De l'Origine et des progrès d'une science nouvelle (1768)," in the series, " Physiocrates," ed. by Eugène Daire, 1st pt., P. 1848, p. 342, the same year, it will be observed, as the appearance of " Just. et Ch." On the other hand, *l'Egalitaire,* a "journal de l'organisation sociale," appearing in May 1840, echoed the same thought. " *Droit et devoir,* parties d'un même tout, principe indivisible: voilà en deux mots tout l'ordre social." But *l'Egalitaire* deduced from this formula not constitutional monarchy, but Babouvism.

[80] " Just. et Ch." 41.
[81] *Id.* 41.
[82] *Id.* 47.

that men who had been listening to Lamennais, Eglantin, Leroux, and had actually sent Louis-Philippe scurrying away for shelter, would be persuaded by such assertions? Was he hoping that the prestige of his position would lend conviction to his arguments? It seems almost unbelievable that he should have expected even a courteous hearing. The publication of this famous philosophical bull is one of the best symptoms of the state of academic philosophy of this period.

III

Besides its political affiliations, the philosophy of Cousin had definite esthetic preferences. Cousin was himself what might have been called a classicist, were one to judge from the lectures on the beautiful. For he believed [83] that the reason and not the sensibility was the faculty which perceived the beautiful. He believed moreover that above the beauty of the world there was an ideal beauty. " The ideal resides neither in an individual nor in a collection of individuals. Nature or experience furnishes us the occasion to conceive it, but it is essentially distinct from nature. For him who has once conceived it, all the aspects of nature, however beautiful they be, are not the simulacres of a superior beauty which they do not realize. Give me a beautiful action, I shall imagine a still more beautiful one. The Apollo himself admits more than one criticism. The ideal retreats unceasingly as one approaches it. Its last term is in the infinite, that is in God; or

[83] *VBB* 138.

to speak more truly, the true and absolute ideal are nothing other than God Himself."[84] Art thus is not an imitation of nature.[85] Its aim is rather an expression of a Platonic ideal.[86] Whence follow certain startling conclusions. "True beauty is ideal beauty, and ideal beauty is a reflection of the infinite. Thus, art is itself essentially moral and religious; for, unless it fails to obey its own laws, its peculiar genius, it expresses throughout its works the eternal beauty. Enchained on all sides to matter by inflexible bonds, working upon inanimate stone, upon uncertain and fugitive sounds, upon words of a limited and finite significance, art communicates to them, with precise form which is addressed to such and such a sense, a mysterious character which is addressed to the imagination and to the soul, snatches them away from reality and carries them off gently or violently into unknown regions. Every work of art, whatever be its form, small or great, pictures, sung or spoken, every work of art, truly beautiful or sublime, throws the soul into a graceful or severe reverie which lifts it towards the infinite. The infinite is the common end towards which the soul aspires on the wings of the imagination as of the reason, by the road of the true and the good. The emotion which the beautiful produces turns the soul in this direction; it is this beneficial emotion which art procures for humanity."[87]

[84] *Id.* 167.
[85] *Id.* 175.
[86] *Id.* 179.
[87] *Id.* 186.

In spite of certain resemblances between Cousin's vocabulary and that of the Romantics, there is no intimate logical connection between their æsthetics. Cousin's theories led him to praise the works of Corneille, Racine, Boileau, Lesueur, Poussin, Le Lorrain, Champagne. It led him to make the absurd statement that " great beauty was absent [from the sculpture of the middle ages] and taste was lacking."[88] In architecture he admitted little if anything after the Renaissance, forgetful of the architecture of Louis XVI, though, let us grant, sensitive to the vulgarity of such buildings as the Madeleine. The influence of Royer-Collard's professed love for the 17th century is obvious in all of Cousin's æsthetic judgments. He loves the calm and the dispassionate, the grand line, organ tones, sublimity, impressiveness.

Cousin's theory of ideal beauty is derived from Winkelmann and Quatremère de Quincy. Winkelmann had said in the French translation, " Supreme beauty resides in God. The idea of human beauty is made perfect by its conformity and harmony with the supreme being, with this being which the idea of unity and indivisibility makes us distinguish from matter. This notion of beauty is as a substance abstracted from matter by the action of fire, like a spirit which seeks to create for itself a being in the image of the first rational creature formed by the intelligence of the divinity. . . . All beauty becomes sublime by unity and simplicity: beauty imprints the quality of the sublime on all which acts and

[88] *Id.* 241 n. 2.

speaks."[89] Similar doctrines were found by Cousin not only in Plato and Plotinus, but also in his contemporaries in Germany. Both Hegel and Schelling had seen a supernatural significance in Beauty. While the former had esteemed it as a sensuous manifestation of the Absolute, the latter had made its production the very purpose of the natural order.

Omitting from our discussion Plato and Plotinus, there was between the Schellingian and Hegelian æsthetics the widest of breeches. For whereas to Hegel the beautiful was necessarily a thing of calm and repose, a whole; to a Schellingian it was a thing of restlessness and might indeed be a fragment. For Hegel's Absolute was a finished product, after all, and its manifestation in sensuous guise would be a manifestation of something as finished as anything sensuous could be. The doctrine of Cousin rested here. The beautiful was an ideal, not a real thing. It was the image of an abstraction, not in any opprobrious sense, but in a Platonic sense, that of Winkelmann. There was no doubt something very elevating in this doctrine, particularly in the opinions of men who could admire whole-heartedly the works of David and his group.

Now Cousin thought that his philosophy was the philosophical expression of the spirit which Mme. de Staël and Chateaubriand had brought into literature.[90] We of to-day would suspect this new spirit to be the spirit of the Romantic movement. And indeed

---

[89] "Hist. de l'art de l'antiquité," tr. by M. Hubert, P. 1781, II 39.
[90] *VBB* iii.

Stendhal in his defence of Romanticism, " Racine et Shakespeare "[91] and Emile Deschamps in his preface to the " Etudes Françaises et Etrangères "[92] consider Cousin as the spokesman for the youth of their time. But what he taught was the very opposite of what " Racine et Shakespeare " taught. What had Romanticism to do with ideal beauty, Romanticism which was so highly in favor of the "natural" with all its inconsistencies and loose ends?

Stendhal was very definite in his opposition to any doctrine of ideal beauty, as anyone might expect who appreciated his affiliation with the logic of Tracy and the psychology of Cabanis. " A very sad thing, which is perhaps a truth, is that *ideal beauty* changes every thirty years, in music."[93]

For Tracy an abstract idea as an autonomous entity was a chimera. For Cabanis the beautiful, which did not especially occupy his attention, could be nothing other than a physiological function. So Stendhal maintained that there was nothing other than a physiological basis for such an æsthetic experience as musical pleasure.[94] The notion that the exquisitely refined beauty of music should grow out of the " tension of the auditory nerves "[95] was quite in keeping with the tenet of the

[91] Ed. Calmann-Lévy, ch. vii 65.
[92] Reprint of the Bibl. du Romantisme, p. 25.
[93] " Vie de Rossini," P. 1824, p. 12. Cf. " Lettres . . . sur le célèbre compositeur J. Haydn," P. 1814, letter XIX and reply, 214; " Promenades dans Rome," P. 1829, II 437; " Hist. de la Peinture en Italie," P. 1817, I 131.
[94] " Rossini " 15; " Haydn," letter XII, esp. 135; " De l'Amour," P. 1822, II frag. 73, p. 222.
[95] " Rossini " 15.

new school that the grotesque and the sublime should be united, as Victor Hugo had preached, *à la Schelling,* in the preface to "Cromwell" (1827). But Stendhal's fiction, if not his essays, is a constant exemplification of this very theory, softening perhaps the word "sublime." I do not maintain that Stendhal held any well articulated theory about the matter, for his interest in metaphysics did not go beyond the Idéologues. Nor did his Romanticism prevent his ridiculing the Romantic high-priest, Schlegel.[96] But if the Romanticists in France are the new school, and if defenders of the new school are Romanticists, Stendhal should certainly be reckoned among them.

The theory of the union of the sublime and the grotesque is paralleled in Schelling's doctrine of the fecund union of the positive and the negative. But accompanying this doctrine of the fertility of contradiction was the doctrine of growth in time. Schelling was one of those men, like Ballanche, who believed that change is not a catastrophe but a blessing. That belief of course was again cardinal in the Romantic creed, for they had to defend their departure from accepted patterns. If change was evil, then Romanticism fell. It is easy to see why Catholics should have opposed Romanticism. It is harder to see how Cousin should have been associated among them.

The *Globe* became one of the champions of the new movement. The *Globe* began to appear during Cousin's imprisonment in Germany and almost immediately took

[96] "Hist. de la Peinture," II 70 n. 1.

up the Romantic cause. Cousin's pupil, Jouffroy, was partly responsible for this attitude, for in an early article on "Modern Eclecticism"[97] he argued that, among other blessings, eclecticism was going to bring about a reconciliation between the Romantic and the Classic in literature, a typically Cousinian task. But already one of his colleagues had gone further than that and had stated that—properly defined—Romanticism should triumph.[98]

The proper definition of "Romanticism," for the *Globe,* turns out to be political and explains why Cousin, in spite of his written words, can be classed among defenders of Romanticists or admired by them. For the one point on which such different writers as Stendhal, Hugo, Manzoni, Nodier agree, says this article, is their hatred of routine; their one common goal is liberty. In Romanticism only is there "life, activity, a forward movement." In another article signed *L. V.*, "L'Indépendence en matière de gout" (2 Apr. 1825), the Romanticists are treated as the encyclopedists of the literary revolution. In "The Situation of Romanticism on the First of November 1825" (29 Oct. 1825, II 919), Romanticism is said to be "no more a *genre* than Protestantism is a religion; its beliefs, its theories, are all negative; and it is between routine and independence, between immobility and movement, that one must choose. . . . In a word, because during one epoch

[97] *Globe* 9 Apr. 1825; I 458.
[98] "Du Romantique," signed "O" in the *Globe* of 24 Mar. 1825, I 424. Des Granges says that "O" was Duvergier de Hauranne in his "Le romantisme et le critique," 236.

things were well done in one manner, is it impossible at another epoch to do well differently? And whereas all changes, ought literature alone to remain immobile and *petrified?* There is the whole question." Whatever definition of Romanticism may be given by various critics, the doctrine itself is simple " freedom, the direct imitation of nature; it is originality."

What has become of Cousin's abstract beauty?

Obviously it would be next to impossible for beauty to reside in a non-temporal idea and at the same time for art to occupy itself with a direct imitation of nature, as Cousin saw. The *Globe* must not be burdened with the responsibility of orthodox eclecticism. Yet it was the paper of Cousin's philosophic and political party. There can be no denying that. Furthermore Jouffroy espoused Romanticism fairly warmly. To him Romanticism was simply the reasonable consideration of the purpose of works of art. The beautiful, he maintained [99] was indeed lodged in order and proportion, as the Classicists had maintained. But there are two kinds of order, that which is the result of habit, the daily repetition of the usual aspect of things, and that which is the adjustment of means to end. Believing that all things have their peculiar end, Jouffroy inferred that to some degree the beauty of an object or a work of art depended on its adaptation to its end. Once, he says, that the public understands the end of the drama to be amusement, it will accept tragedies in prose and plays in which the unities are disregarded.[100] But there

---

[99] " Cours d'esthétique " 69.
[100] *Id.* 74.

is a higher kind of order, which is the relating of an object to our emotions in such a manner that we sympathize with it. In Jouffroy's own words, " The beautiful is that with which we sympathize in human nature, expressed in natural and perceptual symbols.[101]" Our sympathy results from the fact that all creation, however material, is, as in Leibniz, the manifestation of an inner activity, a force.[102] This brings about a true unity of nature, in spite of the hierarchy of beings from the stone to man. The notion of Cousin, that in the contemplation of an invisible and abstract form—whatever that may mean—there is an experience of beauty, thus finds a direct contradiction in the æsthetics of his pupil. Moreover, Jouffroy insists that in a work of art the expression must be in natural symbols and not in mere convention.[103] But for all this he was not a passionate Romantic. He was almost incapable of passion in any form. Yet to read some of his letters is enough to show one that he had in him all the raw materials of the most fervent of the new school. "As for me," he wrote for instance to Boucley (18 July, 1822), "I take an infinite pleasure in suddenly breaking the direction of my destiny, and in brusquely making a new life for myself; the material inconveniences which may result from it are as so many powerful motives which push me towards it and double the charm which attracts me. I love to

[101] *Id.* 184.
[102] *Id.* 250, 276.
[103] *Id.* 250.

despise them, to disdain them, to crush them under foot, to offer them as a sacrifice to the dignity of my liberty."[104] It might be Byron or Chateaubriand talking.

The sympathy which the early Romantics found for Cousin and which Cousin found for them later, comes not from any logical coherence between their ideas and his, but from political reasons. Both Cousin and the Romanticists were being accused by the Classicists of anti-nationalism.[105] Whatever Cousin's ideas might imply, the reactionaries and the ultra-liberals would not permit them to imply classicism. Neither his followers nor his opponents could tolerate that. That is as profound a reason as I have been able to discover why he should have been aligned with one group rather than with the other.

IV

The most important of Cousin's pupils were two men who departed most widely from his doctrines, Theodore Jouffroy and the Abbé Bautain, whom with Damiron he had selected as the most interesting of his early

[104] " Corresp. de Th. Jouffroy," P. 1901, p. 333.

[105] See the mock "Campagne Littéraire" with its quotation from the *Constitutionnel* in the *Globe* of 2 Feb. 1826, III 96. Curiously the liberals of the *Minerve* took much the same attitude as the Catholics. They were troubled by their devotion to Mme. de Staël, but did not grow enthusiastic over the new movement in literature. Their plan was for the Germans to study the French " savans artifices de la composition et du style," and for the French to enrich themselves with German " grandes et belles idées." See *La Minerve Française*, 1818, IV 57, an article on German literature. Cf. the discussion of Romanticism and classicism in Balzac's " Illusions Perdues."

auditors.[106] The Abbé Bautain's importance was shown not so much in the development of philosophic ideas, as in their application. He attempted the introduction of what he thought were Kantian notions into the theology of Rome. The result was held to be destructive of orthodoxy and he was made to recant. Jouffroy had a similar experience with religion, but since he was not in orders he was not subject to papal discipline.

Bautain's road to philosophy led through Strasbourg where the interest in Kant and mysticism were equally strong. His particular doctrine, *fidéisme,* was an attempt, as he said himself, to explain scientifically the teachings of Christianity.[107] He refuted, as he thought, not only the philosophies of Condillac, of the Scottish school, of Cousin—the three main philosophies of the time—but also Lamennais's version of the doctrine of common-sense. This doctrine it was safe to refute, for its author had been condemned a few years before—in 1832 and 1834—for indifferentism and for freedom of conscience. Bautain held that Lamennais's doctrine was not a true philosophy, for it established no scientific principle and prevented the acquisition of one. Moreover, it nullified the possibility of evidence; it degraded human intelligence; and it destroyed voluntary assent in questions of morals. It was not Catholic, for it substituted common-sense for the authority of God; it claimed that faith was owing to common-sense whereas it is due to God alone; it confused special revelation and

---

[106] *PE* 345.

[107] See the dedication of his "Philos.-Psychol. Expérimentale," Strasbourg et P., 1839.

THE RISE OF ECLECTICISM 235

sacred tradition with a " pretended general revelation." It was not in accordance with Christian morality, for Christian morality urges man to shun the crowd, and affirms that common-sense is as nought before divine wisdom.[108]

Bautain's attack on the schools of Condillac and of Cousin are not less severe, though much briefer. The doctrines of Condillac, he maintained, were outworn. His statue was not recognized as a faithful portrait of themselves by men of the nineteenth century. Activity is the rallying cry of the new schools. Since sensationalism does not satisfactorily explain activity, it is easily refuted.[109] The Scottish school, the school of Royer-Collard, is cast off for similar reasons; it does not explain enough. Though concerned with the Ego, it tells us nothing about the soul. It does not explain why the soul is joined to a body, and so on. As for Eclecticism, it is rejected by Bautain because of its vagueness and incoherence.[110] It gives no absolute criterion of truth and falsity, good and evil,[111] for all points of view and all actions have their legitimate place in the universal scheme. Cousin, who declaimed against the baseness of sensationalistic ethics, sees himself the apostle of a theory in which " it is the result which decides right and wrong; it is success which proves legitimacy." [112]

[108] *Id.* lvii. The reader will notice the corroboration of our remark in the section of Ch. IV on Royer-Collard, that the doctrine of common-sense was a " democratic gesture."
[109] *Id.* I xxi.
[110] *Id.* I xxxiii.
[111] *Id.* I xxxiv.
[112] *Id.* I xxxv.

If none of these philosophic creeds will help in his difficulties, Bautain, like other men, must needs construct one of his own. He proposes to replace Lamennais's philosophy with what was a more bitter attack on the efficacy of the reason than Lamennais had ever dreamed of. Like Jouffroy, he had known the sting of argument, had perhaps felt his faith totter after returning from Cousin's lectures. Jouffroy decided to follow the reason where it led him. Bautain was incapable of such conduct. A severe illness is said to have shown him the weakness of his philosophical beliefs,[113] and to have been a more potent philosophical weapon than formal debate. It performed the same function in his life as the news of Mme. Chateaubriand's death did in her son's.

Having been moved by this illness, or by some other powerful force, such as the personal need of faith, to accept the Church's doctrine *in toto*. Bautain began by pointing out that even rationalistic beliefs rest upon certain principles which are assumed, and hence rest upon faith. He pointed out what Kant had pointed out, that when it comes to fundamentals in metaphysics, such as the existence of God, the reason can prove anything—contradictory things if it will. Why then put any credence in it? It is much more to the point to put credence in the teachings of tradition. Tradition seems to Bautain to be the only alternative to rationalism—largely because he felt that in demolishing the other reigning philosophies he had demolished all other possible philosophies. His account of tradition is not dif-

[113] Ferraz; *Op. cit.* 319.

ferent from Bonald's. God has implanted language in man, which when comprehended reveals His divine commandments and His being.[114] The question might be asked how we are to distinguish between the Hebraic-Christian tradition, and the Indian, the Chinese, the Egyptian, the Hellenic-Roman traditions. But such a question, though answered by Lamennais's doctrine of common-sense, is not touched by Bautain. He seems to feel that the mere proof of the reason's impotence in fundamental problems is implication that tradition, divinely inspired, is self-illuminating and self-critical.

The Vatican did not share Bautain's enthusiasm for his doctrine. Close upon its condemnation of Lamennais, in 1840 to be exact, the Abbé Bautain was asked by Gregory XVI to recant. He was asked to subscribe to the following propositions:

(1) Reason can prove with certitude the existence of God and the infinity of His perfection. Faith, gift of Heaven, is posterior to revelation; it cannot therefore be proposed to an atheist in proof of the existence of God.

(2) The divinity of the Mosaic revelation is proved with certitude by the oral and written tradition of the synagogue and Christianity.

(3) The proof drawn from the miracles of Jesus Christ, perceptible and striking to eye-witnesses, has in no way lost its force or its power for subsequent generations. We find this proof in all certitude in the authenticity of the New Testament, in the oral and written tradition of all Christians. It is by this double

[114] Bautain; *Op. cit.* II 206.

tradition that we should demonstrate it to those who reject it or who, without admitting it as yet, desire to believe in it.

(4) We have not the right to expect of an unbeliever that he admit the resurrection of our divine Saviour, before having given him certain proofs of it; and these proofs are deduced from the same tradition by the reason.

(5) Upon these divers questions, reason precedes faith and ought to lead us to it.

(6) However weak and obscure the reason may have become because of original sin, there remains to it sufficient clearness and force to guide us with certitude to the existence of God, to the revelation made to the Jews by Moses, and to the Christians by our adorable Man-God.[115]

Bautain subscribed as requested.

What he subscribed to was in part the truth of what Lamennais had been teaching in his early years. The one sort of testimony which Gregory XVI adduced was tradition and the one explanation of tradition which he had to offer was the explanation offered by the Traditionalists. Tradition was the passing on of revealed truth. The main point of Traditionalism was of course omitted by the Pope, for obvious reasons, that is, the identity of tradition and language. So Bautain, with his philosophy of faith behind him, declared that faith told him that faith was weaker than reason, just as he had once taught that reason told him that she was weaker than faith.

[115] "Enchiridion" 1622.

Besides having to subscribe to the articles mentioned above, Bautain had to promise never to teach that the reason, unaided by faith, could not demonstrate the existence of God or the immortality of the soul—two Kantian principles—nor provide motives of credence for the toughest minded sceptic. It was a triumph in words for Bautain's rationalistic enemies. In the century of science the Church had no intention of appearing less rationalistic than the general run of mankind.

Bautain spent the rest of his life as a teacher of theology in Paris, doing his utmost to ruin the prestige of philosophy, his own undoing.

The direction of his fellow, Jouffroy, was, as we have suggested, in a direction opposite to that of Bautain. The famous passage from his posthumous "Nouveaux Mélanges Philosophiques" (P. 1842, 111-116) which describes his conversion to scepticism, as Wm. James calls it in his "Varieties of Religious Experience," shows a reader how deeply he felt the need of philosophic enlightenment and how real a guide it was in his life.[116] He had none of Cousin's ambitiousness, in spite of the prominence of his name and his teach-

---

[116] For a Fr. appreciation of this passage, see Caro's "Théodore Jouffroy," *RDM*, 1865, p. 340. This is one of the best accounts of J.'s personality and opinions which I have found. Cf. also Taine's "Philos. Classiques," 208. It should be mentioned that Dubois, who knew J. personally, insisted that he died a Christian, believing in God and the immortality of the soul. His reasons for this statement include the following: "He repeated a score of times that the philosophy comprehended and hidden under the symbols of Christianity would not be surpassed; he loved and depicted with love the ceremony of Christian worship." See Dubois; *Op. cit.* xlviii.

ings. He was content to be an editor and a teacher. He is undoubtedly one of the most attractive figures of this period.

In 1819 he wrote to his friend and fellow pupil, Damiron, that all the prayers in the world could not make life pleasant. "Life will remain for me," he said, "and for all those who enjoy it, what it ought to be, a little hell constructed expressly for the reign of virtue where happiness cannot slip in."[117] This sentence might be used as the keynote of his philosophy, a philosophy which can account for virtue but not for happiness, for accuracy but not for truth.

Like Bautain, he is convinced of the relative impotency of the reason. That absolute truth exists, he does not deny[118] but he insists that the possession of it is a prerogative of God alone. Human beings believe that they participate in the knowledge of absolute truth[119] but whether they are justified in their belief is a question worth studying. They are justified if the intelligence of human beings is so made as to reflect reality faithfully.[120] It is obvious that we believe in our intelligence; the fact, says Jouffroy cannily, that we distinguish error from accuracy is truth enough that we do not mistrust it.[121] But again the question of our right to this belief arises and there we meet an obstacle. The only judge of intelligence is intelligence itself; it

[117] Lair; "Corresp." letter of 5 Jan. 1819, p. 228.
[118] "Du Scepticisme," in "Mél. Philos." 231.
[119] *Id.* 233. Cf. "De l'organisation des sciences philos.," in "Nouv. Mél." 216.
[120] *Id.* 235.
[121] *Id.* 236.

would be strange to convict a man of perjury on the testimony of a liar.

The basis of all reasoning is " a blind act of faith "[122] just as it was in Bautain minus the blindness. Belief turns out to be instinctive, doubt rational, a result which would have led Jouffroy to some of the conclusions of our contemporary Freudians, anticipated in a measure by Schopenhauer, if not by earlier thinkers. Jouffroy in his published works does not seem to have developed his result beyond this essay on scepticism. But there are hints here and there of an anti-intellectualistic turn of mind which are worth bringing to light here simply because of their reappearance as full-fledged doctrines later on in the century.

In the first place the very notion of eclecticism is an admission of the individual's impotency in philosophic research. It is not anti-intellectualistic in the sense of attacking the intellect as such, but in the sense of attacking the individual's intellect. To the eclectic, as to Hegel, the individual philosopher sees only part of the truth[123] except when he is an eclectic or an Hegelian. This does not mean that eclecticism and Hegelianism are identical. The eclectics, as far as I know, did not preach the development of systems towards eclecticism, nor even the steady absorption of one system into its opposite in time. Eclecticism might have been produced at any point in history, if the philosopher with sufficient brains had existed to produce it. To continue

[122] *Id.* 238.
[123] " De l'hist. de la philos.," in " Mél. Philos." 252, 260. Cf. " Nouv. Mél." 16.

our exposition, a part of the truth is never enough, and Jouffroy is more frank than Cousin in stating this. For Cousin had his doctrine of spiritualism to inculcate into the minds of the young, whereas Jouffroy was freer to roam as he would.

Eclecticism reposed in part, as we have said, on Reid's doctrine of common-sense. Jouffroy was a much closer student of the Scottish philosophy than his teacher. Having translated both Reid and Dugald-Stewart, he had at least read them. Now the doctrine of common-sense was a candid avowal not merely of the individual's inability to reach complete truth, but of the individual's need to rely on the race even for fragmentary truth. That feeling that the race does not err even when the individuals who compose it do, is prominent in almost all of Jouffroy's writings. He believes in it to the point of making philosophers merely the mouthpieces of the people, as if they were not of the people. Voltaire, for instance, he proclaimed in the *Globe*,[124] would never have been a philosopher if he had been born in the seventeenth century—he means of course in time to be mature at its height. For, he says, " philosophy is the judgment of the people and in the seventeenth century the people believed and did not judge. . . . All the ideas of which Voltaire and his friends are accused, could not have been entertained by them fifty years earlier; they are not their ideas, but the ideas of their time. Luther would have been a saint or perhaps a pope a hundred years earlier." Or again, when he dis-

---

[124] 15 Jan. 1825, p. 267; " Mél. Philos." 46.

cusses in a famous essay how dogmas end,[125] it is seen to be through the interaction of ideas and society. When he reflects on the philosophy of history, he concludes that the object of history is "the development of human intelligence."[126] All that a philosopher can do is to be a precursor and promoter of social doctrines.[127] "What Bossuet called providence," he says,[128] "others destiny, others the force of circumstances, is the fatality of intellectual development." This intellectual development is read in the works not only of philosophers but of poets and of other artists.[129] When he discusses religion, he finds it inextricably bound to politics, customs, ethics, a whole civilization.[130]

Perhaps it is Jouffroy's belief in a common-sense which leads him, as Lamennais's belief in a common tradition led him, to internationalism. "In politics it is no longer a question to-day," he wrote in 1826,[131] "of the balance of Europe, but of the future of humanity. Europe's civil wars are over; the rivalry of the peoples who compose Europe is dying out, as died the rivalry of the Greek city-states under Alexander, and as was effaced the diversity of the French provinces under royal domination. . . . The minister who, first to emerge from the narrow ideas of patriotism, will lead the politics of his country not towards

[125] *Globe* 24 May 1825; "Mél. Philos." 3.
[126] "Mél. Philos." 56.
[127] *Id.* 68.
[128] *Id.* 75.
[129] *Id.* 78. Cf. "Nouv. Mél." 30.
[130] "De l'état actuel de l'humanité," "Mél. Philos." 106.
[131] *Id.* 141.

the worn-out end (*le but usé*) of its aggrandisement and the abasement of its neighbors, but to the profit and in the direction of the union of Europe and of the civilization of the world by the union and by the ideas of Europe, that minister will be the statesman of the nineteenth century. He will make for the power and the glory of his country, precisely because he will have abjured the dogma of patriotism." Such a doctrine had of course been in a narrower form the program of the French Revolution. It was the program of the international revolutionists of 1848.[132]

It might not be out of place to indicate briefly what Jouffroy understood by this "common-sense" which made humanity one solid fraternity. The simplest idea of common-sense is those self-evident principles in which mankind finds the test both of its judgments and its conduct.[133] These principles form a sort of philosophy anterior to philosophy in the strict sense of the word,[134] a philosophy whose solutions are always more inclusive than those of individual thinkers. It does more than either spiritualist or materialist, for it affirms the existence of both matter and spirit; it does more than empiricist or rationalist, for it affirms the validity of both sensory experience and the reason. Thus individual philosophies are not, in Jouffroy's eyes, in contradiction to common-sense, so much as

---

[132] In spite of the evidence of the text which I have cited, Rémusat in his article on J., *RDM* 1844, VII 424, says that the idea of equality and of nationality were profoundly rooted in his nature.

[133] "De la philos. et du sens commun," in "Mél. Philos." 157.
[134] *Id.* 158.

THE RISE OF ECLECTICISM 245

they are less than common-sense. They serve to make articulate portions of that philosophy in which all men believe whether they are thoroughly aware of it or not.[135] This notion of inarticulate philosophies being incorporated in certain consistent modes of conduct had been worked out most attractively by Hegel in his *Phænomenologie,* but Jouffroy shown no sign of having read any German philosopher later than Kant. He developed the idea less perfectly than his German contemporary, being content with a universal philosophy for all mankind, rather than special philosophies for various human types. This attitude is worth noting for in his remarks about Vico and Herder, he blames Vico for finding a universal law for man's development by neglecting the environment and Herder for finding particular laws for various nations by neglecting man's inner nature.[136] Was he not doing just what he had accused Vico of? Or did he feel that the catholicity of his common-sense philosophy eradicated any suspicion of that error?

The origin of common-sense is in the very nature of intelligence, which is both passively receptive of action from without and actively engaged in manipulating the impressions it receives.[137] The whole world affects it and it strives to react to the whole world. The man who had no philosophy of an articulate nature struggles to clarify the vagueness of his impressions, to make them significant. He does this spontaneously, as Cousin

[135] *Id.* 160.
[136] " Bossuet, Vico, Herder," in " Mél. Philos." 87.
[137] " De la philos. et du sens commun," " Mél. Philos." 164.

had already suggested. Though his conclusions are not neat and orderly, they are all-embracing. The philosopher, who voluntarily and deliberately strives to understand the world, is forced to a fragmentary account of things. But this divorce between philosophy and common-sense is not to endure forever.[138] As soon as philosophy turns back upon itself and examines its methods, it will wake up to its short-comings and set about rectifying its errors. The true method of philosophy is not that of Plato, Descartes, Kant, nor even of Aristotle—whom Jouffroy often unconsciously reproduces—but that of Galileo and Bacon.[139] It is the patient accumulation of facts before deduction begins. It was the method which Jouffroy himself attempted in his long study of what he called " psychology."

If common-sense is the repository of the whole truth about the world, unlike the individual reason it enjoys the prerogative of God. It becomes something not unlike Hegel's Absolute, *mutatis mutandis*. Since it is the characteristic of society, it offers Jouffroy an opportunity to develop a metaphysics of socialism for the men of 1848. But he does not accept the offer. Indeed

[138] *Id.* 169.
[139] " Sciences Philos.," in " Nouv. Mél." 97. This point is emphasized because Ravaisson seems to feel that J's. theory of the immediate perception of the Ego—the " cause " of psychic states—precludes the possibility of the Baconian method. (*Op. cit.* 25.) But J. himself says (" Nouv. Mél." 211), " Although we have a perpetual and immediate consciousness of the principle which is we . . . it is nevertheless evident that it is only by the study of these numerous phenomena which it produces or which it experiences that we can acquire an extended and precise knowledge of its nature." (Cf. *id.* 213.)

THE RISE OF ECLECTICISM 247

in some sentences he seems to avoid socialism of any form. "Society," he says, for instance, in his "Problem of Human Destiny,"[140] "is only a collection and the end of a collection can have its justification only in the elements which compose it." But how short a step it was to a veritable mysticism in which individuals are integrated not only emotionally but intellectually in Society, just as souls, according to a thinker like Récéjac[141] are bound together in the Absolute, or as the ethical individual is completed in Royce's Beloved Community. Short as the step was, it was too long for Jouffroy's stride and there remained at the heart of his philosophy an intellectual pessimism.

From the ethical point of view things were perhaps more cheerful. Each man, whether learned in philosophy or not, is held to have within him a conscience which teaches him to distinguish good from evil.[142] It is the business of moralists and jurists to harmonize their opinions and the opinions of conscience[143] and conscience has the right to laugh at ethics and the law in so far as it does not deny the bit of truth that is in them.[144] But it seems that the conscience will have no easy task of making explicit the difference between good and evil.[145] Values do not stalk about the world labelled like figures in a newspaper caricature. But there happen to be in this world certain objects and

[140] "Mél. Philos." 464.
[141] "De la connaissance mystique," P. 1897, p. 275.
[142] "De l'eclectisme en morale," in "Mél. Philos." 390.
[143] *Id.* 392.
[144] *Id.* 393.
[145] "Du Bien et du mal," in "Mél. Philos." 403.

other existents which are either indifferent, helpful, or harmful to our determined goal.[146] (That we have a determined goal is Jouffroy's primitive idea.) Thus good can be defined as the accomplishment of a being's destiny; evil as its non-accomplishment.[147] Consequently good and evil are relative. There is however a certain harmonizing of particular destinies in "universal order."[148] This Aristotelian conception of ethics is taken with peculiar seriousness by Jouffroy and applied in passing to the question of beauty and ugliness.[149]

It would seem that if all things have a destiny to fulfill which is the will of God, good might be more probable than evil. Unfortunately for Jouffroy's peace of mind, all things are an unstable mixture of two antithetical principles, matter and force, whose struggle is life.[150] Moreover in the accomplishment of a being's destiny, there is bound to occur the sacrifice of some other being's.[151] " Whence it comes that no nature here below fulfills its true destiny completely. All things perpetually tend towards it, and are unable not to tend towards it. But this tendency is everywhere frus-

[146] *Id.* 405.
[147] *Id.* 406.
[148] *Id.* 407.
[149] *Id.* 409. J. is not conscious of his resemblance to Aristotle. He utilizes the notion of the ends or destinies of things also in the beginning of the "Cours de Droit Natural," P. 1834, I 2, where it suggests Montesquieu's preface and first chapter of the "Esprit des Lois," though J. himself attempts to refute Montesquieu.
[150] *Id.* 411. (Cf. Cousins's notion of substance and causality.)
[151] *Ib.*

trated; it struggles everywhere and is never entirely victorious." [152]

Yet this ethics is not Manicheism; it is rather Stoicism. For evil is not a positive something. It is merely imperfection. We humans and the lower levels of life alike are struggling to perfect ourselves. We do not succeed, it is true, but we do not completely fail.[153] Perhaps this world is but a transition to another.[154] The analogy of moral and intellectual values, of the good and the true, is complete. In both realms of human interest, that which is sought is never completely found.

Unhappily Jouffroy's opinions on human destiny are lost as are so many of his opinions, but there has been preserved in a stenographic report one of his lectures touching this subject. There he is as Aristotelian as he was in his general moral attitude. Like Aristotle, he investigates the lower levels of existence,[155] finds in their essence—or peculiar character—their destiny and then investigates man with the same purpose. Like Aristotle, he finds that the accomplishment of man's destiny lies in the perfection of his reason.[156] Like Aristotle, he has a vision of a necessary enchainment of events,[157] but unlike him he despairs of influencing it. The gaps in his ethics are however too numerous to be filled in by a process of inference and we can only

[152] *Ib.*
[153] *Id.* 412.
[154] Cf. "Cours de Droit Naturel," I 4.
[155] "Destinée Humaine," in "Mél. Philos." 430.
[156] *Id.* 434; "Droit Nat.," I 38.
[157] "Destinée Humaine," "Mél. Philos." 490.

guess what his conception of man's rational perfection would be. We know that it would be a development away from a religious point of view—which Jouffroy believes gives a true but vague and symbolic account of things—to the philosophic point of view. Christianity is the last of the religions. This is the last sentence in his "Problem of Human Destiny" (p. 491). But how different he thinks life will be when lived rationally, he does not say. Nor does he say why man should be expected to be ever more rational than he was in 1830. He has faith in the world processes which to him, as to so many other philosophers, were impregnated with human values. Thus he can believe that spontaneously there will be produced out of the welter of creation, something more fitting to the ideal which man has pretended to resemble.

It was through the prestige of Jouffroy, as well as Cousin, that the eclectic school grew to important proportions in France, but it was rather the doctrines of Cousin than those of Jouffroy which prevailed among its members. For, with the exception of Jouffroy's notion that in introspection the subject has immediate knowledge of itself and not merely of its "states," there was scarcely an item of his philosophy which would not have caused serious annoyance to anyone who preached it. Philosophy, as we have hinted, was in a precarious position, in danger of attack from clerical and anti-clerical alike. The philosopher, if he was to maintain itself—a condition which all the philosophers naturally accepted without question—must keep midway both parties. "Work on your theses and keep quiet." If these theses were developments of Jouffroy's scepticism, his pessimism, his unconscious Aristotelianism, what good could come of it? Jouffroy did not develop them himself. It was all the more important that no one else do so, for by 1830 eclecticism has become " the official philosophy."

The contributions of such men as Damiron, Saisset, Paul Janet, to the solution of philosophic problems was almost negligible. There was little to do except to repeat in ever greater variety and detail the doctrines of the Master. As Charles Adam put it with finality, Cousin made philosophy a business of teaching, which embarrassed it and impoverished it. In order that it might be generally acceptable, he made it timid, humble before the Church and he enregimented his professors as a bishop does his priests. He borrowed from Catholicism its dogmatism and its discipline with the great difference that Cousin had merely the trammels of a doctrine to teach. He supported his attitude not in the name of a high moral principle, but upon motives of utility and convenience.[158] Severe as this judgment is, it is perhaps not entirely unfair. Cousin was in a position in the educational system of his country to determine who should teach and who should not. One would hesitate to say that he used his position unjustly, but it is certain that he used it. One has only to read Jouffroy's letters to Damiron to appreciate to how great an extent it was necessary for a prospective professor of philosophy to be in Cousin's good graces.

[158] Adam; " La Philos. en Fr.," P. 1894, p. 206.

There was even a story current to the effect that his pride forced Damiron to omit from his edition of Jouffroy's works the young man's attribution of his disappointment in philosophy to his teacher's youth.[159]

Naturally enough, since the eclectics were for one reason or another incapable of aiding the solution of philosophic problems, they turned towards the history of philosophy for their work. Cousin had on many occasions sung the praises of the historians and had with some justice insisted on the necessity of knowing the past if the present was to be properly understood. Consequently one finds the leader of the school himself producing editions of Proclus, Plato, Abelard, Descartes, Maine de Biran, and a translation of Tennmann's *Manual;* his followers studying and translating Aristotle, Spinoza, Kant, Bacon, the Scholastics, the Neo-Platonists.[160] When one turns to the *Académie des Sciences Morales et Politiques,* one finds Cousin's leadership as apparent as in the university. The prizes are no longer awarded for the decomposition of thought and the determination of the influence of signs on the formation of ideas, but for a critical examination of Aristotle's " Metaphysics " (1835), the authenticity of the " Organon " (1837), an exact exposition of Neoplatonism (1829), and the like. This tendency to encourage work in the history of philosophy rather than in the consideration of special problems lasted well beyond our half of the century and produced some of the

[159] Leroux; " Victor Cousin," *Les Contemporains,* n. d. 13.
[160] Cf. Ravaisson; *Op. cit.* 20.

best known pieces of French philosophic research. Whether this interest in the history of philosophy acted to the detriment or to the advantage of French culture is not within our province to determine. But surely it cannot be denied that it owes its existence to the inspiration of Victor Cousin more than of any other one man. Moreover, by strengthening the acquaintance of French readers with the printed word of such thinkers as Kant, Schelling, and Hegel, it was ultimately responsible for the welcome and understanding given in France to the development of their ideas in the work of such men as Renouvier, Bergson, and Taine, to select only the most prominent names. Such people would have found their inspiration without Cousin; that is beyond denial. But they would not have found a public capable of understanding them and willing to accept them.

CHAPTER SIX

THE RISE OF POSITIVISM

Curiously enough the philosophy of the first half of the nineteenth century which was to survive almost in its integrity was not the teaching of an official philosopher at all, but of a man without any recognized position in the learned world, Auguste Comte. Perhaps the secret of Comte's charm for his successors is not his originality so much as his clever use of old material in a new arrangement. As the main points of positivism are known to practically all readers, this chapter will be devoted almost entirely to placing them in their historical setting. Comte must not be imagined to be a lonely figure thinking out great ideas which were ahead of his time. His philosophy, on the contrary, was a much more eloquent expression of the total civilization of early nineteenth century France than that of any other one man, just as Cousin's was an expression of monarchy *à la Louis-Philippe* and Bonald's of absolutism. This is meant in a more or less figurative sense. I have no intention of suggesting that civilizations and political systems have real personalities which express themselves in philosophies.

If one were to scan the civilization of France in our period and to ask himself what its dominant characteristics were, he would be forced to note at least the following: a fairly rapid change of government, the rise of industrialism in the economic scheme, of romanticism in the esthetic, of ultramontanism in the religious, and the increasing success of natural science in the purely intellectual. These symptoms were the results of various ailments and yet were almost all a stimulus to the philosophers of the time. The social question with the accompanying political question busied the Catholic as well as the atheist; the problem of the beautiful or the aim of the arts was as living a problem to the eclectic as to the Catholic; even Ballanche became interested in the labor problem and Enfantin, as everyone knows, in the religious. The very pervasiveness of these problems was characteristic of the period. The critical investigation of human affairs was not so specialized as it is to-day. The scientist thought that he might well be a metaphysician, often, as in the case of Geoffroy-Saint-Hilaire, with lamentable results.[1] The metaphysician, almost without exception, thought that he must be a politician. The politician found religion too tempting to be left alone—see the works of Benjamin Constant. And the religious was as likely as not to produce a book on art. If any of these interests dominated and served as a focus for others,

[1] I refer, of course, to his "law of universal attraction," which one can find expounded in his "Notions Synthétiques, Historiques, et Physiologiques de la Philosophie Naturelle," P. 1838, p. 3. The fundamental idea (p. 21) in that matter is homogeneous, *i. e.,* made up of similar elements and becomes diversified because of space and time. Diversity thus becomes something superficial. The underlying homogeneity seems to the author to account for the universal attraction of like to like.

it was perhaps the interest in social reconstruction. But the interest in science, as we have indicated in an earlier chapter, was almost as great and in some cases more profound. There was a tradition from the days of the Encyclopedia at least, perpetuated in the Institut, that science was the one reliable guide to social progress. It might be fairer to say that after the French Revolution the fashion of looking to political change as a method of moral improvement became prevalent—even among Catholics. The interest was not in social phenomena as such, but in political activity.

Before the Revolution, changing the political structure in accordance with ethical goals was but an unfulfilled desire of certain philosophers who may never seriously have entertained it. After a thousand years or so of a given régime, one voices a hope as a dream and not as a possibility. But after the Revolution, political changes actually took place and convinced people that, given the proper conditions, they could come into power. Hence one finds immediately springing up in the Assembly, the sprouts of what have turned into political parties. It is no doubt unhappily true that these parties were as often as not the vague statement of personal ambitions, left vague and abstract so as to seem impersonal. Such parties had existed under the Monarchy too, but not as political parties. By the time of Louis-Philippe, they were a tradition, and one had every shade of political opinion represented in organized groups of men. We have by now become used to this phenomenon and disillusioned. It no longer seems strange to us to hear one organization maintain that a man whom it has selected has some more delicate sensitivity to the nuances of right and wrong than a man selected by another group. But in the period which followed the Revolution, this was a novelty and was taken seriously, if not by the politicians themselves, at least by their followers. Consequently such apparently abstract systems of thought as Ideology had their political representation, and even Maine de Biran sat in the Chamber.

It was to Comte's credit that he insisted upon studying society as a phenomenon itself and not merely as the dependency of other phenomena. More was involved in this study than appears at first sight. In the first place, there was implied the whole conception of society as an autonomous entity, analogous to the body politic of the Middle Ages. This idea was in essential opposition to the eighteenth century conception of society, formed it may be after the analogy of Newtonian physics in which the individuals were the focus of attention like moving particles, each of which continued its path until interfered with by another. To men living under the Regent or Louis XV, the moral equivalent of the first law of motion must have been especially attractive and indeed Montesquieu, for one, writes politics as if it were what Comte called social physics, and as if he believed with Comte that these laws were only accidentally a part of mechanics and really applied to the whole universe.[2]

[2] Comte; "Système de Politique Positive" (hereafter " Pol. Pos."). 3d ed., P. 1890; I 493.

But if the eighteenth century did not explicitly invent the word "sociology," which Comte introduced in his "Cours de Philosophie Positive,"[3] its thinkers had an important share in turning men's attention to its subject matter. The whole notion of human progress as opposed to individual progress rested upon the presupposition of human solidarity. Montesquieu's interests were obviously in the individual in spite of the superficial appearance of his masterpiece, but he had a vision of societies in the large, for what is the "Lettres Persanes" but a comment on a single society viewed as a structure? It is European *moeurs* as European, not as this European's and that European's, which Rica and Usbek observe. They have a power of generalization which saves them from writing merely travel notes. And in the "Esprit des Lois," which Comte criticizes for its lack of generality,[4] there is, as he had to admit,[5] a submission of whole civilizations to natural laws, such as the law of the influence of climates. Had Montesquieu been able to study his subject with more disinterestedness, there is no reason why he should not have been as self-conscious a sociologist as Comte. The Physiocrats had a less definite conception of society as a unit, studying rather the groups within society than society itself. But in Dupont de Nemours's plea for the study of economics we find the significant sentence, "There is a natural, essential and general *order,* which contains the constitu-

[3] Hereafter "Cours." Ed. Schleicher, P. 1908, IV 132.
[4] "Cours" IV 129.
[5] *Id.* IV 127.

tive and fundamental laws of all societies; an *order* from which societies cannot break loose without being so much the less societies, without which the political state would have less consistence, without which its members would be more or less united and in a violent condition; an *order* which one could not abandon entirely without producing the dissolution of society and soon the destruction of mankind." [6] As we say, the new science is not so much sociology as economics. But the quotation is interesting as a plea for the positive treatment of social problems. Dupont de Nemours, by the way, attributes the founding of this new science to Quesnay's articles, " Fermiers " and " Graines " in the *Encyclopédie*.[7] More than Montesquieu and the Physiocrats, Condorcet was, as Comte admitted, very close to Positivism in his " Esquisses." [8] In Germany, there were Lessing's " Erziehung des Menschengeschlechts " (1780) and Herder's " Ideen zur Philosophie der Geschichte der Mensheit," both to be well known in France later on. In Italy there was Vico, studied with profit by Ballanche and popularized by Michelet. Each of these men had, to be sure, his own peculiar attitude towards the study of society, but no one could deny that, with the possible exception of Lessing, they did not attempt to formulate its laws.

[6] " Physiocrates," 1st pt., P. 1846, ed. Eugène Daire, " De l'origine et des progrès d'une science nouvelle " (1768), p. 337.

[7] Cf. Comte; " Cours " IV 138, where the founder of positivism pays his respects to these men.

[8] " Cours " IV 132. Cf. his " Plans des travaux scientifiques nécessaires pour réorganiser la société " (1822). Repr. in " Pol. Pos." IV, app. 107.

One has only to compare their work with that of Bossuet or St. Augustine to see how the movement towards positivism was making itself felt. Comte is not entirely conscious of his predecessors, but does not refrain from citing Kant and Herder as evidence of the tendency towards the positive treatment of society,[9] although he later said,[10] "I have never read in any language either Vico, or Kant, or Herder, or Hegel, etc., I know their various works only through some indirect accounts of them and very insufficient certain extracts."

But there was another current of sociological study, what Comte called "social statics," which went back, as he knew, to Aristotle.[11] Social statics was the analysis of society into its units and the description of the units. "In a word," said Comte,[12] "social dynamics studies the laws of succession, while social statics seeks those of co-existence." It was social anatomy, if one will.[13] In the work of the Christian political scientists of the Middle Ages, there is all the insistence one could desire upon the organic unity of the body politic. For them the tradition of social unity dates from St. Paul and for some of them, such as Dante and the Papal group in general, social unity is suprapolitical: it is international. Thus society for such thinkers becomes humanity, very much in Comte's sense of the word,

[9] "Considérations sur les sciences et les savans," 2d art., in *Le Producteur*, 1825, I 365.

[10] "Cours" VI, préf. personelle xxvi, dated July 1842.

[11] "Cours" IV 126.

[12] *Id*. IV 192.

[13] Lévy-Bruhl; "Philos. d'Aug. Comte," 4th ed., P. 1921, p. 287.

THE RISE OF POSITIVISM 261

after due allowance has been made for religious differences, the importance of which must not be underestimated. Comte was as generous to the Catholics as he was stingy to their opponents, and attributed willingly to Maistre's "Du Pape" not only his general appreciation of the Middle Ages, but also his interest in social *order*.[14]

There was in the third place, a philosophical approach to Comte's theory of social or human solidarity. This was through Lamennais's treatment of the doctrine of common-sense. Reid's doctrine in Lamennais became traditionalism, it is true, but after all that was a difference of application, not of meaning. We have seen that in Royer-Collard's treatment of Reid, common-sense was an escape both from the doctrine of innate ideas and of sensationalism; it amounted almost to a kind of transcendental ego. But it was a transcendental ego which in Lamennais became incorporated in humanity as a whole and uttered opinions which when heard became the standard of truth. The personal relations between Lamennais and Comte were close.[15] It is not true that in Comte the voice of the people is the voice of God, but it is true that the needs of humanity become, if not creative of truth, at least determinative of truth's progress. For instance, he makes the development of science a function of human needs. Science passes through the theological stage, because man would have been discouraged by the pre-

[14] "Cours" IV 96 n.
[15] See Gibson; "The Abbé de Lamennais and the Liberal Catholic Movement," 73, 95.

mature apprehension of natural law.[16] Again the unity of knowledge must be realized, for a reason which is certainly much more influential than one derived from logic, because the human understanding demands unity.[17] This makes thought and its discoveries a biological phenomenon with a certain survival value; they develop as in Lamennais in humanity as a whole, much as instincts develop in the individual. Yet, let it be noted in passing, this accords but weakly with Comte's fundamental intellectualism, in which he makes all human institutions depend on human beliefs and sees no reform possible in society until a reform has been effected in human thinking.[18] Thinking cannot both be a guide to "life" and a by-product of living. Both of these ideas are in Comte, confusing his argument. They are never completely untangled. It is impossible to say which of them he considered the more important, for both unhappily are influential in his philosophy.

Not only is science a development of the human understanding, but a study of its history will practically take the place of psychology.[19] Comte saw little value in the introspective psychology of Cousin and his group. The intellect, he believed, could not grasp itself in its activity. Hence one must substitute for it the intellect of the race, which is expressed in the history of human beings. This again is in accordance with Lamennais's special brand of Traditionalism.

[16] "Cours" IV 353.
[17] *Id*. IV 351.
[18] *Id*. I 26.
[19] Cf. Lévy-Bruhl; *Op. cit.* 53.

II

The notion that society was unified is thus seen to have a triple root, one part in the work of secular social reformers, one in the ecclesiastical tradition, one in the philosophical doctrine of common-sense. This doctrine was accompanied by another which Comte believed of capital importance, the law of the three states. Briefly, the law of the three states describes the progress of the human mind. Historically, human beings are supposed to have begun interpreting the world about them in anthropomorphic terms, reading a will into the operation of even the least human forces. From this early " theological stage " science progressed to a higher stage, in which forces, essences—attraction, the ether, and the like—were employed to do the work of the theological will. Such entities were considered by Comte to be more abstract and less crude than the entities invoked in the earlier period; the use of them denotes a "metaphysical" turn of mind. The great fault of the metaphysical mind is its desire to explain rather than to describe. The progress towards unbiassed description is the next phase of human development. This period once attained, man becomes positivistic. It should not be forgotten that the law of the three states is not only descriptive itself; it is normative. Not only does science move from theology to positivism, but in doing so it moves from worse to better.[20]

[20] This law was discussed by C. in print in his article, " Considérations philos. sur les sciences et les savans," *Producteur*, 1825, I 289. The same exposition will be found in " Cours " I,

Men so unlike Comte as Damiron, the eclectic, had the same fervent admiration for the pursuit of science.[21] But few of his contemporaries limited its method so narrowly, especially few of his contemporaries among men of science. "Positivism," said Geoffroy-Saint-Hilaire,[22] "the word has been invented, but in what does the idea which it expresses consist?" Other scientists seem to have taken the same attitude. Yet Comte was not the originator of the famous law. Before him his master, Saint-Simon, had made the opposition between theology and metaphysics, on the one hand, and positivistic science on the other. This opinion, he said, he had received from his friend, Burdin, a physician, author of a "Cours d'études médicales" (P. 1803), who, moreover, had the same goal as both Saint-Simon and Comte, viz., social reform. Cuvier, from whom Burdin admitted he had received his greatest inspiration, later formulated a similar law; and Turgot earlier in the eighteenth century had framed one so close to Comte's in both letter and spirit—which was republished in 1808—that there can be little doubt in the minds of fair-minded readers of where Comte's came from.

1st lesson. He maintains that "several of the fundamental ideas" of the book were expounded in his "Système de politique positive" privately printed (100 copies) in 1822 and reprinted in 1824. See "Cours," *avertissement de l'auteur,* I xii. Cf. "Plan des travaux scietifiques," May 1822 and "Cours" IV 344: "La grande loi que j'ai découverte en 1822."

[21] Cf. his "Hist. de la Philos. en Fr.," 149: "La science est grosse de religion, etc."

[22] "Notions synthétiques," P. 1838, 64 n.

In his "Plan of the Second Discourse on Universal History,"[23] Turgot writes as follows:

"Before knowing the linkage of physical effects among themselves, there would be nothing more natural than to suppose that they were produced by beings intelligent, invisible, and like ourselves; for what should they have resembled? Everything which happened without man's having a share in it, had its god, to whom fear or hope soon rendered a cult. And this cult was again constructed according to the attitude which one would have for men of power, for the gods were only more powerful and more or less perfect men, according to whether they were the work of a century more or less enlightened about the true perfections of humanity.

"When the philosophers recognized the absurdity of these stories, without having acquired nevertheless true enlightenment on natural history, they thought to explain the causes of phenomena by abstract expressions, such as *essences* and *faculties,* expressions which, however, explained nothing, and about which one reasoned as if they had been *beings,* new divinities substituted for the old. One followed these analogies and multiplied the faculties to account reasonably for each effect.

"It was only later, while observing the mechanical action which bodies have one upon the other, that there was drawn from this mechanics other hypotheses which mathematics could develop and experiment verify."

This plan was published, as we have said, in 1808 although the discourse itself was delivered at the Sorbonne in 1750.

At the same time that Turgot was formulating this law of the development of the sciences, the editors of the *Encyclopedia* were theorizing about the beginnings of science and its method. They pointed out (Ed. of

[23] "Oeuvres de Turgot," ed. Eugène Daire, P. 1844, II 656.

1751, p. i) that the arts and sciences are mutually helpful; that (p. iv) agriculture and medicine, since they are absolutely necessary to life, developed first, and that physics, " the study of nature," was the first science because it might be useful to satisfy man's curiosity. The " Discours " then says, " All the properties which we observe in [terrestrial] bodies have relations more or less perceptible to us : the knowledge or the discovery of these relations is almost always the only object which we are permitted to attain, and the sole which consequently we ought to set before ourselves. It is not then by vague and arbitrary hypotheses that we can hope to know Nature; it is by study and reflection upon phenomena, by the comparison which we make between them, by the art of reducing as far as possible a large number of phenomena to one alone which may be regarded as their principle " (p. vi).

The link between Turgot and Saint-Simon is, I think it is fair to say, not so much Burdin as Condorcet. That Condorcet was often inspired by Turgot is easily seen from their correspondence. Saint-Simon acknowledges Condorcet as one of the four men who most influenced him, as one of the four men whose works he will try to synthesize. Undoubtedly one of the best known of Condorcet's contributions to science is his " Esquisse d'un tableau historique des progrès de l'esprit humain " (P. An III). It was of course known by Comte, who fully appreciated its method.

Now Condorcet's " Esquisse " practically begins with the statement, which Comte duplicates, that the progress of the human mind as a whole from generation to generation, follows the same law of development as that which governs the progress of the individual's faculties (p. 3). Comte expresses psychological recapitulation thus:

" The point of departure being necessarily the same in the education of the individual as in that of the species, the divers principal phases of the former ought to represent the fundamental epochs of the latter. But, each of us, looking back upon his own history, remembers, does he not, that he was successively, as far as his most important ideas are concerned, *theologian* in his infancy, *metaphysician* in his youth, and *physicist* in his manhood." [24]

Following this opinion of Condorcet's he almost immediately points out the formation of the ecclesiastic class in primitive society, in whose care was entrusted the beginning of science (p. 27). Their feeble knowledge of astronomy and medicine, their total scientific possessions—Condorcet here agrees with the *Encyclopedia*—was corrupted by superstition. Even in the third period, the agricultural, science was ecclesiastic and hence superstitious, not so much because of any inherent

[24] " Cours " I 4. Cf. *Id.* IV 331. The notion that the individual is somehow society in microcosm, is after all as old as Plato, who uses the resemblance largely as the matrix of his Republic, though to be sure in Plato the element of progress is not present. This kind of recapitulation should be contrasted with what might be called the " exfoliation " of the individual in Hegel's " Phänomenologie," in which the individual, being developed, becomes the Absolute by the simple relegation of time to the realm of Appearance out of the realm of Reality. I do not know whether Comte actually derived his idea from someone else or not. At all events biological recapitulation was a familiar thesis by his time, having been expounded by Kielmaier in 1796 and popularized by Cuvier in his lectures on the history of natural science.

reason, as because of the pride of the priestly caste and their desire to monopolize learning (p. 62) and to dominate over their weaker subjects (p. 65). Greece, however, shook off the yoke of the priests (p. 76) and permitted human genius to assert itself. Here begins what was for Turgot and Comte the metaphysical period.

"However their sages, their scientists, who soon took the more modest name of philosophers or friends of knowledge, of wisdom, lost themselves in the immensity of the too vast plan which they had embraced. They wished to penetrate the nature of man and that of the gods, the origin of the world and that of humankind. They tried to reduce the whole of nature to a single principle, and the phenomena of the universe to a unique law. . . . Thus instead of discovering truths, they forged systems; they neglected the observation of facts, to abandon themselves to their imagination; and not being able to base their opinions on proofs, they tried to defend them by subtleties" (p. 77).

If now we turn to Turgot, not to the "Plan" referred to above but to the discourse itself, we find:

"Spectator of the universe, man's senses, while showing him the effects, leave him ignorant of the causes; and to search by the examination of the effects their unknown causes is to guess an enigma, to imagine one or several words, to try them successively until one meets one of them which will fulfill all the conditions." [25]

"Men, forgetful of the earliest traditions, struck by sensible phenomena, supposed that all effects independent of their action were produced by beings similar to themselves, but invisible and more powerful, which they substituted for the Divinity." [26]

And finally, "The [Greek] metaphysician, faltering upon the most important truths, often superstitious or

[25] "Deuxième Discours sur les progrès successifs de l'esprit humain," *Oeuvres* II 600.
[26] *Id.* 601.

THE RISE OF POSITIVISM

impious, was scarcely anything more than a conglomeration of poetic fables, or a tissue of unintelligible words, and their physics itself was but a frivolous metaphysics."[27]

With the coming of Aristotle there was, continued Condorcet (p. 102), a division in the sciences. According to Turgot, " Aristotle, the most inclusive, the most profound, the most truly philosophical of all antiquity, first carried the torch of exact analysis into philosophy and the arts; and unveiling the principles of certitude and the force of sentiment, he subjected to constant rules the procedure of the reason and even the dash of genius." Condorcet credits the age of Aristotle with the introduction of observation (p. 107), which unhappily lacked experimentation to give it greater solidity. It lacked also the printing press, which would have kept its records from destruction at the hands of the Christians. After depicting the gloominess of the Dark Ages, Condorcet pays a tribute to the scholastic philosophers, whose function was to sharpen the distinction between words, but unfortunately not to advance natural science (p. 178). " Everywhere the authority of men was substituted for that of reason. Books were studied much more than nature, and the opinions of the ancients rather than the phenomena of the universe " (p. 183). Thus arose the debates of the Platonists against the Aristotelians (p. 203) and the subtleties of moral science (p. 212), both of which were weak in principle and the second vicious in its aim. Europe became hypocritical and tyrannical and suddenly science began its

[27] *Id.* 604.

real progress against what went before. Comte's positivistic period began.

Mathematics headed the list (p. 215), then physics and astronomy (p. 216), then natural history and chemistry (p. 218). In Turgot (p. 608) the list is mathematics, astronomy, and chemistry. The three men, according to Condorcet, who stand foremost in the reform of science are Bacon, Galileo, and Descartes (p. 229). In Turgot they are Galileo, Kepler, Newton, Bacon, and Descartes (p. 610). And in Comte we read, after he has pointed out the difficulty of assigning a definite date for the beginning of positivistic science; "However, since it is fitting to fix an epoch to prevent the wandering of our ideas, I shall indicate that of the great movement impressed upon the human mind two centuries ago, by the combined action of the precepts of Bacon, the conceptions of Descartes, and the discoveries of Galileo, as the moment when the spirit of positive philosophy began to speak in this world, in evident opposition with the theological and metaphysical spirit."[28]

Saint-Simon's version of the law of the three states is not so clearly defined as Turgot's and it is doubtful that Comte could have derived his formulation from his master. It appeared first in 1803 when he published "Lettres d'un Habitant de Genève."[29] The little book-

[28] "Cours" I 10; cf. I 28.
[29] The date varies according to different bibliographers, for the little booklet was published without a date. Henri Fournel, in his "Bibliographie Saint-Simonienne," P. 1833, gives it as 1802, but notes that 1803 is given by Beuchot's journal. Quérard gives 1803.

let pretended to be promulgating a new religion divinely inspired in a dream. This religion, in which Newton seemed to occupy the place of Christ and Robespierre that of Satan, is the pursuit of man's happiness through the development of science, the goal of the *Encyclopedia*. Saint-Simon points out the familiar correlation between science and art—astronomy and navigation, for instance—which everyone seems to think has a peculiar significance. He then classifies the sciences, as Comte will, as follows: astronomy, physics, chemistry, physiology.[30] All of these sciences, moreover, are controlled by mathematics, as in Comte, and the list, also as in Comte, is arranged in order of growing complexity. In fact, Saint-Simon believed here that the reason why astronomy was the first science to be developed was exactly the simplicity of its phenomena.[31] Progress in these sciences consists in the substitution of observation for imagination; for in the beginning of astronomy there was a tendency to mingle facts observed with facts imagined. Just what type of imaginary facts were intermingled in early science, Saint-Simon does not say, but he cites as his main example of scientific progress the passage of astronomy from astrology and of chemistry from alchemy.[32] Physiology, he maintained,[33]

[30] "Lettres d'un Habitant de Genève," 49. Cf. Comte; "Sommaire appréciation de l' ensemble du passé moderne," repr. in "Opuscules de Philos. Soc.," P. 1883, p. 40; also in "Pol. Pos." App. IV.

[31] "Habitant" 53. Cf. Comte; "Cours" I 10; "Considérations . . . sur les sciences," 2d art., *Producteur* 1825, I 350; "Plan des travaux," "Opuscules" 103.

[32] "Habitant" 55.

[33] *Ib.*

is in the same stage as astrology and alchemy—more or less Comte's opinion too—and will not in its turn became a developed science until the physiologists have chased from their numbers "the philosophers, moralists, and metaphysicians." In physiology he sees the hope of society, for it is much more informative about man than all the so-called moral sciences. "The revolutionists," he says,[34] "have applied to the Negroes the principles of equality; if they had consulted the physiologists, they would have learned that the Negro, according to what his organism tells us, is not susceptible to the equal condition of education, to be educated to the same level of intelligence as the European."

It will be gathered from this that Saint-Simon began his career with the following principles, (a) the founding of religion on science, (b) the improvement of society through scientific progress, (c) the classification of the sciences in order of "complexity," (d) the foundation of the sciences in order of complexity, (e) the progress of the sciences through the purgation of "imaginary" facts.

Saint-Simon has little to add to his theory ten years later, when he writes his "Mémoires sur la science de l'homme" (1813),[35] which is sometimes referred to as the *locus classicus* of his formulation of the law of the three stages. He makes his adhesion to sociology, or "the science of man," firmer by attaching it more definitely to the other natural sciences. He names the four

[34] *Id*. 68 n. 1.
[35] In the large edition of Enfantin's and Saint-Simon's works, this is dated 1813. Fournel gives 1811.

THE RISE OF POSITIVISM 273

men whom he thinks to be not only the precursors of this science, Vicq-d'Azyr, Cabanis, Bichat, and Condorcet,[36] but also to have said between them all that needs to be said on the subject. Here too he definitely attributes to Burdin the inspiration of his theory. According to a conversation held fifteen years earlier— 1798 or 1800 according to the exact date of the "Mémoires"—Burdin believed that all the sciences began by being conjectural, "the great order of things called them all to become positive. Astronomy began by being astrology; chemistry was only alchemy at its origin; physiology, which for long has been swimming in charlatanism, is based to-day on observed and discussed facts; psychology is beginning to found itself on physiology and to rid itself of the religious prejudices upon which it was originally founded."[37] Again he repeats that science began with conjecture because in primitive times there were not enough facts to serve as a basis.

A new school of social science was to be founded, of which Saint-Simon was to be the philosopher and Burdin the physiologist.[38] The latter seems actually to have set to work, for he published contemporaneously with Saint-Simon's "Lettres d'un Habitant de Genève" his five volume work on medicine. But one looks in vain in this treatise for a formulation of the law of the three stages. It is one thing to say that science begins by being conjectural and progresses into becoming positivistic; it is quite another to say that science be-

[36] "Mémoires," ed. of 1858, pp. 242, 252.
[37] *Id.* 255.
[38] *Id.* 270.

gins by being " theological "—anthropomorphic—passes through the stage of being metaphysical, and ends by being positive.

The exact relation between Cuvier and Comte, as regards this matter, is not clear. Burdin, as we have suggested above, thanked Cuvier in his preface to the " Cours d'Etudes Médicales " (P. 1803, I xiv) as one from whose lessons he has greatly profited. It is probable that the lessons were lessons in anatomy rather than in scientific method, yet Cuvier had a theory about the progress of science which may very well have been expressed by him in his lectures before it was published. In a lecture of which there is a copy in the *Globe* of December 30, 1829 (VII 825),[39] he pointed out that the history of science can be divided into three periods. The first he calls " religious." " Science here is secret and the privilege of a few men who transmit it hereditarily." The second he calls " philosophic." Here science is isolated from religion and cultivated by sages who no longer communicate it as priests in symbolic form but spread it about freely. The third he calls the period of " the division of labor," in which science split into its various branches. He pointed out that its initiators, Bacon and Descartes, no longer expected facts to fit into the framework of Aristotelianism; they made experiments and calculation."[40] It is the course of wisdom not to insist upon the influence of Cuvier but rather to consider his ideas on the subject a curious coincidence. For in his " Reflections on the present de-

[39] Repr. in " Hist. des sciences naturelles," P. 1841, I 10.
[40] " Hist. des sciences Naturelles," II 272.

velopment of the sciences and their relation to society," read before the Academies in 1816, where he might have been expected to " anticipate " the positivists most clearly, he adopted more or less the same account of the beginning of science as that which was given in the editors' opening discourse of the *Encyclopedia.* " The early savages plucked in the forest certain nourishing fruits, certain salubrious roots, and thus satisfied their most pressing needs; the early shepherds perceived that the stars followed a regulated course, and used it to guide their journeys across the desert's plains; such was the origin of the mathematical sciences, and such of the physical sciences." [41] He added nothing to this to account for scientific progress. He may have derived the inspiration for his later theory from his inductive study of the history of science. It is hardly likely that he read either Saint-Simon or Comte.

From a consideration of these texts, it seems fair to say that the idea of the three stages explicitly phrased by Turgot was passed on to Condorcet, who expanded it into his history of human progress. From Condorcet it went to Burdin and Saint-Simon and perhaps to Cuvier. Comte undoubtedly derived the idea and the main details of its amplification from Saint-Simon and the phraseology from Turgot. But if this affiliation be doubted, at least enough has been said to demonstrate that the idea was by no means new in Comte, as anyone with sufficient malice might have guessed who noticed his insistence upon his originality.

[41] Cuvier; "Receuil des éloges historiques," P. 1819, I 2.

Comte's unconsciousness of his predecessors ends by becoming amusing. In his articles in the *Producteur* to which he refers readers of his "Cours de Philosophie Positive,"[42] and which appeared in 1825, no mention is made of either Saint-Simon or Turgot. That he should have forgotten Saint-Simon was human enough, considering the relations between them, but there was little excuse for not mentioning Turgot. It is only justice to say, however, that it is one thing to suggest a law in a literary manner and quite another to verify it in a scientific manner and to apply it. Comte loses none of his glory for having had predecessors. His "Cours de Philosophie Positive" remains as impressive as ever. In fact one can but the more admire the man who saw the implications of a law which its authors but dimly suspected.[43]

III

The termination of our intellectual history in positivism seemed to be well substantiated by the work of scientists in Comte's time. The discoveries in chemistry, physics, and biology were occupying the public imagination more than the discoveries in philosophy. Cousin, who by the '30's was the official philosopher, was not so anxious to discover new metaphysical ideas

[42] "Cours" I 3 n. 1.

[43] I am somewhat inclined towards the position of M. Dumas, that there is little in Comte that was not previously in Saint-Simon. If one has not the patience or the facilities to read the originals, one should study his excellent "Saint-Simon, père du positivisme," *R. Philos.*, 1904, LVII 136, 263.

THE RISE OF POSITIVISM 277

as to reconcile old ones. The Catholics were naturally limited to exposition. The Idéologues were to all intents and purposes dead.

This seemed to the French to be true of Germany too. For though Schelling was still alive, he was producing next to nothing. Hegel alone held the field, but his philosophy, if it reached France at all, was by way of eclecticism and it was not until much later that the real Hegel became widely known beyond the left bank of the Rhine. The Germanophile *Nouvelle Revue Germanique* in 1830 reported, "To-day the reign of Schelling is over; but the influence he exerted during a succession of years has left profound traces."[44] And in its report on the Leipzig Fair of the same year, it says,[45] "The enthusiasm for speculative philosophy is no longer what it was in the time of Kant, Fichte, and Schelling; cured of the mania for theories, people are turning with a certain resignation towards experience and history. The school of Hegel alone is an exception; but it interests the public only slightly and its influence is purely local and personal." What this meant, of course, was that people were buying books in natural science or literature.

But literature was looked upon as a product of philosophical positions, rather than as their seed. Science alone was left to produce philosophies and it was this coupling of philosophy with science which gave Comte his peculiar strength later on. His notion com-

[44] *Nouv. R. Germanique*, 1830, IV 371.
[45] *Id.*, 1830, VI 274.

prised two distinct elements, (a) the catholicity of the scientific method and (b) the futility of all metaphysics. One might believe in one or both of these principles; they were not mutually dependent.

As a matter of fact, all of Comte's contemporaries, except the Traditionalists, believed in the first. Cousin, for instance, whom Comte was to belabor for his lack of scientific precision, advocated introspection in psychology because it alone was scientific and was based on no hypotheses. For him the *cogito ergo sum* of Descartes was a perfect example of scientific empiricism. Jouffroy, too, spent years collecting psychological facts on which to found his philosophy. Stapfer, who was influential in turning Maine de Biran's attention towards Kant and who organized an educational system on Kantian principles, praised Jouffroy for pointing out that Reid had made " mental science " (*science de l'esprit*) like the other sciences, and that by making the similarity between physical and philosophical researches complete, he had given to philosophy the only method—that of science—which had ever resulted in anything worth while.[46]

The Catholic objection to the catholicity of scientific method was that in spiritual matters something more was needed than experimentation guided by the human reason. One of their articles, in which this objection among others is elucidated, was called " Of the Abuse

---

[46] Stapfer; " Mélanges philos., littér., hist., et relig.," P. 1844, p. 194. Cf. Jouffroy; " De l'eclectisme moderne," *Globe,* 9 Apr. 1825, V 458, which maintains that among other blessings eclecticism gave the modern world observation in science.

of the Experimental Method applied to Ethics and Philosophy."[47] In it the author objects to the use of the "scalpel of analysis" on the heart of man. "All is simple, all is limited in the visible world; all is complex, all is infinite in the mental world: to transport the experimental method there is a folly more dangerous and no less laughable than if one wished to interest the moral conscience in the application of docimasy or in the solution of the square of the hypothenuse."[48] There was an *arrière-pensée* in the author's mind, for he was really attacking the contemporary psychologists who seemed to separate conscience from the totality of consciousness and hence to violate the unity of the human soul. But this aside, he furnished an excellent example of the kind of distrust which the Catholics had for the experimental method elsewhere than in the traditional sciences.

The futility of metaphysics was not so widely preached. It is, needless to say, here that the Catholics agreed that certain metaphysics, namely those unsupported by revelation, were futile. The eclectic group on the contrary believed in it strongly, advocating merely that it be founded on "the psychological method." The Idéologues and their descendants pretended to be as anti-metaphysical as Comte, and Saint-Simon acknowledged the importance of their work by including Cabanis in his quartette of really great men. Maine de Biran, however, did not share their distrust

[47] By Comte Edouard de la Grange, *Le Conservateur*, 1820, VI 115.
[48] *Op. cit.* 117.

for metaphysics. It was this, even more than the details of his theory, which finally alienated him from his original masters and set him apart historically. Curiously enough it was a scientist, the elder Ampère, whose influence perhaps counted most in producing this effect.

There was in spite of the similarity a difference between the Idéologues' attitude towards metaphysics and the Positivists'. The Idéologues had different reasons behind their opposition. They were inclined to look upon metaphysics as something clerical, something which smacked of incense and which was therefore reactionary and anti-republican. It was associated in their minds with mysticism and neo-platonism and other beliefs which they felt were obscurantist. Thus, as we have tried to show, they believed in substituting for it the analysis of sensations. The Positivists, on the other hand, had a much greater respect for the Church than they had for revolutionary Philosophers. No one is in ignorance of both Saint-Simon's and Comte's regard for the noble organisation which distinguishes its appearance on earth and for the discipline which that organisation entails. When Condorcet expresses the opinion that the Middle Ages were a time of ignorance, Saint-Simon reproves him and rejoices that his friend Oelsner was able to show him Condorcet's error.[49] The *Producteur,* at this time as much positivistic as Saint-Simonian, always treated Bonald and his group with the highest respect. Hence the Positivistic campaign against metaphysics must not be thought of as inspired by anti-clerical motives.

[49] " Mém. sur la science de l' homme," 287.

The Positivist would probably have agreed with the Idéologue in defining metaphysics, but the denotation of their definitions would have differed. The Positivist, when he objected to the study, often thought of the school of Cousin instead of thinking of St. Thomas. Strictly speaking, he had no right to object to metaphysics at all, and sometimes he was careful to indicate when he was exceeding his rights. Laurent's review of Cousin's "Fragments Philosophiques"[50] for instance, accepts Tracy's definition of "sensation" rather than Cousin's, but the *Producteur* warns the reader in a foot-note that this is a purely personal opinion and not the opinion of the magazine. The business of the *Producteur* was "to examine philosophic doctrines only in relation to their application and their social utility."[51] It was the abandonment of metaphysics rather than its annihilation which was their program, for to them it was a human interest now outlived, of no more contemporary interest than primitive war-dances.

The Positivists were not however free from a metaphysics of their own.

Their very insistence on the futility of metaphysics suggests one. By what name it is to be called is of small moment; it had affiliations with both phenomenalism and materialism,[52] but lest these names be too vague we shall point out a few of its main characters.

[50] *Producteur*, 1826, II 325.
[51] *Id*. IV 21.
[52] Cf. Saisset; "La philos. positive," *RDM* XV 187.

Comte's early associates all hated the search for causes and "explanations." Laurent, in the article mentioned above, writes like Comte himself against psychology, because whereas physiology "stops where phenomena are wanting, psychology abandons observation to mount by the inductive path to *causalty,* to *substance,* that is to say, to ontology." Comte, who must be taken as an authoritative source for the dogma of positivism, does not differ much in his attitude towards psychology. He admits that such a phenomenon as perception is *sui generis* and hence impossible of further analysis.[54] But along with "irritability" perception is a mark of animality and the study of their laws determines biology, not psychology. This does not mean that Comte believes in a kind of Leibnizian *petite perception* which is somehow incorporate in animal tissue. On the contrary, he rejects this belief with violence, calling such an " organic sensibility " a " sensibility without consciousness, of which the definition alone is directly contradictory."[55]

The first fact which Comte admits as established in the matter of psychology is the arrangement of the senses in order of specialty, beginning with touch, which is the " universal sense," as Democritus had suggested two thousand years before, and continuing through taste, smell, sight, and finally hearing.[56] It will be noticed, he adds, "that this gradation coincides

[53] *Producteur,* III 330 n.
[54] " Cours " III 370.
[55] *Id.* III 377.
[56] *Id.* III 390.

exactly with the importance of the sensation, if not for intelligence, at least for sociability." It will also be noticed, let us add on our own account that this classification coincides with the classification of the sciences from the most general to the most particular.

The second fact which Comte admits is the distinction between "the passive and the active state of each special sense,"[57] which distinction he attributes to Gall, and which we have seen utilized especially by Laromiguière. A sensation is passive when it occurs in spite of or without reference to our will, he says, but makes no effort to analyse his extraordinary opinion any further and adds that the study of sensation as it would be carried on to-day by a "physiological psychologist" is the only positive study.

This seems a rather summary dismissal of the elementary facts of consciousness, but Comte is equally cavalier when he treats of the more complex. Thus the positive study of "the affective and intellectual functions" consists in the "experimental and rational study of the divers phenomena of internal sensibility peculiar to the cerebral ganglia devoid of all external apparatus."[58] What this study amounts to is what he calls "phrenological physiology,"[59] which is simply a branch of physiology. His insistence upon this item is of vastly greater moment to us than its meaning. It would be next to impossible to infer just what the experimental and rational study of phrenological physiology would

[57] *Ib.*
[58] "Cours" III 404.
[59] *Id.* III 405 n.

consist in did not Comte mention with admiration such
names as Gall and Broussais and presuppose the indissolubility of sensitivity and organic matter.[60] The
two names indicate in a measure the direction which the
Comtean psychology would pursue and the presupposition indicates the limits of the pursuit. With all
due respect to contemporary psychologists, who would
perhaps shudder at being bracketed with Gall and
Broussais, one must admit, I think, that what Comte
was aiming at was something very like behaviorism.[61]

This suspicion becomes strengthened when one reads
his attack on the school of Cousin or rather Jouffroy
who, as we know, followed the Biranian method of
introspection. He declares in the first place,[62] following
Broussais, that such a method limits psychology to
the study of "healthy adults," thus eliminating child
psychology, psychopathology, animal psychology. Second, and here we have certainly a more striking anticipation of contemporary arguments against introspection, it can never study its data as they occur. It
can study them only after their occurrence. Moreover
it tends to obscure the affective side of our mentality,
which Comte believes—in this part of his "Cours"—

[60] Cf. *id.* III 419. "Two philos. principles, which need no discussion, serve as the unshaken basis of the whole of Gall's
doctrine, to wit; the innateness of the various fundamental dispositions, either affective or intellectual; the plurality of the
faculties essentially distinct and radically independent of one
another, although effective acts ordinarily demand their more
or less complex cooperation."

[61] Cf. "Cours" III 409, where he praises Destutt de Tracy
for having seen that "ideology is a part of zoology."

[62] *Id.* III 408.

to constitute "the principal motive power of human life." The affections and passions are far from being the result of intelligence; they are its stimulus.[63] That is why, he concludes, the study of psychology must be linked on the one hand to the fundamental biological researches, and on the other to the extended study of natural history, animals, men, and humanity at large.[64]

Continually combating the introspective study of psychology, Comte has already laid down a few dogmas of interest. The affective ground of intelligence, which harmonizes but little with the intellectualism of his total philosophy, is but one. He proceeds next to demolish, as Hume had before him,[65] the unity of the Ego, so dear to Biran and the Eclectics. He appeals to *les savants positifs* who have recognized the multiplicity of "human nature." The "abstract and indirect" notion of the Ego comes from the "continuous feeling" of the whole organism. But that feeling is shared by the animals. "A cat, or any other vertebrate, without knowing how to say *I,* is not in the habit of mistaking another for himself." In the higher animals, the feeling of personality is perhaps even more pronounced than in man, for they lead a non-social life,[66] a reason which approaches Comte's theory of the egoistic consciousness to that of Royce and Baldwin.

[63] *Id.* III 411.
[64] *Id.* III 409.
[65] He appreciates the work of Hume, who with Adam Smith and Ferguson, he says ("Cours" III 418) has most closely approached positivism. He forgot that H.'s demolition of the Ego was based on introspection.
[66] *Id.* III 413.

These indications of a psychology became more pronounced when Comte wrote his "Politique Positive."[67] He then developed the social aspects of psychology rather than the physiological. Just as he had seen in his law of the three states the history of both the individual mind and the group mind, so now when he analyses the human consciousness, he thinks of it in terms of society. He speaks here of faculties and dispositions with the freedom of his hated eclectics and other "metaphysicians." But he thinks to save himself from their errors by extending the scope of his inquiry into the products of the human mind, the arts and sciences, instead of limiting it to the scrutiny of sensations, images, and the like as they occur. He is a victim of the illusion that the arts and sciences are fixed, so to speak, and have left legible traces like the remains of prehistoric animals in the rocks. That stability gives him a feeling of confidence when he interprets them and eradicates any suspicion that he might have of betraying his positivistic faith.

The opinion that such a theory is metaphysical does not seem without foundation. Is there no metaphysics in the innateness of psychological phenomena, in the non-existence of the Ego, in the multiplicity of mentality, in the union of individual and social history? If Comte is non-metaphysical, it is simply that he has neglected to develop fully his metaphysics. He needed merely to scrutinize a few of his statements and to ask himself on what they were based in order to begin a

[67] Cf. Lévy-Bruhl; *Op. cit.* 233.

seventh volume to his "Cours," which might be called, following Spencer, "First Principles." Along with the metaphysics involved in his psychology, is the metaphysics of positivism itself. What is this universe in which "causes" are illusory and yet in which events follow one another according to "law"? It was no serious matter for Hume to deny the validity of our knowledge of causation, because he was not an atheist and saw, as he said himself, that the invalidity of causal laws made miracles possible. But Comte faced greater difficulties. He was in no position to substantiate miracles. Nor could he logically plead with Spencer that ultimate causes might exist but were unknowable. For to Comte the idea of a cause is an idea which men must reject, as something that belongs to their adolescence. Yet he never met this difficulty and, as far as metaphysics went, he remained simply a member of the opposition.

IV

The focus of both Saint-Simon's and Comte's philosophy was social reorganization. Even the arts and sciences in the eyes of these men existed not for the sake of beauty or truth, but for the sake of what they called Society. In Saint-Simon's early book, "Lettres d'un Habitant de Genève," he had said (p. 46),

"My friends, in England, there are many scientists (*savants*): the educated English have more respect for scientists than for kings; everyone knows how to read, write and do sums in England. Well, my friends, in that country, the workmen in the cities and even those in the country, eat meat every day.

"In Russia, when a scientist displeases the Emperor, his nose and ears are cut off and he is sent to Siberia. In Russia the peasants are as ignorant as their horses; well, my friends, the Russian peasants are ill nourished, ill clothed, and are beaten to no small extent."

It is the scientist, he goes on to say, who can ameliorate the lot of man and it is man's privilege to exact that he use this power (p. 48).

This attitude was adopted by the Positivists in general. In the *Producteur,* to which Comte contributed his early articles, Buchez has an article, "Some Reflections on Literature and the Fine Arts."[68] After depicting what he believes to be the leading ideas of the classic and romantic schools, he says, addressing artists in general:

"It is idleness which must be attacked and combatted in all its forms; people are proud of it; they must be made ashamed of it. Amuse them no longer with the laughable side and the wretchedness of the poor; no longer feed their pride with the picture of their physical or mental superiority, but show them that all which is blame-worthy is their fault, that they are its first cause. Let their rest be troubled by your clamor and become unbearable; ridicule these elegant idlers who gallantly lose their time in horse racing and contracting debts. Make us laugh at the expense of charming women and charming soldiers, and at these captains of industry ashamed of their profession, clumsy imitators of the vices of high society. Oh, of what importance are salons to you? Your voice will be heard in the present and the future; you have in your hands a power which nothing can weaken and which can only increase. To attack that which is falling, to hasten the fall of that which ought to perish, and to raise all that grows by science and labor, there is the task of the fine arts;

[68] *Producteur,* 1826, IV 189.

until this day they have scarcely ever ceased to do the opposite; they must leave this road and take possession of the new and rich mine which is open to them."[69]

The following are the closing lines of a poem to Shakespeare from Louis Blanc's *Revue du Progrès:*[70]

> "A ton ombre applaudit mon coeur de proletaire,
> Mais, O mon grand William, ne fallait renier
> Ce peuple où tu naquis paysan, braconnier . . . .
> C'est pourquoi je te dis: poète *impopulaire!* . . . .
> Il te fallait heurter aux portes des palais,
> Non avec l'éperon de gentilhomme anglais,
> Mais prenant dans tes mains le fouet et la lanière;
> En poète insoumis, enfant de sa chaumière,
> Flageller à grands traits tous ces rois imposteurs,
> Dont ton crayon hardi nous dessine les moeurs;
> Dévoiler le leurs cours les plates fourberies,
> Des courtisans gagés les obliques roueries,
> Et pour leçon alors mettant le châtiment,
> De tes drames, Shakspeare, oblige dénoûment,
> Du peuple soulevé, devant tout un parterre
> Faire clamer la voix et rugir le tonnerre! . . . .
> Voilà, dans tes écrits, dont la gloire renaît,
> Ce que tu devais faire et que tu n'as pas fait."

This hideous bit of advice would not have seemed any more outlandish to Comte than it did to Louis Blanc. Blanc, in fact, in the prospectus to his review, says among other things, "If the man of learning seeks new processes, let it be to diminish the poor man's labor and not his wages. If the poet is inspired, let it be to shame the selfishness of cowardly stupidity or to glorify the grandeur and the august joys of self-devotion."[71] Liberals under the bourgeois monarchy were likely to share that feeling.

We shall treat of Comte's esthetics below. For the moment we are content to indicate what his social pro-

---
[69] *Loc. cit.* 209.
[70] 1841, VI 121.
[71] *R. du Progrès*, 1839, I 14.

gram is, that program which all life must be determined to realize. The development of sociology implies for him a politics, just as the development of astronomy implies an improvement in navigation.

Perhaps one of the primitive ideas in his system is the inherent sociability of human beings, an idea founded, he believes, in the researches of Gall.[72] This, he insists, is one of his main differences with the philosophers of the eighteenth century, who saw in the creation of society the satisfaction of self-interest. The first trait which characterizes the social animal, man, is the influence of the passions upon the intellect,[73] although the intellect is always to be looked upon as the more reliable judge in human affairs. The second trait is the indubitable ascendancy of the self-regarding instincts over the nobler inclinations of man.[74] It is this trait which assures, curiously enough, the successful operation of charity, and similar social attitudes. For we cannot be expected to consider, says Comte, other people as if they were we. Thus the increase of sympathy involves an increase of intelligence[75] and social amelioration will always tend towards the education of man's intellectual activities.[76] In this way Comte hopes that the fundamental antagonism between man's dislike for thought and its indispensableness for his happiness can be eliminated.

[72] " Cours " IV 284.
[73] *Id.* IV 288.
[74] *Id.* IV 290.
[75] *Id.* IV 292.
[76] *Id.* IV 293.

Comte's striking difference from his contemporaries comes to light in this theory of individual sociability. The Idéologue, at the other extreme, with his sensationalism more or less modified, and the vestiges of the ethics of self-interest, was prone to look upon society as a collection of individuals, complete in every way, even when in isolation, and politically similar. For him the amelioration of the individual's lot could be attained directly by the respecting of his " rights " and the exacting of his duties. In Comte's theory, however, the individual is not the social atom. " The scientific spirit," he says,[77] " does not permit us to look upon society as being really composed of individuals." The social atom is instead the family which Comte, like Bonald and Hegel, considers the intermediary link between the individual and society. It is in family life that man begins to emerge from pure egoism[78] towards altruism, by obedience not to any external law enforced by the state, but by obedience to one of the most powerful of his own instincts. " It is incontestable," he says,[79] " that the *ensemble* of domestic relations in no way corresponds to an association strictly speaking, but that it composes a veritable *union,* attributing to this term all its intrinsic energy." It is by respecting the rights of the family that we may escape from the anarchy which, Comte thought, characterized his epoch.

As a corollary of this theorem, Comte deduced the inequality of the sexes,[80] just as he had asserted earlier

[77] *Id*. IV 294.
[78] *Id*. IV 295.
[79] *Id*. IV 310.
[80] *Id*. IV 300.

the inequality of individuals.[81] Woman, he believes, "is fundamentally inferior" and "secondarily superior" to man from the social point of view.[82] She has produced nothing of great importance in the arts and sciences and has no aptitude for government.[83] But, he insists, woman has a deeper sympathy and sociability than man,[84] which gives her the rôle of modifying man's intellectual efforts when they are "too cold or too coarse."

It is in Comte's remarks on the family that we have the clearest vision of his political ideals. The family unites, he thinks,[85] the happiest combination of authority and discipline and altruistic devotion. The authority which Bonald and Maistre placed in the Pope, Comte sees symbolized in the position of the Father, who is no more a tyrant than the monarchs of the counter-revolutionists were. Indeed, Comte's similarity to the Traditionalists is practically complete, lacking only the outward acceptance of Catholic dogma to make it identical. Comtism has been called an "inverted Catholicism." As a matter of fact, it is not at all inverted. It is Catholicism of the Bonald-Maistre type expressed in more or less novel and secular language. The supremacy of the spiritual powers, the belief in tradition,[86] the inequality of individuals, sexes, and ages, the so-

[81] *Id.* IV 296.
[82] *Id.* IV 300.
[83] *Id.* IV 301.
[84] *Id.* IV 302.
[85] *Id.* IV 304.
[86] *Id.* IV 306.

cial irreducibility of the family are all in "Législation Primitive." That Bonald and Maistre found a pretended sanction for these ideas in the teachings of the Church corroborated by observation, whereas Comte found his verification for them in pretended observation alone, is an accident of biographical importance only. Life in a society organized by the Traditionalists or by Comte would have been much the same, except that neither Bonald nor Maistre aspired to the triple tiara.

Society as a whole in Comte's system is an organism, just as it was for the political scientists of the Middle Ages. On the analogy of the individual organism in which there is presumably a division of labor for the benefit of the whole, society is made out to be a complicated animal whose parts work for a good which is theirs but indirectly.[87] In spite of the "naturalness" of such a phenomenon, it does not always prevail, and the efforts of social benefactors should be directed towards the coordination of individual labor,[88] by apportioning to each man the work for which he is fitted—as in the Republic of Plato—either by nature or education.[89] Lest this lead to over-specialization and the disintegration of society, the government must constantly keep its wards in mind of their common solidarity,[90] aided by the inherent tendency of society to develop the same sentiment.[91]

[87] *Id.* IV 309.
[88] *Id.* IV 315.
[89] *Id.* IV 316.
[90] *Id.* IV 319.
[91] *Id.* IV 321.

The importance of solidarity is more clearly appreciated when one remembers that society, as Comte understood it, is industrial, the result of an evolution through theological and metaphysical times.[92] The solidarity of the Catholics was supernatural. It depended not upon economic but upon religious principles and was an eternal truth. The effect of its realization would have been sensibly the same as that of Comte, but as neither Traditionalist nor Positivist was debating the pragmatic value of his theory, the differences were emphasized rather than the similarities. And whereas in the Catholic solidarity the individuals were at least as equal as the children of a just parent can be, in Comte's there was a very practical subordination of man to man in the mere earning of his daily bread. It was as comforting to be told that one's misery was a social necessity as it was, in the time of Marcus Aurelius, that one's broken leg was a result of immutable physical laws. In both cases one had no further transcendental recompense to make his evil tolerable. In the Catholic system there was, to be sure, a similar element in the theory of inherited guilt, but it was somewhat mitigated by the chance of rehabilitation.

The Comtean state would not have been without its spiritual head. In his early essay, " Considération sur le Pouvoir Spirituel " (1826), he had indicated the necessity of finding a substitute for the work done by the Church in pre-revolutionary Europe. Had spiritual power prevailed, he says, Europe would have avoided,

[92] *Id.* IV, ch. 51.

first, what he calls "the divagation of intelligences," *i. e.*, free individualistic thinking unordered by a common purpose; second, the almost complete absence of public morality; third, the growing belief in a purely "material" point of view; fourth, bureaucracy.[93] These evils, Comte believes, were rooted in the necessity of things as a preliminary to the new order. The new order, however, would, as we have said, not differ greatly from the old, for it would see restored to the spiritual power the "government of opinion,"[94] which means for Comte the control of education. But since education to his mind signifies the adaptation of men to the lives which they must lead and to the peculiar function which they must fulfil,[95] it appears that the spiritual head of the state would play the rôle of Plato's philosopher-kings, the rôle which Comte had said in his "Philosophie Positive" was the very life of the social organism. His "Politique Positive" gives us an idea of what the control of opinion might be like, but

[93] "Pol. Pos." IV App. pp. 184-187. My interpretation of the phrase, "divagation of intelligence," is justified by C.'s condemnation of Lamennais for espousing the cause of freedom of worship.

[94] *Id.* 193.

[95] C.'s definition of education is, "Le système entier d'idées et d'habitudes nécessaire pour préparer les individus à l'ordre social dans lequel ils doivent vivre, et pour adapter, autant que possible, chacun d'eux à la destination particulière qu'il doit remplir." ("Pol. Pos." App. IV 193.) In "Pol. Pos." I 303, C. adds that the spiritual power shall control the fine arts as well as education, basing his argument on the phenomenon of medieval art and the failure of the *fêtes décadaires,* which latter were, of course, managed by the temporal power.

into that we shall not venture here. For it should be clear that Comte's state is, as we have said, a translation of the Catholic state.

To one who is sensitive to the charms of undirected thought and the apparent good it has produced in the arts, if not in the sciences, Comte's program will seem uncouth and barbarous. Indeed had he himself been a man in whose life the arts had counted, a man who could appreciate the revelations of, say, a Delacroix in regard to his manner of working,[96] he would never have thought of coupling governmental control with intellectual fertility. At the very time in which he was methodically producing or gestating his work, Delacroix was writing, " What makes a man extraordinary is at root a manner he has peculiar to himself of seeing things. . . . Thus there are no rules for these great souls: *they* are for the people who have only the talent which is acquired."[97] What would the arts have gained by directing the talent of this man?

V

The beautiful in Comte's mind is associated, as it was in Cousin's, with the true and the good. Any ob-

[96] " Je n'aime pas la peinture raisonnable; il faut, je le vois, que mon esprit brouillon s'agite, défasse, essaye de cent manières, avant d'arriver au but dont le besoin me travaille dans chaque chose. . . . Si je ne suis pas agité comme un serpent dans la main d'une pythonisse, je suis froid; il faut le reconnaître et s'y soumettre; et c'est un grand bonheur. Tout ce que j'ai fait de bien a été fait ainsi." (" Journal d'Eugène Delacroix," P. 1893, I 112.)

[97] *Id.* I 102, dated 27 Apr. 1824.

ject, he maintained, is good in so far as we consider its utility for the satisfaction of our public or private needs; beautiful relative to the "sentiment of ideal perfection which its contemplation may suggest to us," true in its relation to "the whole of appreciable phenomena," abstraction being made of its utility or its beauty.[98] The definition of the beautiful in relation to ideal perfection we recognize as an inheritance of Winkelmann and the revival of interest in classic art. But the ideal which Winkelmann—and his school—and Comte are speaking of are two different things. Comte's psychology, as we have suggested, is a development from the theories of Gall and Cabanis. There is no place in such theories for ideals which dwell apart from matter as the neo-platonic tradition seemed to teach. On the contrary, he asserts that all arts are imitative since "reality always furnishes the natural source of ideality."[99] "In our infancy, individual or collective, as among the animals, a servile imitation, limited even to the slightest acts, constitutes the first manifestation of our esthetic aptitudes. But, in spite of the pretentions of a puerile vanity, representation now receives the name of art only in so far as it is embellished, that is to say, perfected, so as to become at bottom, more faithful, making stand out better the principal traits which an empirical mixture distorted at first."[100] Comte is not aware of the metaphysical difficulties of his position because he is not aware of the need for metaphysics.

[98] "Cours" VI 10; cf. "Pol. Pos." I 283.
[99] "Pol. Pos." I 288.
[100] *Ib.*

"Ideal" to him is, as we understand him, simply an adjective of intensity. It is the word "perfection" which he is interested in emphasizing. This becomes clearer when we read what he has to say about the arts themselves.

The true aim of art, he suggests, is to "charm and ameliorate humanity."[101] It is not, it will be noticed, to do anything for the artist. This aim is consonant with Buchez's "Reflections" cited above, and with the works of both Catholic and eclectic estheticians. But humanity is to be charmed and ameliorated only by that which strengthens the social order. This is accomplished by the action of the beautiful on our emotions, which are, he says, unfortunately a greater stimulus to action than our ideas. These emotions, sympathy and antipathy, are aroused by the contemplation of moral and immoral types, but in order to make them more effective tools of social reform, the types must be exaggerated. In this exaggeration the "ideal" finds its place. "The ideal" becomes in Comte's lexicon synonymous with a "consistent exaggeration." He says frankly[102] that unless good and evil are presented in art as respectively better and worse than they are in reality, art will fail to achieve its social purpose. The art, *par excellence,* is obviously poetry.

Poetry, in the recognition of its types, touches philosophy, but in their utilization touches politics.[103] It is therein that it becomes the instrument of the positivistic

[101] "Pol. Pos." I 280.
[102] *Id.* I 284.
[103] *Id.* I 285.

movement. For positivism will encourage the exercise of the affective and speculative faculties as the one means of happiness and will be helpless without poetry.[104] This does not mean that poets are to be the unacknowledged legislators of Comte's world. He repudiates such an idea almost with horror. "Although a vain pride already inspired the ancient poets with certain errors analogous to the pretention of our contemporaries, art was never regarded as the regulator of the polytheistic society in spite of the ease with which the dominant beliefs lent themselves to esthetic treatment.[105] Whenever artists have attempted to lead society, he believes, misfortune has followed. Their true function is to stimulate desirable emotions—presumably at the order of the state—to be an intermediary between the affections and the reason.[106]

Since the arts other than poetry have a less obvious message, they are put in a group lower in importance than poetry. Our two "esthetic" senses are sight and hearing,[107] each of which has special arts to cater to its needs. Hearing, as might be guessed, has the art of music, which Comte places immediately after poetry. It is "more popular and more social"[108] and demands a smaller training either to produce it or to enjoy it. Sight has three arts, architecture, sculpture, and painting, arranged in order of increasing esthetic importance.

[104] *Id.* I 276.
[105] *Id.* I 279.
[106] *Id.* I 287.
[107] *Id.* I 293.
[108] *Id.* I 294.

For esthetic importance, Comte thinks, depends on an art's ability to express spiritual beauty (*la beauté morale*). Architecture is to all intents and purposes limited to the expression of material beauty.

Up to the present time, continues Comte, the esthetic genius has had no opportunity to fulfil its proper rôle.[109] Antiquity, in spite of the amateurs who short-sightedly praise it, was but a preparation and the middle ages, though much more favorable to the development of the arts, were not a period of genuinely great art, because their customs were moribund.[110] They were spontaneous expressions of the social mind, but the social mind itself was not yet free.

Yet freedom is all important if the fine arts are to achieve their natural greatness. The positivistic régime assures it, for the positivistic régime is the goal of human evolution. When it prevails, the social conditions for the completest operations of humanity shall prevail as well.[111] Bit by bit art is becoming the interest of humanity at large and everything goes to show that in the future the greatness of our esthetic productions will be unsurpassed.[112] They will achieve greatness under direction of the spiritual powers in the state. They will be fortified by the fundamental basis of science.[113] But they in turn will act upon the sciences, curiously enough, in that upper margin of "theoretical liberty"

[109] *Id.* I 295.
[110] *Id.* I 297.
[111] *Id.* I 298.
[112] *Id.* I 299.
[113] *Id.* I 301.

THE RISE OF POSITIVISM   301

to embellish what we know of the truth.[114] Art will be the instrument used by positivism to turn the minds of the young towards contemplation, which will serve them in their scientific work later on.[115]

Convinced that works of art *en masse* spring from the social mind, Comte believes that individual works of art spring from the individual's mind with the same spontaneity.[116] Hence he is opposed to the instructions received in art schools which "stifle the esthetic impulse under technical labor."[117] The artist, on the contrary, needs only the same universal training as other human beings receive. Thus he will no longer belong to a race apart and will address his works to all his fellow-men.[118] This is a possibility because the artist is the same intellectual type as the scientist. "Studying the intellectual types which have not been able to find a suitable environment, one easily recognizes that the same minds would have cultivated with equal success either philosophy or poetry. Diderot, he says in a passage which recalls one cited above from Jouffroy, "would doubtless have been a great poet in a more esthetic time, as Goethe an eminent philosopher under a different public impulse."[119] That Goethe was a contemporary and compatriot of Kant, Fichte, and Schelling, is not taken into consideration.

So utilitarian a conception of art has its immediate parentage in Saint-Simon, but it traces its ancestry back to the ecclesiastical art of the middle ages without a

[114] *Ib.*
[115] *Id.* I 302.
[116] *Id.* I 307.
[117] *Ib.*
[118] *Id.* I 308.
[119] *Id.* I 310.

break in the chain. Readers who are familiar with the writings of M. Emile Mâle appreciate the greatness which can come from an art strictly disciplined by a non-esthetic group of censors. The smallest details of a Book of Hours were regulated by a power superior to the artist. Art flourished with a peculiar strength and abundance. It is that goal achieved by the Church at which Comte is undoubtedly aiming. But the positivistic church had not as yet the universality and the authority of the Church of Rome. Could it have attained them, there is little reason to doubt that the program of Comte was practical. *A priori* there is no ground for believing that the *Grand-Etre* should not inspire as many poets, painters, and architects as God. The one problem was to make humanity believe in it. And Comte thought that he has solved that problem.

Comte is as far from agreeing with the romantic artists of his time as either Catholics or Eclectics. The philosophical estheticians had one fundamental idea which the more progressive artists could not accept. The idea of a single type of beauty. The question was a practical one. One of the romantic ways of justifying novelties was maintaining a kind of esthetic nominalism. The romanticists sometimes maintained that the idea of beauty changed from age to age, or from country to country, or from individual to individual. The classicists, on the contrary, interested in conforming to certain French traditions, defended their conservatism by maintaining that Beauty was one and indivisible and eternal. Stendhal saw the necessity of attacking that thesis above all others. He attacked from the point of view of Idéology. Emile Deschamps, writing much later—1828—continued the same tradition in his own way. Insisting on what appears to be the opposite theory, namely, that there is no real distinction between classic and romantic, that good and bad literature are the only kinds there are, he argues that romantic literature is simply the production of certain *genres* as yet untried in France, the lyric, the elegiac, and the epic.[120] But he maintains as strongly that it is only possible and useful to compare writers of the same century[121] and later speaks like a true romanticist of the revolution which is taking place in all the arts.[122] Such arguments which urge a liberalism in appreciating the new and different works of art, indicate the same feeling that Stendhal had, the feeling that the beautiful is manifested in divers ways. In fact, it was one of the most convincing arguments that the new school could have found.

But, like all relativistic and pluralistic theories, it ran into difficulties when it approached the question of criticism. The approval and disapproval of works of art, which is one of the most usual pastimes of critics, demands a standard and a standard is an awkward tool for a relativist or pluralist to handle. The philosophers had standards, but they were standards as often as not inapplicable to the art of their time or so detached from genuine esthetic interests as to be valueless in criticism. The German romanticist had his

[120] Pref. to "Etudes françaises et étrangères," p. 12.
[121] *Id.* 16.
[122] *Id.* 35.

philosophy already for him. The French, on the other hand, had German philosophy as interpreted by Mme. de Staël, idéology, eclecticism, catholicism, or positivism. The romanticists often laughed at the German philosophers.[123] Deschamps, as we have said, accepted Cousin as the philosopher of his age, although Jouffroy would have done much better, and Cousin proclaimed himself as the representative in philosophy of the same school as that which Mme. de Staël and Chateaubriand had opened in literature. If Stendhal may be counted among the romanticists, idéology may be given a place in the new movement. Catholicism had a certain influence through Lamennais's effect on Hugo and Lamartine perhaps. But positivism, in spite of its bid for favor, was as much beyond the artistic pale as it was beyond the scientific. The reason for the small rôle played by philosophy in French romanticism is that the romanticists were primarily men of letters, interested in purely esthetic enterprises. When they entered politics, they seemed to forget their romanticism. Their solidarity was very imperfect and it would not

[123] The predecessors of the French romanticists among the philosophers, like Ballanche and Mme. de Staël, had a great respect for Kant. Later the sentiment changed. See Counson's "De la légende de Kant chez les romantiques français," in *Mélanges Godefroid Kurth*, Liège 1908, II. Chateaubriand turned his back decisively on Kant ("Génie" I, ii, ch. ii). This may have been because of Joubert's influence. Hugo's *mot* about K's wig, reproduced by Counson, is too well known to be repeated. See his "Littérature et philos. mêlées," 1819, in *OC, Philos.* I (1819-1834); P. 1882. "Up to 1880," says Counson (p. 333), "Kant remains for him [*i. e.*, Hugo] the most learned pedant and the most trifling."

be difficult to point out that beyond a very limited extent there was no " movement " at all in the sense of conscious concerted action. The attempts which have been made since 1830 to see one definite philosophy in French romanticism gain their strength from oversimplification of facts. Unhappily they have distorted history beyond tolerance and changed it into polemic.

Such an account of positivism as we have given here does not do justice to its effect in France and abroad, where it captured the imagination of men more or less tired of metaphysics and religion and yet incapable of abandoning all metaphysical and religious activity. Its importance in France is seen in even academic French philosophy; in England it worked its way into literature and social life; and in South America it is still a potent force. But its larger development came in the second half of the century. In the first half it remained in France an obscure philosophy announced by an unrecognized thinker. Yet of all the indigenous philosophies of the time, it alone was to survive. Comte and to a lesser extent Maine de Biran remain, out of all the philosophers we have mentioned, influences in the present day.

CONCLUSION

There are but few remarks which are needed to conclude the historical study of any nation's ideas, for the study should be self-concluding. But it is permissible to draw together the threads of discourse, if only to attain an esthetic end.

The first half of the nineteenth century, which is the period we have been discussing, begins and ends with the ascendancy of a Bonaparte. This is symptomatic of the disease which was afflicting the unhappy country. Whereas other nations, such as England and the United States, may be said to have been creating for themselves a divine mission which they could later maintain was pushing them on to conquest and glory, France was wasting her energies in political reform, in the vain hope of making people better and happier by governmental means.

The same futility characterizes the philosophies of the period. The same element of tragedy, of self-defeat marks them. The Catholics, hoping to protect the Church, end by being excommunicated; the idéologues are disgraced by the man whose success they help make possible; the eclectics begin as the new school of French philosophy and end as a group of timid schoolmasters, safe in the study of the past; the positivists, split into two camps, begin as the champions of natural science and end as the champions of a religion much more fantastic than the metaphysics which they existed to oppose.

French philosophers of this period, unlike their German contemporaries, were either in the political opposition or in opposition to the mass of their countrymen. Almost without exception they held some political position; they were always on the defensive. This brought their thoughts close to the ground and gave them that appearance of shallowness which has kept them out of the histories of philosophy. What this really means is that they did not construct philosophical systems. Yet the importance of a philosopher is not to be measured by the number of pages which he receives in a history of philosophy. Such standards are determined largely by an uncriticised tradition. It is to be measured rather by the intimacy which he has with the civilisation in which he works; by the effect he has upon that civilisation or by the clearness with which he expresses that civilisation's interests.

By such standards our philosophers take on a striking importance. Plato, Aristotle, and Plotinus had relatively little contact with their times. They wrote delightful books; they influenced aliens beyond any other three men, furnishing material for almost all succeeding thinkers. But what had they to say to Greece or Rome that could be absorbed by Greece and Rome? Cousin, in spite of his shallowness, changed the educational system of France. The traditionalists voiced the aspirations of all Catholicism. Positivism had as its end the reconstruction of French society as it existed after the Revolution. There is something admirable in this wrestling with actual problems—however distant those problems may seem to us now. A real history of ideas ought to see that the importance of a thought is to be measured by the stimulus which calls it forth. One is not forced either to write or to read histories.

The philosophies of this period, like those of all periods, have a great lyrical element. They are, as Mr. Santayana might say, bad poetry. Their value, for everyone but their founders is to a large extent like the value of a painting. But there are some people who try to refute paintings as if they were arguments, just as there are some people who swallow a scientific theory as if it were a cool and succulent oyster. Undoubtedly all these thoughts have some mysterious significance in the scheme of things, if there is a scheme, and undoubtedly each thinker could provide a good reason for maintaining that his particular prejudice has a peculiarly close relation to the Truth. But it is certain that the biographical element played a preponderant part in its development. What determined the evolution of Maine de Biran, if not dissatisfaction with the practical consequences of his theory? Was his mysticism more logical or "truer" than his early ideology? Was Cousin's spirit of compromise more logical than Bautain's fidéism? Can there be much doubt that Cousin's eclecticism was born from his desire to be a figure in the political as well as the learned world? Can there be much doubt that Bautain stopped short of agnosticism by his frank desire to stay a Catholic? It could be maintained that such reasons lie behind all philosophies. We are content here to suggest that they certainly lie behind those of our period.

The main interest of our period for students of the history of philosophy is that of any spectacle in which human beings play a rôle. Historical curiosity is useless; its satisfaction serves no ulterior end. No one was ever the wiser in a practical way for knowing history; no one was ever the more intelligent for ignoring it. History is simply another means of sophistication and as such invaluable. It should be the mother of tolerance and the scourge of fanaticism. But, unhappily, it is seldom either, for it can be known only through bad translations.

If this interpretation of a part of French culture is interesting to read and if, as I hope, it has introduced new thinkers to the American public, it can ask for little greater success. It has no pretentions of being complete. It has been written from a special point of view which is apparent to the most casual reader. But as long as the point of view is obvious, it will be easy to check the accuracy of the exposition. That perhaps is all that can be asked of an expositor. For is there any recipé for leaping out of one's training and natural endowment and surveying things in utter detachment?

APPENDIX

Azaïs

The teachings of Azaïs were peculiarly adapted to the Empire because they had that obvious symmetry of construction, apparent common-sense and clearness which appeal to men who have not the power of intellectual analysis nor of deep emotion. They lacked all the difficulty of sensationalism and the liberalism it seemed to involve. They lacked the hard uncompromising discipline of Catholicism. Apparently founded upon natural science, they were nevertheless phrased so that a child could grasp them and think that he was grasping something elusive. Apparently implying profound moral issues, they taught the simple morality of the Decalogue. They had all the naïveté of Plato's science and none of the grandeur of his philosophy. They were in fine outwardly noble and almost sublime, inwardly trivial or downright false.

Their formulator began life as an obscure enough student in the Congregation of the Doctrinaires, where both Daunou and Laromiguière were taught. Sent to the Collège de Tarbes, he wrote a letter in despair to his father, the musician, pleading to be released. The letter was intercepted and the writer made secretary to the Bishop.

This new assignment, while it made Azaïs more contented, did not incline his mind more favorably towards holy orders. He refused to enter the Church and became instead organist in the Benedictine Abbey of Cevennes.

By this time the Revolution had broken out. To a man of Azais's pacific nature, it was bound sooner or later to become intolerable. He stood it as long as he could, but finally published a violent pamphlet against it. The 18th Fructidor saw him condemned to deportation, but he found concealment in the hospital of Tarbes among the Sisters of Charity.[1] He had always found help in the friendship of women.[2] Years later he said of his behavior at this time, "I was irritated like all the other proscripts, that Napoleon had prevented us from stopping the torrent of revolution; and I did not see that no dam could at that moment have been erected, that in the moral and physical situation, every essentially monarchical institution was impossible. . . . The Revolution had to work itself out, and at the same time to be mastered; which made inevitable nay, even desirable, the power of a revolutionary soldier."[3]

At Tarbes he had time to think these thoughts through to the best of his ability. But like so many people of his time, he thought more about himself than about anything else. If he was interested in good and evil, it was because he had suffered evil and hoped for good. Nothing was more striking to his eye than the contrast between the peace which now surrounded him and the turmoil from which he had escaped. This contrast,

[1] "Des Compensations dans les destinées humaines," 4th ed., P. 1825, I 388, n. 1.
[2] Guadet; "Azais, sa Vie et ses Ouvrages," P. 1846, ix.
[3] "Jugement impartial sur Napoléon," P. 1820, p. 37.

he says,[4] sharpened his idea of a balance in man's vicissitudes. "I had seen before chagrin, bitterness, ennui, often despair, in the lap of fortune; I had been stirred by violent troubles when I lacked for nothing. On the contrary, in my new situation, in the asylum from misfortune and indigence, I was at peace, I was happy; and if any noise penetrated my retreat, it was usually the accents of gaiety and innocence. I listened to the games of poor orphans gathered together by charity."[5]

This thought to him was a conversion like that of St. Augustine in the garden at Milan. But instead of being a revelation of the living God, it was a revelation of the Platonic formula that pleasure is what builds up and pain what tears down and of the utilitarian formula that pleasure is good fortune and pain bad.

He began to write, not as he says for publication, but for his inner happiness.[6] The result was his "universal system," built upon the principle of compensation as a base. It read into the universe characters of good and evil much in the manner of the early Greeks. His fame began to grow. It was at this time that Madame Cottin, the novelist, ran across him, was carried away by him, and saw in him a latter-day Plato.[7]

In 1806 he made his appearance in Paris, where he was given a position as *maître d'étude* in the Prytanée of St. Cyr, which he later changed for a class in geo-

[4] "Compensations" I 370.
[5] *Ib.*
[6] *Id.* I 395.
[7] See "Souvenirs et Corresp. de Mme. Récamier," 273; Sainte-Beuve; *CL* XI 488; Guadet xxvii.

graphy. Here he expounded his universal system in a manner which he later found unsatisfactory.[8] But everyone who has written of him sees at this period the height of his success. His most sympathetic biographer, Guadet, speaks of his "brilliant audience" and his contemporary, Damiron, of his great vogue and his real talent in speaking and discussion.[9] As late as 1839 the Abbé Bautain grouped him with Maistre, Bonald and Ballanche as an "homme distingué."[10] That he owed a large part of his success to the benevolence of Napoleon is indubitable, although he says later that Napoleon always repulsed him and that only the "honorable and obstinate good will" of Montalivet, the father of Louis-Philippe's Minister of the Interior, kept him alive.[11]

His reasons for denying Napoleon's favor were not difficult to understand. In 1815 Azaïs had published an extravagant eulogy of the Emperor, "De Napoléon et de la France," which he admitted had caused him to be distinguished by the subject of his praise.[12] He was made Rector of the Academy at Nancy during the Hundred Days, after having held the posts of Inspector of Printed Books (Inspecteur de la Librairie) in Avignon in 1811 and in Nancy in 1812. After Waterloo of course he lost his post. There was nothing for him to do then but to appeal to the pity of the world. The

---

[8] "Compensations" I 413.
[9] "Hist. de la Philos. en Fr.," 95.
[10] "Philos." lxiii.
[11] "Jugement impartial" vii.
[12] *Id.* viii.

world had pity. Mme. de Staël's influence and that of a group of scholars won him a pension of 6000 francs from Louis XVIII. Could he have done less than repudiate his relations with Napoleon?

In his garden in Paris he continued to expound his doctrines. His mildness, his simple eloquence, his universal and ill-founded formulæ, attracted to him a small group of auditors. He began to publish his own books and invited readers to call at his hermitage, as he called it, 3 rue Duguay-Trouin, to discuss them in private. "Mon ermitage . . . sera ouvert avec empressement à tout homme que la verité intéresse, et je serai plein d'estime, de déférence, de reconnaissance, pour tout homme qui m'aidera à perfectionner le Système de la Vérité."[13] But by then his vogue was gone and he was on the high-road to the oblivion where he would now rest had not a German candidate for the doctorate dragged him out of it.[14]

Azaïs's philosophy is interesting in that he founds a highly optimistic ethics upon a consistent materialism. Believing, as he does, that all ideas are material,[15] the literal functions of the brain in the central part of which resides the soul, he does not deny their value either as a means towards the good life nor as an element of goodness attained. With him it is not a question of ideas being "nothing but" brain states; their physiological origin is not an evaluation of them.

[13] "Compensations" III, précis 108.
[14] Josef Schweiger; "Der Philosophe P-H. Azaïs," Bonn 1913.
[15] "Compensations" III 209.

Ideas like everything else are material. Hence the world can be interpreted according to a law which applies to the physical as well as to the mental realm. That law is what accounts for the dualism which exists in objects. Objects tend to expand. But when one expanding object meets another expanding object, one must either dent the other or completely annihilate it. The fact that such catastrophes do not occur daily is a result of the harmony in the world. There is, that is to say, a compensation between expansion and compression.[16] Since expansion, if left unchecked, would involve the explosion of the expanding object, and since an explosion is not taking place, the universe must be infinite in extent.[17] For only infinity, by which is meant limitlessness, can insure the world against dissolution.[18]

Just as in Germany Schelling was reading the drama of self-consciousness into Nature, so in France Azaïs was reading the simple ups and downs of Nature into consciousness. They were equally successful and had nothing but facts to contradict them. In Azaïs, music, physics, psychology, astronomy, botany, and all the other arts and sciences join hands in a beautiful harmony; in Schelling the same trait is noticeable. But whereas the German is expanding the Ego to make physics into psychology, the Frenchman is expanding the non-ego to make psychology into physics.

There is no need of going through the details of this pseudo-science. A fertile imagination can recon-

---
[16] *Id.* 212.
[17] *Id.* III, précis 3; "Explication universelle," P. 1826, I 1.
[18] "Compensations" III, précis 8; "Explic. Univ." I 8.

struct it for itself. Wherever there are two apparently opposing facts, one has simply to read into them compensation. The formula always works. It is its application to man which interests us. As we have indicated above, pleasure is what constructs, pain what destroys.[19] Pleasure is a precise sign of organic amelioration, pain of organic harm.[20] This is the bridge between the moral and the physical realm. Just as there is compensation between expansion and compression, between construction and destruction, so is there between pleasure and pain.[21] Like Plato and the humoralists, health and sickness are the physiological accompaniments of pleasure and pain. Azaïs like them describes health as a kind of harmony which differs from their harmony only in language. He substitutes the words " organic functions " for " humors." [22] Indeed to read this part of Azaïs is to read a modern paraphrase of the Greek physicians.

To speak of ideas, says Azaïs,[23] as if they were distinct and immaterial, is to speak the language of illusion and incoherence. But the faculty of feeling them, which is an activity, is immaterial.[24] Its immateriality may be simply something material highly expanded, like the soul of Tertullian, the pneuma of the Stoics, or the animal spirits of Descartes and his contemporaries.[25]

[19] " Compensations " II, précis 196; " Explic. Univ." I 351.
[20] " Compensations " III, précis 199.
[21] " Explic. Univ." I 352.
[22] Cf. " Timaeus " 87; " Philebus " 31, and even Spencer in the " Data of Ethics."
[23] " Compensations " III, précis 210; " Explic. Univ." II 17.
[24] " Compensations " III, précis 211; " Explic. Univ." II 43.
[25] " Passions," Oeuvres, ed. Cousin, P. 1824; IV, art. viii, ix and " l'Homme " IV 344.

The tradition that activity is somehow correlated with the immaterial dates back at least to Aristotelian physics, for it was a Greek habit to make the corporeal utterly passive and, by implication, the active non-corporeal— or as non-corporeal as possible. Indeed, Plotinus proves that the soul is essentially impassive—like Lucretius's gods—because it is not body. But Azais makes nothing of this point, and of course it is really a flaw in his system. He probably included it because contemporary psychology took it for granted.

No man writing in his time could avoid considering the philosophy of government. Azais no more resisted the temptation than his fellow-thinkers. Here perhaps more than anywhere else he shows himself a man after the Emperor's heart. Believing that wisdom consists in accepting with love the duties of man's station,[26] he urges man to ally himself with others in society.[27] But society must be organized, lest the expansive force of each individual be unrestrained. Like a human being, it must have its chief, the head, the seat of intellectual action, and it must have its inferior organs subordinated to it.[28] Thus only can there be obtained that equilibrium necessary to the health of the whole.

Among the members of the social organism are those who are fixed, the solids, and those who are mobile, the producers, the fluids. As the producers always struggle to achieve the joys of the property owners, and the property owners to retain what they have, the State

[26] " Compensations " III, précis 282.
[27] *Id.* I 27.
[28] " Compensations " III, précis 286; " Explic. Univ." I 348.

has to see to it that the laws are especially favorable to the fixed. For the mobile classes are more numerous and more active, and would soon overwhelm the fixed if unhindered.[29] To retain the needed harmony or balance between classes, it is necessary to have a chief and the chief should be a monarch and an hereditary monarch. He may be absolute if he be wise and good; limited if not.[30] But in all events he must think of one thing only, the balance between the proprietors and the proletariat, the fixed and the mobile.

When, however, a state arises from a colony, the government may then be republican. For this is simply justice due to the many founders of the state. When a number of men have planted a colony, they have thrown their fortunes in together; there is no aristocracy, "fluids form almost all the substance" of the body politic. It is only by rapid expansion that such a body can grow.

"I have just defined," says Azaïs, "the United States of North America."

He shared his Emperor's hatred of England and hence could excuse America from the universal explanation.

This is, in brief, the sum of Azaïs's philosophy. Fantastic as it seems when thought of out of its nineteenth century background, it was not without a certain prestige. I cannot discover that Emerson drew his inspira-

---

[29] "Compensations" III, précis 294; "Explic. Univ." II 362. Cf. "Jugement Impartial" 89.

[30] "Explic. Univ." II 364. Cf. "Compensations" II xiv,—the man in the family.

tion from Azaïs, but his version of a similar doctrine was not at all laughed at among the élite of America. So Azaïs was able to find certain sympathizers. He maintained that Davy in the *Philosophical Magazine* noted the " Système Universel " and called its reasonings " often very ingenious." This mild praise so delighted Azaïs that he reprinted it thirteen years later, feeling himself to be the collaborator of the great Englishman.[31] Mme. de Staël was not wholly unkindly to him and praised six short stories which make up the second volume of " Des Compensations." [32] Broussais, who believed with Azaïs in the theory of phrenology, permitted him in an almost enthusiastic letter to dedicate his " De la Phrenologie " to him.[33] It is certain, in spite of the shame with which Frenchmen mention his name, that he was considered seriously by some men of letters and by many amateurs of philosophy. He was the popular philosopher of the Empire. Under a Napoleonic régime, one could expect little more.

[31] " Constitution de l'univers," P. 1840, App. 415.
[32] " Compensations " II xviii.
[33] P. 1839, Intro. 41.

INDEX

References are given only to those pages which are likely to be of interest. In the case of extended discussions the reference is to the page where the discussion begins.

L'Action Française, 93.

Activity, in Laromiguière, 35, 37, 40; in Destutt de Tracy, 35; in Cabanis, 36; in Maine de Biran, 42, 45; in Stendhal, 67; in Cousin, 204.

Ampere, J. J., and Biran, 52 n. 36; 53; introduction to Kant, 173.

Analysis, and education, 4; and religious ideas, 5; in Ideology, 25; and the Reason, 30.

Ancillon, on Biran, 64.

Mme. d'Anjou, letter to Louis XVIII *re* return of religion, 100.

Arbogast, 4; quoted, 5 n. 6.

Azaïs, philosophy expounded, Appendix; his reputation, 313, 319; and Napoleon, 313; his materialism, 315; and Schelling, 315; compensation, 316; philosophy of government, 317.

Baldus de Ubaldeis, 82.

Ballanche, Ch. III, sec. 3; his reputation, 112; his importance for the history of philosophy, 115; his sentimentalism, 115; agreement and difference with Bonald and Maistre, 116; exposition of his philosophy, 119; change both real and good, 119; rehabilitation, 120; metempsychosis, 120; no eternal hell, 121; growth of religion, 121; personal interpretation, 122; theory of tradition, 123; early reading of Kant, 172.

Bautain, quoted on Ideology, 33; philosophy suggested, ch. V, sec. 4; his philosophic importance, 234; *fidéisme*, 234; attack on contemporary schools, 235; his recantation, 237.

Bernardin-de-Saint-Pierre, and God, 7; and Napoleon, 13.

Bonald, likeness to medieval Catholics, 71; love of unity and permanence, 71; hatred of multiplicity, 71; and Dante, 72; tradition, 73, 79; and Hegel, 73, 75; men elements of society, not independent atoms, 74; language, 76; on Mme. de Staël, 78; Napoleon's attitude towards, 80; on Aristotle and Plato, 81 n. 32; his predecessors, 82.

Brillat-Savarin, relation of his " Physiologie du Goût " to Cabanis, 69.

Buchez, on literature and the fine arts, 288.

Cabanis, contribution to Ideology, 31; physical and mental in, 31; some implications of his theories 32.

Catechisms, Napoleon's, 17; the Citoyen Poitevin's, 18.

Chateaubriand, his philosophical function, ch. III, sec. 2; his conversion, 94; " Le Génie du Christianisme," 95; its fame, 96; his sincerity, 96 n. 60; Napoleon's reaction, 97; reception of " Le Génie " by the Pope, 97; its argument, 98; its effect, 99; similar projects, 100; Ginguené's protest, 100;

Chateaubriand not in the Catholic tradition, 101.
Christianity, and slavery, 98 n. 68.
The Church, and Napoleon, 3; and Ideology, 4; and sentimentalism, 7; and the Monarchy, 8; her pre-revolutionary privileges, 9; scepticism within her ranks, 10; progress of revolutionary campaign against, 11; historical analogies of attempted suppression of, 12; its task according to Lamennais, 132.
Comte, see Positivism.
Condillac, and Bonald's theory of language, 83.
Condorcet, 88; and positivism, 266.
Constant, comment on Mme. de Staël, 112.
Cousin, and analysis, 31; on Laromiguière, 35; on Biran, 64; and Schelling, 190, 208; on sensationalism, 209; his goal political, 199; spirit of compromise, 200; on mysticism, 201; an empiricist in his own eyes, 203; activity in, 204; the human faculties, 205; spontaneity and reflection, 206; cause and substance, 206; political philosophy, Ch. V, sec. 2; hated by both republicans and reactionaries, 211; on French origin of his ideas, 212; charge of anti-Catholicism, 214; his advice to Bersot, 218; "Justice et Charité," 220; esthetic preferences, Ch. V, sec. 3; a classicist in taste, 224; art an idealization, 225; theory derived from Winckelmann, 226; ideal beauty in the Romantics, 228; a political but not an esthetic Romantic, 230; his pupils, Ch. V, sec. 4; made a business of the teaching of philosophy, 251; his influence, 252.

Dante, 72.
Daube, on activity and passivity, 36; 37 n. 9, 38.
Daunou, Napoleon's boast to, 22; the rôles of logic and metaphysics, 39; refusal of position as Councillor of State, 81.
Delacroix, on esthetic inspiration, 296.
Destutt de Tracy, contribution to Ideology, 24; his theory of resistance contrasted with Fichte's, 28; and the will, 29; why his theory died out, 29; and Biran, 47, 48; fundamental paradox of his philosophy, 68; on Kant, 175.
Dietrich of Niem, 83.

Eclecticism, Ch. V. See Cousin.
Effort, in Maine de Biran, 46; in Rey Régis, 46 n. 28.

Fontanes, Napoleon's admission of defeat to, 22; on the prerequisites of the Neo-Christian apology, 93, 97; letter to Joubert re the Pope's reception of "Le Génie," 98.
Franklin, 7.

Geoffroy-Saint-Hilaire, his cosmology, 255.
Ginguené, review of "Le Génie," 100.

Habit, Maine de Biran's memoir on, 45, 47.
Harris, quoted, 50 n. 34; 65.
Hegel, and Bonald, 73, 75; and Maistre, 75 n. 14.
Mme. Helvétius, 15.
Hoene-Wronsky, 174 n. 56.

Ideology, and Napoleon, 4; the fortunes of, Ch. II; fate of the word, 23; synopsis of its tenets, 24; and Condillac, 24; Destutt de Tracy's contribution to, 24; his description of,

INDEX

24; and zoology, 25; popular reaction to in the Empire, 26; and sensationalism, 26; why it died out, 29; Cabanis's contribution to, 31; and passivity, 32; in Laromiguière, 35; doctrine of habit, 44; Biran's break with, 57.

Institut de France, suppression of the Second Class of, 19, 21; Napoleon's membership, 20; its *raison d'être*, 39.

Jouffroy, philosophy expounded, 239; contrast with Cousin, 239; impotency of the reason, 240; basis of reason a "blind act of faith," 241; and Reid, 242; internationalism, 243; meaning of "common-sense," 244; its origin, 245; like the Absolute, 246; ethical point of view, 247.

Kant, and Biran, 51, 52 n. 36; their categories, 54; introduction into France, Ch. IV, sec. 2; reputation during the Revolution, 165; philosophic interest in, 168; in the *Spectateur du Nord*, 170; Villers's early article on, 170; in Lyons, 171; Ballanche, 172; Ampère, 173; Hoene-Wronsky, 174; Kinker, 174; Destutt de Tracy, 175; Laromiguière, 176; Villers's book on, 177; its reception, 179; effect on Mme. de Staël, 180; Degérando, 181; and the Abbé Bautain, 234.

Lamartine, letter to Maistre on appearance of "Du Pape," 92.

Lamennais, Ch. III, sec. 4; the unity of his thought, 126; basis of his theory, 127; equation of "religion" and "Catholicism," 129, 131; its substantiation, 130; homogeneity of tradition, 130; the task of the Church, 132; his ultramontanism, 133; the ordinances of 1828, 134; *Mirari Vos*, 137; "Paroles d'un Croyant," 140; its philosophy, 141; rights and duties, 143; theocracy, 144; liberty and solidarity, 144; internationalism, 145.

Language, divine origin of a commonplace in the eighteenth century, 83 n. 39.

Laromiguière, his philosophy, Ch. II, sec. 2; and Kant, 34; his writings, 34; his charm, 35; and L. J. J. Daube, 36; the basis of his epistemology, 37; intelligence in, 38; on system, 39; on the will, 40; basis of his fame, 40, 40 n. 12; and Napoleon, 41; his retirement, 42; Biran's article on, 59; on Kant, 176.

Lerminier, quoted, 22.

Louis XVIII, influence on the counter-revolutionary movement, 71.

Loyson, quoted on Bonald and Maistre, 86 n. 45.

Maine de Biran, his philosophy, Ch. II, sec. 3; earliest philosophical ambition, 42; why interested in activity, 43; memoir on habit, 44; early views of activity and passivity, 45; and causation, 46; and effort, 46; and Destutt de Tracy, 47, 48; memoir on the decomposition of thought, 48; and Rousseau, 50; and Kant, 51; comments on the "Profession de Foi du Vicaire Savoyard" ethical not epistemological, 51; the Ego in, 52; his categories and Kant's, 54; their "deduction," 55; his misgivings thereon, 55; his Philosophical Society, 56; misgivings upon the introspective method, 56; break with Ideology, 57; article on Laromiguière, 59; spontaneity of attention, 59; his growing piety, 60; the autonomy of the will, 60; his mystic way, 60; the last phase of effort, 62; his influence, 63; contrasted with Nietzsche, 64; estimates of his work, 64.

Maistre, his philosophy expounded, 85; an eleatic like Bonald, 85; hatred of time and change, 85; relation to the Christian tradition, 86; evil and disobedience, 86; hatred of diversity, 88; longed for medieval unity, 89; his ultramontanism, 90; invective against Voltaire, 91; his prophecies, 91; reception of " Du Pape," 92; his voice now heard in " L'Action Française," 93.

Napoleon, attacks revolutionary culture, 1; friendship for the Church, 3; restoration of the Cult, 13; and Ideology, 14; and science, 15; aim in founding the University, 16; Imperial Catechism, 17; remark to Queen Louise of Prussia, 18 n. 35; and unity, 19; remarks to the Professors of Pavia, 19; and the Institut, 20; boast to Daunou, 22; admits spiritual defeat to Fontanes, 22; and Laromiguière, 41; and Bonald, 81; rewards Chateaubriand, 97; his " classicism," 110.

Neo-Christianity, Ch. III.
Nicholas of Cusa, 82.
Nietzsche, and Biran, 64.

Parlor-Christians, 98.
Passivity, in Ideology, 32; revolt against, in Laromiguière, 40; in Maine de Biran, 42; 45, 47.
" Persian Letters," 10.
Philosophy, and the Revolution, 2; attitude of the people towards, 2; and anti-clericalism, 8, 10, 11; Mme. de Staël's definition of, 107.
The " Physiologies," 69.
Political parties and the Revolution, 256.
Positivism, its rise, Ch. VI; a philosophical summation of early nineteenth century French culture, 254; study of society as such, 257; antecedents, social dynamics, 258; social statics, 260; and Lamennais, 261; law of three states, 263; and Turgot, 265; and Condorcet, 266; Saint-Simon, 270; Burdin, 273; Cuvier, 274; and metaphysics, 277; Catholic objection to, 278; and Ideology, 280, 291; not free from " metaphysics," 281; nor from " psychology," 282; and behaviorism, 284; social program, Ch. VI, sec. 4; the domination of " social utility," 289; inherent sociability of human beings, 290; inequality of the sexes, 292; the family, 292; and Catholicism, 292; society an organism, 293; and industrial, 294; the spiritual power, 294; definition of education, 295 n. 95; esthetics, Ch. VI, sec. 5; definition of the beautiful, 297; aim of art, 298; poetry, 298; other arts, 299; freedom and the arts, 300; parentage of the theory, 301; and romanticism, 302.

Reid, influence on French philosophy, Ch. IV, sec. 1.
Revocation of the Edict of Nantes, 12.
Régis, and Biran, 46 n. 28.
Robespierre, and sentimentalism, 6; and the Clergy, 7.
Rousseau, " Profession de Foi du Vicaire Savoyard " quoted, 49; and James Harris, 50; and

INDEX

Bonald's theory of language, 83; the master of Mme. de Staël, 102; not a unified personality, 102; and Lamennais, 142.

Royer-Collard, his teaching expounded, 157; anti-sensationalism, 158; the *via media*, 159; sensation and perception, 161; causality, 162; principle of induction, 163.

Sainte-Beuve, on Biran, 64; the "parlor-Christians," 98.
Saint-Martin, 7; 83 n. 36.
St. Thomas Aquinas, 82.
Schelling, introduction into France, 184; hostility of the pre-Cousinian notices, 186; possible explanation of, 187; in the *Archives Philosophiques,* 188; in the *Globe,* 189; and Cousin, 190; first translation into French, 191; Barchou-Penhoën, 192; Cuvier, 192; his charm, 193; Lèbre on, 194; Cousin's debt to, 207; his esthetics contrasted with Hegel's, 227.
Sentimentalism, 6; and the Church, 7; in Ballanche, 115.
Shakespeare, lines to, 289.
Simon, on Biran, 64.
Mme. de Staël, Bonald's opinion of, 78; her philosophy expounded, Ch. III, sec. 2; and Chateaubriand, 102, 110; and Rousseau, 102, 111; theory of knowledge, 104; the antithesis between our aspirations and our capacities, 104; springs of action non-rational, 105; notion of philosophy, 106; harmony between her philosophy, religion, and politics, 108; a woman without a country, 109; or party, 109; cause of her hatred of Napoleon, 109; her "enthusiasm," 110.
Stapfer, and Biran, 52 n. 36; and Kant, 173.
Stendhal, and Ideology, 65, 67; and idealism, 66; and the teachings of Cabanis, 66; on the "Génie du Christianisme," 66; activity, 67.

Theodosian Code, 12.
Traditionalism, Ch. III; its effects, Ch. III, sec. 5; its condemnation, 147; its ineffectiveness, 149; minimum effect on literature, 150; and on painting, 151.

Unity, and Napoleonic government, 19; in Bonald, 71; achieved in the Middle Ages, 89.
The University, Napoleon's aim in founding it, 16; contrasted with the Ecoles Centrales, 17.

Villers, early article on Kant, 171; book on Kant, 177.
Volition, in Maine de Biran, 47; its autonomy, 60.
Voltaire, Maistre's invective of, 91; Jouffroy's comment on, 242.

Date Due

NOV 9 '60